THE REFORMATION AND REUNION

THE REFORMATION
AND REUNION

By

C. SYDNEY CARTER, D.D. (Oxon)

Fellow of the Royal Historical Society.
Principal of Clifton Theological College, Bristol.

With an Appreciation by the Rt. Rev. E. A. KNOX, D.D.,
and a Foreword by the Rt. Rev. F. S. GUY WARMAN,
Bishop of Manchester.

LONDON
THE CHURCH BOOK ROOM,
7 WINE OFFICE COURT, E.C.4

Printed in Great Britain by
PAGE & THOMAS, LTD., 131, FINSBURY PAVEMENT, LONDON, E.C.2.

CONTENTS

Visible and Invisible Aspects of the Church—Other Reformed 'Confessions'—Rogers on the 'Articles'—Græco-Russian Church—'Notes' of the Church—Question of Episcopacy—Views of Elizabethan Churchmen — Article XXIII. — Case of Robert Wright—(b) On Eucharist—Elizabethan views—on Real Presence—Lutheran and Helvetian views—Reservation—Bp. Sparrow's "Rationale"—Bishop Cosin's teaching—The Archbishops 'Opinion' 1900—The Sacrifice of the Mass and Article XXXI.—Reformed condemnation of the Mass—Doctrine of the Eastern Church—on Eucharist—Dr. Covel's account—Cyril Lucar—(c) On Authority of Holy Scripture—Wyclif's translation—Bible Reading in medieval days—Wycliffe's views—Luther and Melanchthon—Origin of word 'Protestant'—Scripture the supreme and final Rule of Faith—Testimony of Caroline divines—Reformed 'Confessions' on appeal to Antiquity—Roman Teaching—Bellarmine—Council of Trent—Eastern Orthodox Church—Anglican Teaching.

Minor diversities of usage and Ceremonies—Anglican 'Ornaments,' Rubric—The Scotch Reformed Worship—The Swedish Church Worship and Usages—Worship of Danish and Norwegian Lutheran Churches — Luther's 'Order of Divine Service'—Worship of the Swiss Churches—Of the Dutch Reformed Church—Of the French Reformed Church—Peter du Moulin—Bingham's Evidence.

With the Swiss Reformers—Foreign Reformed Congregations in England—The Puritan Controversy—The Caroline Position and Divines—John Dury—Case of Archbishop of Spalato—Eighteenth Century Illustrations—Fr. Courayer—Non-Jurors and Greek Church.

Findings—Intercommunion with 'Old Catholics'—Effect of Tractarian Teaching—Kikuyu Federation—South India Scheme—Negotiations with English Free Churches. Remarks.

AN APPRECIATION

By the Rt. Rev. E. A. KNOX, D.D.

THE imprimatur of the University of Oxford on the historical correctness of Dr. Carter's presentation of the Reunion Problem cannot fail to command the attention of all who desire to form a sound judgment on that question. But why are we asked to spend time on reading such a historical disputation? Cannot we form a judgment for ourselves without turning over musty archives of the past? The answer is to be found in the very fact that the question is not novel but centuries old. For centuries devout men have not only " prayed for the peace of Jerusalem," but laboured also to give effect to their prayers. Yet the question is with us still, and it is only by patient study of the past that we shall learn what the real hindrances to Reunion are. For the unity of the Church of Christ is not a problem but a fact. It is the will of God, and who hath resisted, or can resist, His Will? The disunion is not in the Church of God, but in the Churches or visible Communions and takes shape in forms of government, modes of worship, and expressions of doctrinal belief. These are the questions that divide the communions one from another.

The value of historical research is that it brings clearly into light the difference between reconcilable and irreconcilable divisions. On one side lie the disputes between the Churches of the Reformation. They are not only reconcilable, but in process of reconciliation. Their differences arise from variations in interpreting

vii

the Scriptures, which all of them accept as a revelation made by God to man for the purpose of showing to man his helplessness arising from sin, and the provision which God has made for the remedy of that helplessness in the One Mediator between God and man.

On the other side stands the irreconcilable division caused by the claim of the unreformed Church whether Western or Eastern, based on tradition, to be the only true Church and to supplement the provision made by God through Sacrifices offered by a God-ordained Priesthood. At the present moment enormous efforts are being made to draw the Church of England from its position among the Reformed Churches into the fold of the unreformed, and to arrogate for it the supplementary powers which Rome and Constantinople claim. The merit of Dr. Carter's work is the clearness with which he establishes the novelty and modernity of this claim, so far as the Church of England is concerned, and its utter inconsistency with the teaching of centuries of Anglican Divines. It is the historical precision, the wealth of incontestable documentary evidence, that makes Dr. Carter's work invaluable. It should be carefully and prayerfully studied and mastered by all who sincerely pray that the whole Catholic Church may be drawn together in " unity of spirit, in the bond of peace and in righteousness of life."

E. A. KNOX,
Bishop.

viii

AUTHOR'S PREFACE

PROBABLY the feeling was never stronger than it is today for the removal of all unnecessary barriers which have for so long separated those who agree in calling upon the name of Christ as Lord and Saviour. Churches and Communions with varying origins and histories which have for generations been separate and alienated from each other are drawing together and joining in Conferences for Reunion, at which they have the opportunity of examining that which they each hold to be fundamental and vital in their Creeds and principles. Attempts are being made in a spirit of mutual respect and appreciation of differing views to discover formulæ of concord which, without violating conscientious convictions or traditional and cherished heritages, may achieve a longed-for rapprochement resulting either in formal Union or at least in full inter-communion between Christians and Churches historically long divided and still at variance.

It is both unwise and shortsighted, even if it were not practically impossible, in all such efforts to neglect the task of looking back in order to trace the exact position and origins of the various branches of the Church of Christ. For it is most important to discover by an historical retrospect the extent of their past relationship and connection with each other, especially in view of the serious and far-reaching breaches in Christendom during the period known as the Reformation. That great Movement, both as a religious and political force, seriously affected almost all the Nations of Europe and in general threw them into two distinct and hostile camps, the main dividing line of which was their attitude to the Papacy and the unreformed Roman Church.

The chief purpose of this investigation is concerned with those organised societies of Christians who repudiated the temporal and spiritual claims and authority of the See of Rome. It is an attempt to discover from authorised and original sources how far they were in agreement in their doctrines and practices. It is also an endeavour to estimate to what extent the various National and regional Churches, opposed to Rome, differed in their attitude to the previous Medieval Faith and worship, as well as in their regard for traditional Catholic doctrine and ceremonial. Further, in view of the present important ' middle ' position claimed for the Anglican Church, it is a question of real practical interest to trace the actual share which the English church and people took in this widespread revolt from current orthodoxy, and examine their points of contact with the similar movement on the Continent.

The later evidences of, and attempts at fellowship in the succeeding centuries, not only with the Reformed but with the Unreformed Churches, have also been examined in the light of the fundamental principles adopted by the Reformers generally, and also with relation to the present-day efforts towards Reunion.

It would appear from recent pronouncements that the question of the importance of an episcopally ordained Ministry is still the crux of the Reunion problem. We may say that this has been the case now for nearly a century, since the Tractarians contended for the medieval theory of the Ministry, which, in its rigid form of the essential nature of episcopacy, can be traced back to St. Cyprian's teaching.

Ten years ago with the issue of the " Memorandum on the Status of the Existing Free Church Ministry," which was signed by such eminent Church of England representatives as the two Archbishops and ten diocesan bishops, this barrier seemed to have been removed. No practical effect, however, has so far been given to this important Declaration—that Free Church nonepiscopal ministries " are real ministries of Christ's

Word and Sacraments in the Universal Church." On
the other hand, a new claim has been recently advanced
that the mere public advocacy of this 'Declaration' in
the hope of securing closer fellowship with the English
Free Churches, is an uncharitable 'offence' towards
Anglicans holding the Tractarian theory of the Ministry.
To question that " episcopacy is not among the essentials
of the Church," is, we are told, " to give offence to a very
large number " of Church-people, and also to 'damage
severely' approaches which have been made to the
unreformed Eastern Orthodox Church."*

An imperious demand to impose silence on a crucial
and vital point of this character cannot certainly be
acquiesced in on the sole ground of 'charity' or of
'offence.'

For obviously an accusation of 'want of charity' and
'giving offence to others' comes with equal, even if
not with greater force, against those who thus *publicly*
deny what the Archbishops and bishops of our Church,
just quoted, in effect assert—that episcopacy is *not* of
the essence of the Ministry—since they positively declare
non-episcopal ministries to be " real ministries of Christ's
Word and Sacraments in the Universal Church."

It is the purpose of the following pages to show from a
careful, comprehensive and critical examination that
this declaration is in accord with the traditional historic
position held by our own divines, in common with
their Continental Reformed brethren, since the Reformation up to the rise of the 'Oxford Movement.'

In recent years this historical fact has been questioned
or denied by prominent Churchmen like Bishop Gore,
who declared that the Church of England " has always
acted in such a way as to satisfy those " who hold that
episcopacy is of " the esse of the Church " (*Basis of
Anglican Fellowship*, p. 34), or the late Dean Hutton,
who actually asserted that it " was historically speaking
absurd " to doubt that this theory of episcopacy " was
not part of Reformation teaching " (" Church Congress"
Speech, 1922).

These pages should convince the unprejudiced inquirer

---

* " Times," June 23, 1934.

that such statements are devoid of any true historical foundation, and that it was the consistent attitude and policy of our Reformers and leading Churchmen to seek for Unity, not on the basis of any uniform obligatory form of Church *Order* or polity, but on the profession of a common orthodox *Faith*.

It may be added that this investigation formed one of three theses which were presented to, and accepted by the University of Oxford in 1933, as constituting " an original contribution to Christian theology " meriting the degree of Doctor of Divinity.

In order to avoid burdening the text with frequent references to authorities, at the end of each quotation there is a number in a bracket, and thus its source will be found in an Appendix listed under the separate chapters.

I am much indebted to the Bishop of Manchester for his sympathetic and discriminating FOREWORD, and to Bishop Knox for his incisive and generous APPRECIATION.

My sincere thanks are also due to Miss E. L. Lillingston for valuable help in translating foreign liturgies, as well as to my friend Major R. J. Norris for his very real assistance in correcting the proofs.

C.S.C.

LENT, 1935.

FOREWORD

VERY willingly do I respond to the request of my friend, Dr. Carter, that I should write a foreword to this book. It is a careful historical study of the Reformation period and of the years that immediately followed. It is not intended to be a complete study, but it covers a field which has very special interest and importance today. We believe, as Lambeth 1920 reminded us, that God wills unity, and we are trying to work towards it. Of all the movements towards unity there comes first in the minds of most of us the re-uniting of our English Christian communions and as far as they may be a welding into one of the Reformed communions on the Continent of Europe. Rome stands apart and until her outlook changes it must be so. But the reunion of the churches of the Reformation ought not to be ultimately impossible. Our prayers and our efforts move towards that ideal, while at the same time we maintain our loyalty to Christ, to His Gospel, and to truth. Any movement towards unity must take account of the original causes of disunion, and the real differences between the communions concerned. This book is an effort to help to that end and it seems to me, so far as I am competent to judge, a fair and accurate and well-documented account. Gladly therefore, do I commend the book.

If I am asked why we should trouble ourselves about the past, why should we not deal only with the present as it confronts us, I have my answer ready. I believe the study of history has its value in every department of human thinking and activity. It not only gives us valuable guidance, but it helps our frame of mind. First, it prevents hasty action, it compels thought and care in all effort at progress. Again the mistakes of the past would never have been made, the catastrophes would not have happened, if only careful planning and thinking had not all too often yielded to the precipitate and thoughtless impulse of the moment. Real progress comes slowly, it has come slowly in the past, it will come slowly again still.

But progress comes and the second great service that the study of history renders lies in the fact that it guards us from despair. Defeatism is all too common in these days, men's hearts fail them for fear, sometimes even in the most noble of quests, the highest of ambitions. There is danger that in our despair we should become deaf to the call to unity and the cause of the Kingdom should suffer. History is sometimes a tangled skein, but prayer and patience and persistent effort have unwound it in the past and we need courage to believe that they will do so in the future. The study of history helps to that courage.

In his first chapters, Dr. Carter sets out the history, helps to provide a remedy for despair, to guard against haste and then, in the last chapters of the book, he reaches his conclusions and draws his inferences. Every student of history does the same. Those of Dr. Carter deserve our respect and our consideration, for they have the backing of his learning and of his studious research, but he will not expect all who read his words to reach the same conclusions and draw the same inferences. He knows that on some points upon which he touches, he and I have in the past stood on different sides and yet he is kind enough to ask me to write this Foreword to his book. I believe he is not only kind but wise. There are differences amongst those who are united in thanking God for the many blessings we owe to the Reformation. Of course there are, for the revival of learning of necessity meant reasonable freedom of thought. There is danger today of hardening and narrowing in this respect, both amongst ourselves and in relation to those from whom we differ more greatly.

All too slowly we learn the lesson of our unhappy divisions and sometimes we are prone to accentuate them. Unity must always involve tolerance, a certain freedom within the larger loyalty. I am I hope no partisan, indeed as the years go by partisanship becomes to me more and more distasteful. It still cripples the Church in its task of winning the world for Christ. The task of the Church of Christ is great indeed, the challenge to it insistent. May God speed the day when all who love the Lord Jesus Christ shall be one in Him and realise their membership one of another. If we read this book with that thought in our minds in the study of its history we shall discover afresh the need for patient effort and indomitable hope amid the baffling problems of the world and the Church, and not least among them the problem, nay, the task of the reunion of the divided Church of Christ.

I wish this book a happy and useful life, born as it is just at the time when we are beginning to think of the three hundredth anniversary of the placing of the English Bible in our Anglican churches.

GUY MANCHESTER.

CHAPTER I

INTRODUCTION

The Reformation Movement in General.

THE ideal of the Papacy as the one great spiritual
and unifying influence in Christendom had
been sadly shattered long before the XVIth century.
The theory was a noble and beneficent one, and
in the semi-barbarous periods of the Middle Ages,
so full of national and tribal warfare, and of selfish
violence and misrule, it proved a powerful controlling
force towards order and national tranquility. It also
fostered a spirit of Christian brotherhood between man
and man and nation and nation. The definite claims of
the Pope, as head of the Universal Church, to dominate
and dictate to the different civil governments, and, as
Christ's Vicar, to act as a sort of spiritual Father to
kings and potentates, would in the hands of a powerful
reforming pope like Gregory VII, have proved a great
regenerating force. In theory the pope was to be accepted as the supreme ruler in Christendom, the arbiter
of its quarrels and the one who would decide on appeal
all international questions concerning peace and war.
He also was to be accepted as the one authority able to
see that justice and equity were administered in the
Courts of the various Nations. The Church was to be
the champion of the weak against the strong, of right
against might. It was to regenerate the brutal semi-
barbarous society of the time, not only by its proclam-
ations of Christian ideals and practices, but by its moral
discipline and spiritual jurisdiction over princes and

1

rulers. The Church, in short, was always to insist on the superiority of things spiritual to things temporal.

Certainly the conditions of the Middle Ages sadly needed such an authoritative and unifying force, and this partly accounts for the easy way in which the early popes were able to extend their claims to superior or supreme jurisdiction in Western Christendom, notwithstanding that these claims were built up on shameless forgeries. The manifest gain of possessing one recognised central authority was so attractive that the origins of the papal claims were not, in that uncritical age, carefully examined. Consequently Pope Boniface VIII, in 1303, dared to promulgate a Bull declaring that " it was absolutely necessary to salvation that every human creature should be subject to the Roman Pontiff " (Bull Unam Sanctam).

The pope was thus regarded as the supreme Head of the Church and therefore to be a member of the Church it was necessary to be in communion with the See of Rome. In fact, we may safely say that during the Middle Ages the idea of an independent National Church which owed no allegiance to the Pope as the Vicar of Christ on earth—the successor of St. Peter and thus the earthly head of the Church — was quite inconceivable in Western Christendom. Unfortunately, noble and beneficent as this ideal was, in practice it was completely discredited by the selfish and sordid methods of rapacity, deceit and treachery by which it was maintained. The popes claimed a temporal power, and accordingly they soon subordinated their spiritual aims to their ambitions and avaricious material interests as temporal Sovereigns. They engaged in European wars and did not scruple to exploit their spiritual claims in order to extort money from the faithful to accomplish their worldly designs. The ambition of most of the popes of the Middle Ages was to be, as a Venetian contemporary declared of Pope Julius II, " lords and masters of the game of the world." But just as popes used kings as pawns in their own game, so in their turn kings used popes, and the spectacle of the " Babylonish Captivity " (1305-77), when the papacy was completely dominated by the French monarchy, was a rude shock to the noble ideal of the Pope as the "spiritual father of Christendom." The supremacy of the papacy as a great moral power over the conscience of mankind, or as an impartial arbiter between nations, died in the Captivity of Avignon. This was practically illustrated by a current rhyme of the time which declared " Now is the Pope become French and Jesus become English, now will be seen who will do more, the Pope or Jesus."

We may also safely say that the ideal of the supreme universal dominion of the Pope received an inglorious interment during the papal Schism (1378-1417), when the two or three rival claimants for the papal See were levelling curses at the followers of their rivals.

Concurrently with this exploitation of Papal supremacy there was the alarming growth of practical and doctrinal abuses and corruptions in the Church. The simple worship and pure Scriptural beliefs of the early days of Christianity had been almost obscured by the multitude of ' dark and dumb ' ceremonies and superstitious practices and beliefs which abounded, and which were fostered and confirmed by current medieval doctrines. The extravagant homage given to the Blessed Virgin Mary and the Saints virtually amounted to a form of polytheism when each saint, as Erasmus declared, was regarded as a sort of deity possessing special powers. The excessive worldliness and ignorance of so many of the clergy had become a scandal admitted by all earnest churchmen. Various spiritual revivals, like the Dominican and the Franciscan in the XIIIth century, and the Lollard in the XIVth, had done something, but not very much, to check it for a time. The evil started from the top, since most of the popes of this pre-Reformation period were notoriously corrupt and venal and possessed few claims to real piety. The Papacy instead of being a commanding spiritual power receiving the well-merited homage and respect of Christendom, was regarded rather in the light of a vast agency for collecting money to defray the expenses, and satisfy the worldly aims and ambitions of the Papal Curia. Roger Bacon, in the XIIIth century, gives a most doleful

3

account of the general corruption of the Court of Rome in his day—" Laceratur enim illa sedes sacra fraudibus et dolis injustorum, perit justitia, pax omnis violatur, infinita scandalia suscitantur. Mores enim sequuntur ibidem pervissime regnat superbia ardet avaritia, invidia corrodit singulos luxuria diffamat totam illam curiam, qula in omnibus dominatur " (¹). Is it any wonder that he adds that " the whole clergy is intent upon pride, lechery and avarice."

Conditions had certainly not improved two centuries later when Colet denounced the bishops as being more like wolves than shepherds and ' as the slaves of vanity and avarice, who sold the sacraments and absolutions " (²).

Erasmus had described the clergy as those "whose brains are the rottenest, whose intellects the dullest and hearts the blackest he could conceive of." " They bray out the psalms," he says, " in churches like so many jackasses, they do not understand a word of them " (³).

With the medieval theory of the ' Treasury of Merits', as a sort of storehouse of the alleged supererogatory works of Christ and the Saints at the disposal of the Pope for the benefit of the faithful on earth and in purgatory through the purchase of Indulgences, a false mechanical idea of religion was undoubtedly encouraged. This demoralising system was also fostered by the doctrine of purgatory and of the power of the priest to deliver souls from its torments by the celebration of sacrifices of Masses. In fact, salvation had come to be almost exclusively dependent on the gift of the Church and normally all grace and pardon came through the sacrifice of the Mass and the sacrament of penance, both of which were dispensed exclusively by the priest. " God," said a medieval writer, " is more compassionate and generous through the priest than of Himself, for He does more kindnesses through him than through himself " (⁴). The very widespread belief in the power and efficacy of images and relics, and in pilgrimages to celebrated wonder-working shrines fostered the crudest superstitions. For instance, the " True blood of our Lord " was

4

exhibited at Hailes Abbey, while amongst the 5,000 relics at Wittenberg were pieces of the rods of Aaron and Moses and some ashes of the "Burning Bush." Even the earth of which Adam was formed was preserved for veneration!

Moreover, there is evidence that it was not only the simple and ignorant who were deceived in this way. For Bishop Latimer, who certainly was a learned priest, declares that for many years he thought "that divers images of saints could have holpen me and done me much good and delivered me out of my diseases" (⁵). Again the practical failure and the widespread corruption of the Monastic system had been a cause of complaint and scandal amongst churchmen for centuries. In defiance of the rule of poverty, the monasteries had amassed considerable wealth and were large feudal landlords, while the abbots and monks themselves too often lived lives of idle pleasure-seeking and luxury, if not of actual vice. Attempts at reform had always proved futile and ineffective. For one thing there were too many vested interests to be overcome. The monasteries were no longer, as at one time, homes of learning, literature, industry and pre-eminent piety. One of the most careful, competent and reliable authorities for this period of history tells us that all attempts to restore true discipline became increasingly difficult, so that "where the monk of 1200 had quietly declined discipline," the "monk of 1500 flatly refused obedience." He adds, that while there was "some real downward progress", "the monachism of 1500 was condemned, not so much for its actual sins of omission and commission, as for its gradual loss of faith in its own professed ideal, a faithlessness bred of centuries of failure" (⁶).

There is little doubt that the main cause of the corrupt state of the Church was the ignorance of Holy Scripture. The lay people generally were almost entirely ignorant of the Bible, except possibly for a few short extracts to be found mixed up with "uncertain stories and legends" in some popular book of devotion. There was, we should recall, no authorised translation of the Bible in English, and the versions attributed to

Wycliffe had been condemned as heretical. In fact, in spite of the statements of Sir Thomas More and modern Roman apologists like Cardinal Gasquet, there is little doubt that the medieval Church regarded the possession of the Scriptures in English as a mark of heresy. Sir Thomas More defended this view by declaring that the withholding of the Scriptures from the laity was of necessity, because of the "false translations." But Erasmus is frank enough to confess that men had been burned at the stake for advocating the circulation of the Bible in the vernacular, and he declares that "the theologians are careful that the sacred Scriptures shall be known to few lest their authority and their gains should be interfered with" (7). Jean Gerson, in the XVth century, had condemned the popular reading of the Scriptures because the common people had "not the wit nor the learning" to understand them and "so they ought to seek the law from the mouths of the priests." But it should not be forgotten that a Roman Council (of Toulouse) had in 1229 definitely forbidden the laity "to have the books of the old and new testament, except perhaps if anyone wishes to have for devotion the Psalter, or Breviary, for the divine offices or hours of Mary." Even amongst the clergy there was deplorable ignorance of the Scriptures. St. Thomas Aquinas, in the XIIIth century had complained of the inexperienced priests who could not speak Latin, and very few of whom "have learnt Holy Scripture," while Bishop Hooper in the XVIth century found that not half the clergy of his diocese could repeat the Ten Commandments. There is nothing gained by trying to paint too black a picture, and probably the nearest approach to truth on this question of the knowledge and circulation of Holy Scripture in pre-Reformation times is found in the careful and well-balanced statement of Dr. Coulton, who declares, from the fullest knowledge of the subject, that—

the best medieval writers knew their Vulgate very well, a great many more knew parts of it well enough—The average priest knew nothing outside the Service Books and not even all that was inside, the lower priesthood, as Roger Bacon and other equally credible witnesses testify, understood little or nothing

6

even of their Church offices . . . the most educated and ambitious of the laity seldom got far beyond the Psalms and the Sunday Gospels and Epistles. A few of the richest possessed Bibles in French or Psalters in French or English, but as soon as a general desire for vernacular translations arose it was opposed by the ecclesiastical authorities, and for the rest of the Middle Ages vernacular Bibles were either explicitly condemned or lay under a strong suspicion of heresy ([8]).

Many prominent and earnest churchmen, while absolutely loyal to medieval Catholic doctrines, deplored this degenerate condition of the Church, and were under no illusions as to its cause. Dean Colet fearlessly told Convocation in 1512 that the—

Church is become foul and deformed . . . . so that we seem able truly to say All things that are in the Church are either the lust of the flesh, the lust of the eyes or the pride of life. To sum up all in a word, every corruption, all the ruin of the Church, all the scandals of the world come from the coveteousness of the Priests ([9]).

Erasmus, one of the most prominent figures of the Renaissance Movement, and devoted to the Roman Church, used equally strong language ; and, as we have seen, he laid the chief blame on—

impious popes, who gave dispensations for the not preaching of Christ, adulterate the Gospel by their forced interpretations and undermining traditions and by their lusts and wickedness grieve the Holy Spirit and make their Saviour's wounds to bleed anew ([10]).

But while prominent and trustworthy churchmen felt compelled to speak thus strongly and despondingly, we cannot doubt that there must have been multitudes of genuinely pious people leading devout and holy lives. For Dr. Owst, in his recent valuable researches, has proved that during the XIVth and XVth centuries especially, the power of the medieval pulpit was considerable. Fiery and eloquent preachers denounced with apt illustration, invective and satire the moral abuses and evils, the self-indulgence and luxury of their day. It is impossible therefore to believe that these preachers of morality and righteousness made no impression on their hearers, even though their sermons effected nothing

7

in the shape of a widespread or permanent spiritual revival. We should, moreover, not forget, in this connection, the wonderful effects produced in Bohemia and Austria, by the fervent Apostolic zeal of such powerful and persuasive revivalist preachers as Milicz, of Cremsier. Conrad, of Waldhausen, and Mathias, of Janow, in the latter half of the XIVth century.

Dr. Owst tells us that the pulpit records of these days—

reveal a Church striving by word of mouth, however fitfully, to curb wild passions and vicious habits, to educate the masses in a higher way of life, to reunite a discordant Society in brotherly love and common service, to establish according to its lights a city of God upon earth in every home and community.

That such efforts very largely failed, the increasing degeneration and corruption of Church life affords only too painful evidence, and by the XVIth century things were probably at their worst. We can form a little idea of the low moral state of Society generally at that time from the lament of a leading Jesuit, who was ordered to Germany to counteract the Lutheran Movement. He reported that—

the apostacy of so many countries is to be attributed not to the garbled Scriptures, but to the scandalous lives of the clergy. Would to God there were in this city of Worms but two or three priests not living in concubinage, or guilty of other public or notorious crimes (11).

Like Colet, Erasmus felt that the one remedy for the corrupt state of the Church was a true knowledge of Scripture. He wished the Scriptures to be translated into every language so that the simple people—the husbandman at his plough and the weaver at his shuttle —could read them. " If the ship of the Church is to be saved from being swallowed up by the tempest, there is only one anchor that can save it, it is the heavenly Word which issuing from the bosom of the Father, lives, speaks and works still in the Gospel " (12). It was with this end in view that he published his new edition of the Greek Testament in 1516, with a scholarly Latin translation. The study of the Bible soon led many earnest

8

men both in England and on the Continent, and especially in Germany, to the conclusion that the reforms needed to purify the Church were not merely the removal of moral abuses and crude and ignorant and superstitious practices, but the rejection of doctrinal beliefs which had no Scriptural warrant. Therefore not only in England but also in European lands there arose, in the first quarter of the XVIth century, bodies of earnest doctrinal reformers anxious to restore the pure Gospel teaching and practice which characterised the Faith of the Apostolic and Primitive Church.

Again, it was this same study of Holy Scripture which at length gave men courage to break loose from the false and corrupting teaching and practices of the Medieval Church. Medieval Catholicism as a system was strongly entrenched. It possessed great strength from its unity, its perfected organisation, its practically unchallenged philosophy of life, its great wealth and privileges, its far-reaching temporal powers, and its exclusive supernatural claims. The Medieval Church was a very real force in the life of the people, since they very generally believed in the exclusive claims to supernatural power advanced by the clergy. Moreover, they greatly feared to disobey those who could withhold Indulgences and Absolution and virtually close the gates of Heaven against the sinners and disobedient. God, we must remember, was regarded in these days, rather in the light of an angry Potentate needing to be propitiated with an indefinite number of pilgrimages, fasts, penances, and masses, than as a loving Father longing to pardon penitent sinners on the merits of Christ's one sufficient sacrifice for sin. It is this mistaken view of God which explains Luther's early agony of soul in his desperate efforts to discover a ' Gracious God '.

But although the Medieval Church was apparently so strongly entrenched, the elements of its strength proved to be the seeds of its weakness, because they were supported mainly on the unstable foundations of ignorance and fear. Consequently when the Renaissance spirit of inquiry and investigation, combined with a serious study of the Scriptures, proved that the extravagant spiritual and temporal claims of the Pope had no Scriptural or historical basis, there was a rude awakening and a wide repudiation of papal ecclesiastical authority.

It is the main object of this treatise to discover how far this attack on Medieval *doctrines* as well as abuses, was indigenous in England or whether it was almost entirely the result of a similar movement on the Continent, and more especially in Germany and Switzerland. It is necessary therefore to make a passing reference to the influence of the Lollard movement on the Anglican doctrinal Reformation. For instance, was Lollardy a practically extinct and spent force in the early years of the XVIth century, or was there a considerable body of secret Lollards which formed the fertile soil that produced the large party of later doctrinal reformers? Henry Knighton's Continuator in the beginning of the XVth Century tells us that the Lollards were " then held in such great honour and had so multiplied, that you could hardly see two men passing in the road, but one of them shall be a disciple of Wycliffe " ([13]). This is probably an exaggeration, but it is sufficient to show the importance of the movement at that time. In spite of their severe persecution under Henry IV, the Lollards still continued to be very numerous, and to hold their secret gatherings for worship. There were also evidently a goodly company of them in 1449, when Bishop Pecock endeavoured to confound their heretical teaching in his book the " Repressor of Overmuch Blaming of the Clergy," which, singularly enough, was the ground for his own condemnation for heresy.

But the continuance of Lollardy or ' heresy,' is shown by the prosecutions which are recorded not only throughout the century, but also in the early years of the next. The movement was mainly supported by the lower middle class and had largely been driven under ground, while it had often embraced some crude and radical political as well as religious ideas. But it was by no means stamped out, and in 1525 Bishop Tunstal told Erasmus that Luther's teaching was merely a revival of Lollard views —" there was nothing new in it, but that it simply put new weapons in the hands of *already existing* bands of

10

Wyclif heretics " ([14]). Moreover, the fact that over 170 manuscripts of Wycliffe's condemned hand copied translations of the Scriptures have survived to our own day is sufficient evidence of the very numerous and widely scattered followers of Wycliffe's teaching. It would also give us good reason to assume that this teaching must have persisted to the time when the later Reformation movement had begun. Dr. Gairdner has declared that the Lollards remained a latent power in the land and " that they mingled with and domineered over the Reformation though they did not bring it on " ([15]). Even if we may question the truth of the *first* statement, there is no reason to doubt the accuracy of the *last*, since the early doctrinal Reformers seem to have had no direct association with Lollardy or its teaching.

We should therefore be inclined to say that the scanty evidence we possess points to a considerable number of secret disciples of Wycliffe's teaching still flourishing at the time of Luther's revolt, and of the revived study of the New Testament in England. This fresh interest in the Scriptures was due mainly to Dean Colet's lectures on St. Paul's Epistles and to Erasmus's edition of the Greek New Testament, in 1516. Foxe relates the great stir made to put down heresy which was spreading widely " in divers and sundry quarters of this realm " in 1520 and 1521. And, as he says, " this was before the name of Luther was heard of in these countries among the people." These ' heretics ' were called the ' known ' or ' just fast men ', a name which had previously been bestowed on the Lollards whose opinions they held. Foxe declares that their teaching, which was that of the Apostles, had been received of a great number long before Luther's day, and that—

the Church of England has not lacked great multitudes who tasted and followed the sweetness of God's Holy Word, almost in as ample manner, for the number of well disposed hearts, as now . . . the fervent zeal of those Christian days seems much superior to these our days and times ; as manifestly may appear by their sitting up all night in reading and hearing, also by their expenses and charges and buying of books in English . . . some gave a load of hay for a few chapters of St. James or St. Paul in English.

In spite of the want of teachers and books, Foxe " greatly marvelled to consider how the word of truth did multiply so exceedingly among them " ([16]). There is little doubt that these humble ' known ' men or Lollards, would welcome this new movement and that they accelerated the doctrinal Reformation which it produced and greatly swelled the ranks of its adherents. But they did not apparently contribute any outstanding characters who stood forward as pioneers of this Scriptural Reformation.

A recent scholarly work has endeavoured to prove that Lollardy represents an earlier and a completely different tradition from that of the later type of Continental Protestantism, whether Lutheran or Calvinistic. The latter, it is contended, was essentially a ' High Church ' movement placing supreme value on its connection with historic, Catholic Christianity. This thesis asserts, on the other hand, that Lollardy completely discarded historic Christianity and that Wycliffe is thus the real Father of English Protestantism, and of the old ' English dissenting tradition ' which never accepted the ' High Church ' principles of the Anglican Reformers. This true Protestant ' tradition,' we are told, spread later to America through the English ' Separatists' and it has thus formed the background of American culture ([16]). Far too little definite historical evidence is, however, offered to support this theory, whereas there is ample proof that, in its main essential doctrines, Wyclifite teaching definitely anticipated the special doctrines and principles of the later Anglican Reformers, such as the reading of Scripture in English, the denunciation of pilgrimages, invocation of saints, and of the Real or Corporal Presence of Christ in the Sacrament of the Eucharist.

CHAPTER II

THE ENGLISH CHURCH AND LUTHERANISM UNDER HENRY VIII

THERE is little question that the Renaissance Movement, in spite of the revolution it had created in scholarship, had done very little to cleanse the Church of its moral abuses, and internal corruption. Dr. Gairdner, sympathetic as he is with this Movement, states that—

it may be questioned whether the Revival of Letters, when it reached England, did very much for a reformation of morals. The Humanists were not on the whole remarkable for moral fervour and the new impulse had in it very little of a religious character. In truth it created in many far too much admiration of that ancient Pagan civilisation whose secrets it brought to light (1).

But by its restless spirit of inquiry and its search for knowledge and truth and its revival of accurate scholarship, it had unintentionally promoted a far more radical movement for *reform of doctrine* as well as of worship. In Switzerland this had led to the teaching of Zwingli and in Germany to the teaching and revolt of Luther from current orthodoxy.

We have now to examine how far the later Lutheran Movement affected the English doctrinal reformation. At first the two movements were closely allied, but it would scarcely be correct to affirm that the English movement was entirely dependent on the Lutheran or would never have been heard of without it. Apart from the considerable number of ' known ' men, or secret Lollards, who were almost entirely lacking in organisation, leadership or scholarship, there was a rising body of young scholars at the Universities who were anxious for a religious reformation, even before the Lutheran movement had touched England, which was not till 1517.

Cardinal Gasquet declares that at this date " the Lollards as a body, had been long extinct " in England ([2]). But the fact that Bishop Longland, of Lincoln, arrested nearly 500 Lollards as late as 1521 is sufficient to discredit such a statement. Even though Dr. Gairdner may be correct that " Lollardy was not the beginning of modern Protestantism," it certainly must have played some part in it. In any case the evidence does not support Cardinal Gasquet's contention that English Protestantism was entirely of foreign origin —" the work both of raising the seed and of scattering it over the soil of England, must be attributed, if the plain facts of history are to be believed, to Germans and the handful of English followers of the German Reformers " ([3]). But the " plain facts of history " tell us that this ' handful ' of English doctrinal Reformers anticipated and did not *follow* the German movement. We do not know the exact date when Tyndale went up to Oxford. It was probably about 1504, but in any case it was several years before Lutheranism or Lutheran writings had reached or influenced England. Foxe, in his life of Tyndale, tells us that—

at Oxford Tyndale grew up and increased . . . especially in the knowledge of the Scriptures, whereunto his mind was singularly addicted, insomuch that he lying then in Magdalen Hall, read privily to certain students and fellows of Magdalen College some parcel of divinity. instructing them in the knowledge and truth of the Scriptures ([4]).

From Oxford Tyndale went to Cambridge and there became " further ripened in the knowledge of God's Word." This account makes it fairly clear that Tyndale did not owe his special religious outlook to Luther, but to his own deep personal study of the Word of God. It was in fact the study of the Word of God, more than anything else, which produced the English doctrinal Reformation. There is every reason to assert that Tyndale's spiritual awakening or ' conversion ' was due

14

to the earnest, careful and fearless study of Holy Scripture, to which he had probably been inclined by the lectures which Erasmus, and also Colet, gave on the New Testament. We can imagine with what warm approbation these words of Erasmus would be read by Tyndale and the secret Lollard ' Gospellers '—

" I am content," wrote Erasmus " That my book be deficient in acuteness, if only it be pious. Let it be unserviceable for theological debating, provided it be useful for religious living. . . . Amid the general darkness that prevails . . . in such a conflict of human opinions, to what refuge shall we flee sooner than to that truly sacred anchorage of Evangelical doctrine ? "

It was also about the year 1522 that Tyndale determined to translate the Scriptures into English even *before* Luther's Bible of that year was known either to Tyndale or in England.

It is quite clear that Tyndale, Bilney and Fryth, were earnestly engaged in studying Erasmus' Greek Testament and imparting its precious truths to others before Luther's writings had reached England ; and there is every reason to believe that the English doctrinal movement would have persisted, even though at a much slower and more chequered pace, apart from the work of the foreign Reformers. But at the same time there is no doubt whatever that the writings of Luther exerted a profound influence and acted as a powerful stimulus to the doctrinal reformation in England, so that the special tenets and principles of Luther were, as we shall see, welcomed and accepted by the little company of English scholars who were dissatisfied with the received ' Catholic ' doctrine. There is abundant evidence to show that the two movements worked hand in hand and were closely allied. We know that Luther's writings had reached England as early as 1520, and that his treatises on the " Babylonish Captivity of the Church " and " The Address to the Christian Nobility of the German Nation ", were being read in England in 1521. They had already aroused the attention and condemnation of the ecclesiastical authorities. For on May 12, 1521, a solemn holocaust of Luther's books was carried out by

Wolsey's orders in St. Paul's Churchyard. But it is also evident that this spectacular destruction of 'heretical' books, as well as their strict prohibition, did little to retard their circulation in England. The books of Luther and other prominent foreign Reformers, like Zwingli, Bucer, and Melanchthon, continued to circulate and to find warmly appreciative readers in this country. In 1519 an " Index "of Prohibited Books was published. Henry VIII also wrote exhorting the princes of Saxony to repress, if necessary ' with blood,' " that execrable sect of Luther," while Hugh Latimer, in 1524, in his thesis for his Cambridge B.D., bitterly attacked the teachings of Philip Melanchthon. Lutheran opinions were making distinct headway in the Universities. Conferences for Bible study, probably somewhat on the lines of the modern ' Oxford Groups,' were being held in several of the Cambridge Colleges, and a common meeting place of these disciples was soon nicknamed ' Germany.' At least 27 young scholars, including many leading men, who later were called on to suffer for their faith, like Barnes, Fryth, Bilney, Latimer and Ridley, were soon ardent supporters of this spiritual revival. Oxford was likewise ' infected,' since a number of zealous ' Lutherans ' migrated thither from Cambridge to help Wolsey form his new foundation of ' Cardinal College.'

Tyndale's New Testament published in 1525 was secretly disseminated by these zealous disciples, and even the Archbishop (Warham) became alarmed at the growth of this new movement. " One or two cankered members have," he declared to Wolsey, " induced no small number of young and incircumspect fools to give ear to them." The entire band was therefore arrested and rigorously confined in unhealthy prisons, and in consequence several died. One or two others escaped and several were compelled to recant publicly.

This desire for a spiritual and doctrinal Reformation, although it had a native origin, was undoubtedly fostered and greatly accelerated by the contemporary spiritual awakening in Germany. Moreover, at this stage the Lutheran movement provided much of the driving force behind its English counterpart and was in closest association with it.

It is well, therefore, to notice more in detail the extent to which Tyndale was influenced by Lutheran teaching. Was he a mere follower of, and borrower from the great German Reformer ? We should remember that Tyndale went to London in 1523 with the vain hope of securing the protection and patronage of Bishop Tunstall to enable him to pursue his work of translating the New Testament. Repulsed by the Bishop of London, he spent six months under the roof of the hospitable and secretly sympathetic City merchant, Humphrey Monmouth ; and it was probably during this period that Tyndale found opportunity to read the proscribed writings of Luther. There is little doubt that the clear and fearless Scriptural teaching of these treatises would incline him to look to Luther rather than to Erasmus as his future guide and leader.

In May, 1524, Tyndale left England for Hamburg, and after this date his movements are uncertain until we have proof of his presence in Hamburg again in April, 1525. There has been much speculation as to where he actually was during this year, and most authorities agree in deciding that he was not in Hamburg, for the simple reason that there was then no printer there, and yet it was during this interval that he printed the Gospels of St. Matthew and St. Mark. It has therefore been conjectured that Tyndale employed this time in visiting Luther at Wittenburg. In support of this, there is the fact that one of the articles of accusation brought a few years later against Humphrey Monmouth was—" Thou wert privy and of counsel that the said Tyndale ... went into Almayne (Germany) to Luther, there to study and learn his sect." And it is significant that Monmouth did not deny this charge. As additional support for this theory, we find that Sir Thomas More declares in his ' Dialogue,' that " Tyndale as soon as he got him hence, got him to Luther straight, and that at the time of his translation of the New Testament, Tyndale was with Luther at Wittenberg and the confederacy between him and Luther was well known." It is true that Tyndale denies

17

such 'confederacy'; but More still insisted that he was with Luther when translating the New Testament. Cochlæus, the spy, who was the means of preventing Tyndale from printing his translation at Cologne, also declares that "Tyndale and Roye had both been sometime at Wittenberg"; John Foxe, also, in his Life of Tyndale, affirms that "on his first departing out of this realm, he took his journey into the further parts of Germany, as into Saxony, where he had conference with Luther and other learned men in those quarters" (5).

Uniform testimony from such diverse sources can scarcely be neglected, and we are fairly safe therefore in concluding that Tyndale did visit Luther at Wittenberg at this time, and that from there he went to Cologne with the object of getting his precious manuscript printed there. He was, however, discovered and had to fly to Worms in September, 1525, and from there his New Testament was sent to England in 1526. It seems fairly evident, therefore, that Tyndale had some collaboration with Luther, and it is generally admitted that he had Luther's Bible before him when he was engaged in his own translation. For instance, his Marginal Notes are very largely Luther's. Mr. Demaus, in his careful and scholarly biography of Tyndale, declares that a comparison of Luther's and Tyndale's translations of the Pentateuch reveals two "plain and indisputable facts"—"that Tyndale had Luther's work before him and constantly consulted and occasionally adopted it, and that he never implicitly follows Luther, but translates from the original with the freedom of a man who had perfect confidence in his own scholarship" (6). Bishop Westcott, in his ' History of the English Bible,' corroborates this view and emphasises Tyndale's "complete independence" as a scholarly translator. "From first to last," he declares, "his style and his interpretation are his own, and in the originality of Tyndale is included in a large measure the originality of our English version" (7). Dr. Jacobs, in his valuable work on the "Lutheran Movement in England," is inclined to question this verdict, and he certainly tabu-

18

lates some cases of close resemblance in the two translations, especially in St. Paul's Epistles.

But Tyndale himself, in his ' Epistle to the Reader,' set forth with his first New Testament in 1526, is careful to assert his own originality as a translator. " He had," he said, " no man to counterfeit (or imitate) neither was he helped with English of any that had interpreted the same, or such like thing in Scripture before time" ([8]). There is little question that Tyndale borrowed considerably from Luther, especially in his comments or glosses on the text of Scripture and more particularly in his " Doctrinal Treatises." His ' Parable of the wicked Mammon " is really a Scriptural defence and exposition of Luther's doctrine of Justification by faith. Again a great deal of the ' Prologues ' of the different New Testament books in Tyndale's Bible are translated from Luther's German Bible. But Tyndale always used his own independent judgment and was not afraid of opposing Luther's personal views. This was apparent when he differed entirely from the great German Reformer in regarding the Epistles to the Hebrews and of James to be of apostolic authority. With regard to Hebrews, he was of opinion that it was written by an Apostle or in the Apostles' time or near unto. Seeing " the epistle agreeth to all the rest of Scripture, why should it not be authority and taken for Holy Scripture ? " ([9]).

Similarly, although Tyndale admits that James does not witness to the saving work of Christ, but merely to a " general faith in God," yet in spite of Luther's rejection of it, he declares that " it hath many good and godly sentences in it . . . and ought of right to be taken for holy Scripture " ([9]).

We should not forget that although Tyndale's translation was so vigorously condemned, it became a few years later, though in a slightly different form, the authorised version for general public reading. It is one of the ironies of fate that Tyndale was not permitted to see this triumph. For the ' Great Bible ' issued by Royal authority in 1539 was virtually Tyndale's translation, completed by Coverdale's version of the Old

Testament, including the Apocrypha. The Coverdale portion starts from the Book of Ezra. Coverdale's version was based on the Vulgate compared with Luther's German translation. Thus the official English Bible was considerably indebted to Luther's labours, even though it had on it the distinct hall mark of Tyndale's original scholarship.

It is instructive to notice in passing, Tyndale's very definite repudiation of the popular allegorical interpretation of Scripture—"We have need," he says, "to take heed everywhere that we be not beguiled with false allegories, whether they be drawn out of the New Testament or the Old." Finally, he adds "beware of allegories ; for there is not a more handsome or apt thing to beguile withal than an allegory " [10]. It is also rather surprising to find at this period such a clear enunciation of what is often supposed to be a modern discovery of the ' progressive revelation ' in Scripture. Speaking of the ceremonies of the Mosaic dispensation, Tyndale says, "The ceremonies were not permitted, only, but also commanded of God ; to lead the people in *the shadows of Moses and the night of the Old Testament* until the light of Christ and day of the new Testament were come," as "children are led in the fantasies of youth, until the discretion of man's age be come upon them " [10]. Again in his Prologue to Leviticus he emphasizes this truth—"such ceremonies were unto them as an A.B.C. to learn to spell and read, and as a nurse to feed them with milk and pap, and to speak unto them after their own capacity, and to lisp the words unto them, according as the babes and children of that age might sound them again " [10].*

But although Tyndale probably owed much to Luther, it would be untrue to assert that his opinions and outlook were entirely ' Lutheran.' His agreements with the German Reformer were due more to accident

---

*But we should remember that Tyndale, in expounding this ' accommodation ' view of the interpretation of the Mosaic narratives, was only following in the footsteps of John Colet, who had explained the account of the Creation on lines first set forth by Origen and by Dionysius of Alexandria.

than to conscious design. They arose from the common basic principle of the English and Continental Reformations, of the supreme authority of Scripture in the Church. As Tyndale says of his "Parable of the Wicked Mammon "—" If God's Word bear record unto it, God thanks. If God's Word condemn it, then hold it accursed *and so do all other doctrines* " ([10]).

On the burning question of the Eucharist Tyndale was not 'Lutheran,' although he was anxious to avoid any controversy or appearance of disagreement on this crucial subject. He pleaded with John Fryth—"meddle as little as you can with the presence of Christ's body in the sacrament, that there appear no division among us," and he urged that " the right use should be preached and the Presence to be an indifferent thing "—" To believe," he said, " that the body of Christ is everywhere, though it cannot be proved, hurts no man that worships him nowhere save in the faith of the Gospel " ([10]). But his own view of a spiritual presence to the faith of the recipient, is quite clear.

The bread, broken and eaten in the supper . . . putteth us in remembrance of His death . . . and thus we have Christ present in the inward eye and sight of faith. We eat his body and drink his blood, that is, we surely believe that his body was crucified for our sins, and his blood shed for our salvation ([11]).

Another prominent Reformer who from the first was included in the little band of so-called 'Lutheran' Cambridge men, who met at the 'Germany' or White Horse Inn, was John Fryth. He was a learned young scholar and migrated, with a number of other scholarly young men to Oxford to help in the newly founded 'Cardinal College' which Wolsey had started there.

This little company of learned graduates was soon accused of 'heresy,' and its members were imprisoned. When Fryth at length regained his freedom, he escaped abroad and joined Tyndale. After two years he was rash enough to return to England, and was enticed by a false friend to write his opinions on the Eucharist. This treatise was shown to Sir Thomas More, and he was then accused of heresy, and in the end, in 1533, burned at the stake, for opinions which he had never even taught. It was a peculiarly gross act of persecution and tyranny, since Fryth was, for those days, singularly devoid of the spirit of controversy. He had no desire to denounce the current views of transubstantiation or to interfere with the sincere beliefs of others, if only such teaching were not made a ' necessary article of faith.' He did not apparently hold the Lutheran view of Consubstantiation, but, provided that the sacrament was not worshipped, " he was content to permit every man to judge of the sacrament, as God should put into their hearts, and no side to condemn or despise the other but to nourish in all things brotherly love and to bear another's infirmity " ([12]). Such enlightened and tolerant views have scarcely yet been fully practised, but they were entirely foreign to the spirit of that age, otherwise the pages of Church history would not record the fratricidal crimes of Christians persecuting their fellow believers merely for their conscientious opinions.

Another of Tyndale's early companions at Cambridge, who also welcomed the new Lutheran teaching, was Thomas Bilney—" Little Bilney " as Latimer calls him. But although holding what were then described as ' Lutheran ' views, he does not seem to have come into any personal contact with Luther himself. His conversion was due to his study of Erasmus' Greek Testament—" At last," he says, " I heard speak of Jesus, even then when the New Testament was set forth by Erasmus " ([13]). But we are told that " a perusal of Erasmus's New Testament *and the works of Luther*, taught him other views of religion, and he embraced the teachings of the Reformers except the denial of transubstantiation " ([14]). Yet another early Lutheran sympathiser was Robert Barnes. He was educated at the University of Louvain and then at Cambridge.

He was made Master and Prior of the Augustine monastery at Cambridge. A learned scholar and a great student of Scripture and a D.D., he was converted to Evangelical views through Bilney. He was one of the original band of Lutheran ' gospellers ' who met for discussion and bible study at the 'White Horse,' in Cambridge. We get a striking illustration of the danger of these clandestine gatherings from the statement of Foxe that "this house especially was chosen, because many of them of St. John's, the King's College and the Queen's College came in *on the back side*." Barnes was accused of heresy for a sermon which he preached in 1536, and was ordered to recant by the Vice-Chancellor. He was brought before Cardinal Wolsey for animadverting on Wolsey's ostentatious display of pomp and wealth, as out of harmony with his Christian calling. He was persuaded to abjure his 'heresy,' but he was imprisoned for six months, when by a clever ruse of feigning to drown himself, he managed to escape to Antwerp. From here he visited Luther at Wittenberg and studied with him and was soon in great favour with the leading German Reformers—Luther, Melanchthon, and Justus Jonas. Thomas Cromwell persuaded him to return to England in 1531. He was then employed on several occasions by Henry VIII for political ends in his negotiations with the Protestant Princes of Germany. In furtherance of these designs Henry was induced to engage officially in Conferences with the prominent Lutheran divines with the object of reaching a religious concordat. Barnes was selected, with Bishop Foxe, and Dr. Heath, to take part in these negotiations with Luther and Melanchthon in 1535. In 1539 Barnes went as Henry's ambassador to arrange the marriage between the King and the Duke of Cleves' daughter. But after the abrupt conclusion of this unfortunate matrimonial alliance, Barnes was apprehended and later on was burned for heresy. He was evidently a wholehearted Lutheran and Luther translated his Confession of Faith into German.

A celebrated pupil of Barnes, when he was Prior of the Augustine monastery, was Miles Coverdale. Although it does not appear that he ever saw Luther, his sympathies and religious convictions were strongly 'Lutheran,' and he was on most intimate terms of friendship with the leading 'Reformed' Continental divines. He learned Evangelical truth from Barnes and

23

he was associated with the early ' Germany ' students, such as Bilney, Stafford and Latimer. He had sufficient zeal and courage to give moral support to his former Master, when Barnes was haled before Wolsey for heresy. It seems probable that on the execution of Barnes in 1540, Coverdale left England for Germany. He resided first at Tubingen, where he got his D.D. degree. He then went to Berzabern, in the duchy of Deux Ponts, where he acted as a schoolmaster and pastor for about eight years. He returned to England in Edward VI's reign and was consecrated Bishop of Exeter in 1551, but was deprived by Queen Mary in 1553 and imprisoned, and only released two years later on the personal appeal of the King of Denmark. He then prudently went abroad and soon returned to Berzabern until the accession of Elizabeth. He joined in the consecration of Archbishop Parker but refused the see of Llandaff which was then offered him. He maintained, while abroad, the closest and most affectionate relationship with Conrad Hubert, the Lutheran minister at Strasburg and he calls both Bucer and Peter Martyr his ' most excellent preceptors.' His translations of Scripture were original and not borrowed from Tyndale, but he certainly consulted Luther's German translation, while his ' Ghostly Psalms ' were largely Lutheran. He is another definite Anglican link with the German Reformation.

It is important to notice the extent to which the great leader of the English Reformation—Thomas Cranmer—was influenced by Lutheranism. Although Cranmer was greatly affected by Lutheran teaching, and had married, as his second wife, the niece of Osiander, a Lutheran divine, it would scarcely be correct to describe him as a wholehearted Lutheran in his views. For instance, he never seems to have held the special Lutheran doctrine of consubstantiation, but to have gone from transubstantiation to a ' receptionist ' view, closely akin to that held by the Swiss Reformed divines. He himself attributed his Eucharistic views to the teaching of Ridley, who was converted to them through reading the IXth century book of Ratramnus or Bertram, on the subject—De corpore et sanguine domini—

Cranmer told Brookes, at his Examination, that in 1538 he believed differently, in fact ' maintained the papists' doctrine ' about the Eucharist " until my lord of London, doctor Ridley, did confer with me, and by sundry persuasions and authorities of doctors drew me quite from my opinion " [15]. The nearest approach to Lutheran views which Cranmer made are to be found in what is described as ' Cranmer's Catechism.' In reality this was a translation set forth by Cranmer's order of a Catechism in German (based on Luther's Shorter Catechism) translated into Latin by Justus Jonas. Cranmer had an English translation of the Latin published in his own name, and thus clothed it with his imprimatur. As Strype says " he owned it for his own book," and Dr. Rowland Taylor, Cranmer's Chaplain, admitted it was " not of his own making yet he set it forth in his own name " [16].

The translation from the Latin was not, however, exact, and the English version introduces new matter to the extent of an additional thirty pages. Some of the variations are rather significant in their modification of what could be cited as ' Lutheran ' teaching. Again in the Latin there is the question " Quid est sacramentum altaris ? " This is translated " What is the Communion or *Lord's Supper* ? " In the Latin answer we have, " It is the true body and the true blood of our Lord Jesus Christ, *sub pane et vino*." The English renders this " under the form of bread and wine." But the English translation teaches plainly that " We ought to believe that in the Sacrament we receive truly the body and blood of Christ " and that " we eat and drink his very body and blood, although man's reason cannot comprehend how and after what manner the same is there present " [16]. This statement concerning the inability to define the manner of the Presence, is virtually contradicted by the further ambiguous assertion that " Christ causeth his body and blood to be in the Sacrament *after that manner and fashion*, as it was at that time, when He made His Maundy with His disciples." Again, in explaining the need of self examination before communicating, and especially of forgiving our neighbours, the Catechism declares that in this way " we worthily receive the body and blood of Christ and eat and drink the body and blood of Christ *spiritually* " ([16]). Although these views seem, at least patient of the Lutheran teaching of Consubstantiation, yet Cranmer denied, at his Examination before Martin, that he ever held the Lutheran view of the Eucharist. When twitted by Bishop Gardiner and Dr. Smith about the inconsistency of the teaching of this Catechism with the teaching in his ' Defence ' of his book on the Sacrament, Cranmer replied " In that Catechism I teach not (as you do) that the body and blood of Christ is contained in the Sacrament being reserved, but that in the *ministration thereof* we receive the body and blood of Christ whereunto if it may please you to add or understand this word (spiritually) then is the doctrine of my Catechism sound and good in all men's ears, which know the true doctrine of the sacraments." Even if this explanation of the definite language of the ' Catechism ' may seem rather forced and unconvincing, yet Cranmer insisted that Dr. Smith reported ' untruly of him ' " that in that booke (Catechism) I did set forth the real presence of Christ's body in the Sacrament " And he adds in proof that in 1548 he held no such view, " This I confess that not *long before* I wrote the said Catechism, I was in that error of the real Presence, as in many years past in divers other errors as of transubstantiation, of the sacrifice propitiatory of the priests in the Masse . . ." ([17]). Evidently, therefore, Cranmer never admitted any adherence to Lutheran teaching on the Eucharist, although it is probable that an unprejudiced reader of this Catechism would endorse Archbishop Laurence's statement that " the doctrine of the Eucharist contained in this Catechism is completely Lutheran " ([18]).

Certainly a contemporary foreigner studying at Oxford at the time this Catechism was issued so interpreted its teaching, although we must bear in mind that John ab Ulmis knew no English and may have based his remarks only on hearsay evidence. But in August, 1548, only a month after its publication, ab Ulmis wrote to Henry Bullinger, that—

this Thomas has fallen into a heavy slumber. For he has lately published a Catechism in which he has not only approved that foul and sacrilegious transubstantiation of the papists in the holy supper of our Saviour, but all the dreams of Luther seem to him sufficiently well grounded, perspicuous and lucid.

Ab Ulmis could not read the English translation of this Catechism and it is obvious from his statement about transubstantiation, that the reports which he had heard about its teaching, were grossly exaggerated. In fact only four months later he discovered his mistake, since he then tells Bullinger that the " abominable and silly opinion of a carnal eating had long since been banished and entirely done away with. Even that Thomas (Cranmer) himself . . . is in great measure recovered from his lethargy " [19]. Cranmer, as we have already seen, declared that ' not long before ' he published the Catechism, he held the doctrine of the Real Presence, but it is certainly open to question, from the language employed in it on the Eucharist, whether at that time he did not still hold it. Soames would seem to have accurately summed up his teaching when he says, " it does not plainly assert transubstantiation, and therefore there is reason to believe that when Cranmer published this piece, he was beginning to waver upon the subject of that doctrine " [20].

Mr. C. H. Smyth in his scholarly treatise on ' Cranmer ' labours at much length to prove that the Archbishop entirely repudiated what he describes as the distinctive ' Zwinglian ' view of the Eucharist, because he taught that " Christ's flesh and blood be in the sacrament truly present, but spiritually and sacramentally, not carnally and corporally. And as he is truly present, so is he truly eaten and drunken and assisteth us " [21]. It is singular that there is such a common misrepresentation of the Eucharistic teaching of Zwingli ; although it is probably due to an exclusive attention to his emphasis on the commemorative aspect of the Lord's Supper. But Zwingli taught, in language almost identical with that of Cranmer, a true spiritual and sacramental Presence of Christ in the Eucharist. " I believe," said Zwingli, " that in the Holy Eucharist the real body of

Christ is present to the eye of faith, that is, to those who thank the Lord for the benefits conferred on us in Christ His Son." Again in his address to Francis I, "Christum credimus vere esse in coena, immo non esse Domini coenam nisi Christum adsit . . . verum Christi corpus credimus in coena sacramentaliter et spiritualiter edi a religiosa et sancta mente," " ut Chrysostomus sentit." Consequently Bishop Hooper was substantially correct when, in 1549, he told Bullinger that Cranmer " entertains right views as to the nature of Christ's Presence in the Supper . . . his sentiments respecting the Eucharist are pure and religious and *similar to yours in Switzerland* " ([22]).

But although this digression on Cranmer's Eucharistic views would seem to prove that he never actually held or taught Consubstantiation, yet he was in close and most friendly touch with the Lutheran Movement in Germany. It was before Cranmer was appointed to Canterbury, while he was acting as Henry VIII's ambassador in Germany, specially in connection with the legitimacy of Henry's marriage with Catharine of Aragon, that Cranmer was brought into close touch with Lutheranism. At Nuremburg he met Osiander, the Lutheran pastor, and had frequent conferences with him on theological questions. In fact, an intimate friendship sprang up between them, one result of which was that Cranmer, then a widower, married Osiander's niece. She came over secretly in 1534 and remained in England with him for five years until in 1539, the stringent regulation regarding celibacy for the clergy in the ' Act of Six Articles ' compelled Cranmer to send her back to Germany for a time. A close friendship also had been commenced between Cranmer and Melanchthon. In 1535 Melanchthon had shown his respect for, and high opinion of Cranmer's learning and judgement, in seeking his views on a book on the existing religious controversies. He also commended to the Archbishop a number of eminent and learned foreigners whom Cranmer hospitably received in England. The chief of these were Aless, Gualter, Dryander, Eusebius Mennius, and Justus Jonas junior. In 1548 Cranmer proposed a scheme to Melanchthon which affords us a very clear ' outward and visible sign ' of the concord and fellowship existing between adherents of Reformation teaching in England and abroad. It was nothing less than a sort of international Conference of Protestants—a Synod of all learned divines—to draw up " a common confession and harmony of faith and doctrine drawn out of the pure Word of God," so as to unite better all the Protestant Churches, especially on such controversial subjects as the doctrine of the Eucharist, the divine decrees and Church government. Such a project is evidence in itself that Cranmer regarded the Anglican and foreign Reformers as possessing practically a common doctrinal outlook. He wanted this Synod to meet in England, as the safest place at the time. He invited Bullinger and Calvin, as well as Melanchthon. Calvin pleaded physical weakness and infirmity, although he declared that " if he might be of any use he would not grudge to pass over ten seas for the purpose." Melanchthon fully approved of the proposal and very wisely pleaded against the use of obscure or ambiguous phraseology, that " ambiguities might not hereafter occasion new differences." This common practice of issuing Concordats capable of a double interpretation has proved the pitfall of nearly all religious conferences on Christian doctrine or unity down to the present day. For ' agreement ' has too often been apparently achieved on an unreal basis of equivocal terminology. Melanchthon urged strongly that their conclusions should be expressed with " all the perspicuity and distinctness imaginable." Bucer, on the other hand, was in favour of some obscurity and indefiniteness of expression especially on the sacrament of the Eucharist.

That Cranmer was regarded as a warm friend and apologist for the German Lutherans, was evidenced by the accusations of some of his opponents in 1543. They asserted that " he kept up a constant correspondence with Germany and that he gave a great many exhibitions in Germany and had many pensioners there." Probably this statement implies that Cranmer assisted Lutheran students to come to England, like the modern ' Rhodes scholar,' to study at the Universities. But at all events it is definite evidence of the close fellowship and friendship in religion between Cranmer and the Lutherans.

Another prominent English churchman attracted to Lutheranism was the proto-martyr of Mary's reign, prebendary John Rogers. He had been chosen by the Merchant Venturers of Antwerp as their Chaplain and while there he met both Tyndale and Coverdale, and, according to Foxe, it was owing to his reading the Scriptures with them that he was converted to the Evangelical faith. He moved to Wittenberg in 1536 and for 10 years ministered to a Lutheran church there with much acceptance and ability. In fact, it has been asserted that he was ordained there. . . If this is true, it might well mean that he lacked episcopal Orders? But it is scarcely likely that he would have been rector of a London church and Chaplain in Antwerp without previous ordination in England. Foxe only rather cryptically states of this German pastorate—" he then being orderly called," which may or may not imply episcopal ordination. In 1547 he returned to England and Bishop Ridley appointed him a prebendary of St. Paul's Cathedral. He had inherited Tyndale's manuscripts, and completed Tyndale's Bible by adding the missing Old Testament books from Coverdale's translation. He then set it forth under the name of ' Thomas Matthewe,' since Tyndale's name was ' anathema ' in England at the time.

But not only were there these examples of friendly intercourse and association with Lutherans on the part of prominent Anglican churchmen during Henry VIII's reign, there were also other attempts and approaches made towards Lutheranism of a more official nature on the part of Church and State. The Divorce question was the first occasion which brought Henry VIII into direct friendly contact with Lutherans, through his anxiety to obtain the opinion of Lutheran divines on the legitimacy of his marriage with Catharine of Aragon. As early as 1531 Friar Barnes visited Wittenberg as Henry's Commissioner for this purpose, when Melanchthon's desire to placate Henry actually led him to countenance polygamy as an 'emergency' measure to satisfy the "King's conscience and the needs of the Kingdom." There is little doubt that the political necessities of the Lutherans inclined some, at least, of their leaders to sacrifice their principles to satisfy Henry's scruples, in order that he might be inclined to champion their cause against the Emperor. Henry was therefore invited by the Protestant Princes to be the 'Protector' of their 'League of Smalkald,' on the condition of his acceptance of the Augsburg Confession of Faith. Thus the Elector of Saxony declares that if Henry will advocate in England "the pure doctrine of the Christian religion according to the 'Confession' and 'Apology'," he would vote for him to be received as the "Defender of the Evangelical Faith." Great efforts were made by the Lutherans, aided by Barnes, to win over Henry VIII to their cause. Melanchthon wrote an extravagantly fulsome epistle to Henry, calling him "the most learned of all kings," and declaring that he "ought justly to be loved by all good men on account of his eminent moderation and justice." He also dedicated his edition of his 'De Locis Communibus' of 1535 to Henry VIII, and he asks for the King's friendly criticism. Melanchthon makes in it an earnest appeal for a reformation of *doctrine*, declaring that some of the chief Articles of Christian doctrine have for a long time been "enveloped in densest darkness." He urges the need for "good and wise princes" to apply the remedy, since they are under an obligation to preserve the Church from being rent asunder by adopting some plan for "the propagation to posterity of a godly and sure form of doctrine" ([23]).

It was apparently early in this year (1535) that Henry extended a cordial invitation to Melanchthon to visit England and also suitably acknowledged his flattering attentions to himself. Moreover, courteous words were followed by definite actions. In November, 1535, a Conference was held at Wittenberg between Henry's special envoys—Dr. Barnes, Bishop Foxe and Dr. Heath, and the Wittenberg theologians and also with the Protestant Princes at Smalkald. After protracted discussions it became evident that while Henry desired a political alliance with the Lutherans, he was not prepared to pay their price of conformity in doctrine and ceremonies with their 'Confession.' One of the Lutheran divines fairly accurately summed up Henry's attitude when he said—

the King of England has become a Lutheran to this extent, viz., that since the Pope would not approve his divorce he has forbidden all men in his realm at the peril of their lives to regard the Pope as Supreme Head of the Church, but commanded them to regard himself instead. All other papistical affairs, monasteries, masses, indulgences, prayers for the dead they not only retain in England, but even obstinately defend.

But although Henry was not prepared for a doctrinal agreement with the Lutherans, there were other advances towards a reform of doctrine made at this time which certainly owe much to Lutheran sources, and prove that Lutheran teaching was making considerable headway in England. In 1536 Convocation passed what Thomas Fuller quaintly describes as 'Twilight Religion' or the 'Ten Articles.' Dr. Jacobs has examined these Articles carefully comparing them with Melanchthon's writings, and he discovers a manifest analogy between them. He gives good evidence to show that both the 'Augsburg Confession' and Melanchthon's 'Apology' have been laid under contribution in the formulation of these 'Ten Articles.' A definite strain of medieval Catholic religion was, however, retained in them, thus creating, as Fuller puts it, "a 'medley-religion,' to salve the credits of both parties." The 'Ten Articles' were followed the next year by the issue of the 'Bishops' Book' or 'Institution of a Christian Man,' drawn up with Henry's consent by the Bishops as a sort of exposition of the 'Ten Articles.' It was largely the work of Cranmer, and consequently it was rather more Lutheran in flavour than the 'Ten Articles.' It represents the high water mark of doctrinal reformation in Henry's reign. Froude declares it to be "in point of language beyond all question the most beautiful composition that had yet appeared in the English language" (24). Much of the 'Bishops' Book' is based on Luther's Catechism. For instance Luther's Larger Catechism speaks of the purpose of God's Creation —" He causeth all creatures to serve for the necessities and uses of life—sun, moon, and stars, in the firmament, day and night, air, fire, water, earth and whatever it bears and produces, bird and fish, beasts, grain and all kinds of produce." The Bishops' Book paraphrases this language by saying " I acknowledge and confess that He suffereth and causeth the sun, the moon, the stars, the day, the night, the air, the fire, the water, the fowls, the fishes, the beasts and all the fruits of the earth, to serve me for my profit and my necessity."

Henry still continued to hold out hopes of a religious concord with the German Lutherans and so in 1538 a mission of three eminent Lutherans was invited to England, and protracted conferences were held with Cranmer and a small committee of bishops and divines of the Anglican Church. These German ' Orators ' put the results of these joint labours in writing, and apparently they reached an agreement with the English divines on the main fundamental articles of the Christian Faith. But in spite of Cranmer's efforts, the medieval Catholic party of the ' old learning ' refused to proceed further, and treat of ' abuses ' such as Communion in one Kind, clerical celibacy, and private propitiatory masses, to all of which the Lutherans were strongly opposed. The Orators say " the purity of doctrine cannot be conserved unless these abuses be taken away that fight the Word of God, and have produced and maintained the tryanny and idolatry of the Roman Anti-Christ." They maintained that the three practices they objected to were both unscriptural and unprimitive, and they declare that " the use of both species in the Eucharist has the clear command of Christ and the approval of the holy Fathers and the custom of the ancient Church." As regards Private Masses, they tell the King that " the Mass was nothing else than a Communion and bond in the time of the Apostles and the Ancient Church, and the teaching that the Mass is meritorious to take away sins of the living and the dead is far removed from Scripture and detracts from

33

the glory of Christ's Passion, and destroys the Scriptural teaching that we are justified on account of Christ's merits through faith alone. We do not indeed doubt that your Majesty as a most learned King and most devoted to Gopsel truth, will judge most easily that the private Mass has not been rashly abrogated, but by most just and firm reasons from the Word of God which is not able to err."

They then declare that Clerical Matrimony has been prohibited by the Pope, " but that such prohibition is against Scripture, against the laws of Nature and all honesty and has given occasions to many sins and crimes and vile practices," since " Scripture allows priests equally with any other sort of men, liberty to marry " ([25]). Apparently from a letter of Cranmer's to Cromwell, Henry himself had written a book defending these practices. Cranmer told Cromwell that he had urged the bishops to proceed with the business but that he " perceived they only sought an occasion to break the concord . . . For they manifestly see that they cannot defend the abuses and yet they would in no wise grant unto them," but caused themselves to say that " the King's grace hath taken upon himself to answer the said Orators in that behalf and thereof a book is already devised by the King's Majesty" ([26]). This ' book ' of the King's must refer to the ' Answer ' which Henry wrote to these German Orators which Burnet has preserved in his ' Records ' ([27]). The Lutheran envoys were again invited to England in 1539, but no further agreement was reached. One result of this friendly Mission was the issue of the ' Thirteen Articles ' of 1538 which are believed to have been drawn up at the Conferences and to be based on the Augsburg Confession. These ' Articles ' were discovered during the last century by Dr. Jenkyns, and are now thought to have been used largely by the Reformers in drawing up the Forty-two Articles of 1552. It is at least very significant, as Archdeacon Hardwick points out, " that they omit all the subjects on which the English and German negotiators had failed to reach any agreement." In spite of the abortive nature of these negotiations the appearance of the utmost cordiality was maintained with the Lutherans, since Henry wrote to the Elector of Saxony styling the ' Orators ' ' his blameless friends,' and talked of " their supreme devotion to Christian godliness."

From a close comparison of these ' Thirteen Articles ' with the Augsburg Confession, we find that Article I on ' the Unity of God ' is almost word for word identical with Article I, Part 1, of the Augsburg Confession. The same is true of the second and third Articles on ' Original Sin ' and of the ' Two Natures of Christ.' The Article on ' Justification,' while it contains a much longer exposition, incorporates verbatim the language used in Articles IV and V of the ' Confession ' on ' Justification ' and the Ministry of the Church. Article V on ' The Church ' is also much longer, but it includes almost all of the definition given in Article VIII of the Confession on the same subject. The Article on Baptism (VI) also incorporates the language employed in the very short Article IX of the ' Confession.' Again Article IX on the ' Use of the Sacraments,' although much longer, uses language only slightly different from that in Article XIII of the ' Confession.' Article X on the ' Ministers of the Church ' incorporates practically vebatim the very short Article on this subject in the ' Confession,' while half of the XVth Article of the ' Confession ' is included in the long Article (XI) on ' Ecclesiastical Rites.' Only two of the Articles XII and XIII on ' Civil Things ' and ' The Resurrection of the Body ' have no exact quotations from the ' Augsburg Confession.'

It is quite obvious, therefore, that through the medium of these ' Thirteen Articles ' the German Confession of Faith has left its mark on our existing ' Articles of Religion.'

There is little reason to think that Henry VIII was ever in earnest in wishing to have a religious concordat with Lutheranism. His attempts in this direction were undoubtedly prompted solely from his political difficulties, which made a German alliance most profitable if not essential in his struggles with France and the

Emperor. Myconius, the Lutheran Superintendent of the Church in Gotha, and one of the German representatives, was under no illusions as to Henry's real attitude. He wrote quite clearly in 1538, after the practical failure of the negotiations and Conferences of that year in England with the German ' Orators,'—" Henry wants nothing else than to sit as Anti-Christ in the temple of God, and that king Henry be pope. The precious treasure, the rich income of the Church—these are Henry's Gospel " ([28]). Henry was a son of the Renaissance, and as such was anxious to reform some of the more glaring abuses and superstitions of the medieval religion, but the eagerness with which he promoted the passing of the ' Act of Six Articles,' showed that he fully accepted the distinguishing features of medieval and Roman catholicity. On the first appearance of Luther's writings Henry had proved himself a champion of current orthodoxy by writing a book against the great German Reformer, and he never really receded from this position. In the Act which forbade Papal dispensations in 1534 it was clearly stated that there was no intention of " varying from the congregation of Christ's Church in any things concerning the very articles of the Catholic Church of Christendom," by which was meant the teaching of the Medieval Church. And in his last appeal to the Pope he had declared that " No Princes heretofore have more highly esteemed nor honoured the See Apostolic than we have " ([29]). In spite therefore of his attempt to exploit the Lutherans for his own ends, Henry's real attitude was that, so tersely described by Bishop Hooper, " Our King has destroyed the Pope but not popery." Luther, after the passing of the ' Act of Six Articles ' had denounced Henry in no measured terms as " the blasphemer " who " wants to kill the Pope's body but keep his soul " ([29]).

CHAPTER III

THE ENGLISH CHURCH AND THE 'REFORMED'
CONTINENTAL CHURCHES

WITH the accession of Edward VI the English Doctrinal Reformation as a National or State Movement really begins. So far as Henry VIII's reign was concerned this had been little more than a political affair with one or two spasmodic tentative and half-hearted doctrinal gestures designed to deceive the Lutheran Princes and thus gain their political alliance. But under Edward VI there was a serious and sincere attempt to inaugurate genuine doctrinal changes, although the orientation was no longer mainly Lutheran, but rather ' Reformed.' The cause of this change of policy is easy to understand. Whether the report which was circulated was true or not—that Henry VIII was, at the time of his death, really contemplating further changes in the Reformed direction and was determined to change the " Mass into a Communion, besides many other things "—it is at least certain that he selected for the six councillors to govern during the minority of the young King, mainly those who were definite Reformers. The Duke of Somerset, Edward VI's Uncle, who was chosen Protector, was a stout supporter of Cranmer's views. Burnet tells us that most of the bishops " were weak and ignorant men who understood religion little and valued it less, and so although they liked the old superstition best . . . yet they were resolved to swim with the stream." And he says " it was designed by Cranmer and his friends to carry on the Reformation, but by slow and safe degrees not hazarding too much at once " ([1]).

But this definite determination to inaugurate doctrinal reform led at once to a closer intercourse with the foreign Reformers, while Cranmer's change of views on the Eucharist, which occurred in 1546, to something in accord with those held in Switzerland, threw the balance on the ' Reformed ' rather than on the Lutheran side. But for the past 10 years the connection between the English and foreign Reformers had been growing and deepening. In 1536 a French Reformed Church had been formed in Canterbury and another in London, although the passing of the ' Bloody Statute ' led to a great exodus of the English disciples of Reformed views from England to the Continent. Many of different classes, especially the enthusiastic young men of ability and intelligence, fled at this time to escape serious persecution. They found asylums in both German and Swiss towns and thus bonds and friendships were formed not only with Lutherans but with Zwinglians in Switzerland.

A most affectionate friendship had sprung up between Cranmer and Martin Bucer, and the latter seemed to be in a measure the pensioner of the Archbishop, since Bucer thanks Cranmer for his ' very liberal present ' and speaks of his " excessive liberality towards those whom you consider in any way to labour for the Church of Christ " ([2]). Moreover we see how hopefully the Lutherans viewed the progress of the Reformation in England in 1538 when Bucer tells Cranmer " We count you altogether happy in the Lord, from whose labours has resulted such fruit . . . godly men, who have experience in ecclesiastical matters, consider the progress of the Kingdom of Christ amongst you as most extensive and your exertions to promote it exceedingly successful." Before a year was over Bucer and his friends had a rude awakening as to the real state of religious affairs in England. But it is obvious that he regards Cranmer as a sort of leader and guide of the Reformers and the Reformed Faith, since he intreats him that he would " number him among his true sons and clients and admonish him as a father and a patron should do " ([2]).

But next year on the passing of the ' Act of Six Articles' Bucer writes to Cranmer in a very different strain. " He does not doubt," he says, " That Cranmer will read with benefit to himself this reproof, however severe, which is administered to you for the glory of Christ." " We are," he says, " all of us amazed more than I can express at the sight of these decrees, and at the previous rejection of the terms of alliance between his serene Majesty and ourselves. It would have been too idle to suppose that we should not have been offended by those most severe decrees." He laments the prospect that " all the churches would for the future be entirely in the hands of the followers of Anti-Christ." Bucer, however, still regards Cranmer and his party as " brethren and members of the same body" and prays that he may faithfully retain and rightly explain " the article of justification so that the kingdom of Christ may yet remain amongst you " (²).

With the changed outlook at the commencement of the new reign in 1547 the former close fellowship with Bucer was resumed, and we find the latter writing to Cranmer from Strasburg in September, 1548, to thank the Archbishop for his invitation to him to come to England. His friend, Peter Martyr, wrote from England in December 1548 strongly urging him to accept this invitation, and he declares " such is the splendour of your name, in this country both from report and from your writings, that you cannot but be honourably received." This assurance from a fellow foreigner was fully borne out by the cordial nature of Cranmer's personal plea to Bucer. " Come over to us," he writes, " and become a labourer with us in the harvest of the Lord. We will make it manifest that nothing can be more gratifying or agreeable to us than the presence of Bucer." Shortly after his arrival, Hooper wrote to Bullinger that " Bucer is with the Archbishop of Canterbury like another Scipio and an inseparable companion." Bucer was in England for nearly two years and worked in close association with Cranmer, and the Archbishop found no cause to modify the high opinion he had formed of him, since on his

39

death in February 1551, he told his widow that Bucer's profound learning and piety had been " an everlasting benefit to the Church."

The Emperor Charles V had published the Interim in May 1548, and this was a distinct setback to the Lutheran Cause, since in it the Pope was to be acknowledged as Head of the Church, and the seven Sacraments were to be retained. Bucer therefore welcomed Cranmer's invitation as a happy and timely relief from the well-nigh intolerable conditions then prevailing at Strasburg. He does not disguise his great joy at the changed prospect opening up in England, and he tells Cranmer that there was nothing which would delight him more "than to render assistance to a Church which is nobly recovering itself as yours is and making such happy progress in Christ our Lord." " In the midst of your so great anxieties your reverence," he declares, " has called us from death to life." This statement was not an exaggeration, since we find that in March 1549 Bucer and Paul Fagius were deposed from their office as preachers by the magistrates, and were in danger of falling into the hands of the Emperor. Consequently they were very glad to set out for England and they arrived there in April 1549. The glowing account which they wrote to their brethren in the Ministry at Strasburg, of their reception in England, gives us a good illustration of the close and cordial relationship which Cranmer had already established with the prominent foreign Reformers. Bucer tells his friends—

We yesterday waited upon the Archbishop of Canterbury, that most benevolent and kind father of the Churches and of godly men, who received and entertains us as brethren, not as dependants. We found at his house, what was most gratifying to us, our most dear friend doctor Peter Martyr, with his wife. Master Immanuel (Tremellius) with his wife, and also Dryander and some other godly Frenchmen whom we had sent before us. All these are entertained by the Archbishop of Canterbury.

Four months later Bucer writes again that the " Archbishop of Canterbury treats us with the greatest kindness and familiarity." We can also glean from his correspondence something of the number of religious refugees then in London, when he says " There are six to eight hundred Germans, all godly men and most anxious for the Word of God," and he pleads for a suitable pastor to be sent over to minister to them. Prominent among the " godly Frenchmen " who were being entertained by the hospitable Cranmer was Peter Alexander, a native of Provence. He had been Chaplain to Queen Mary, the sister of the Emperor Charles V, and he came over to England in 1547 on the express invitation of the Archbishop. He was evidently a valuable colleague for Cranmer, and we are told that he was most industrious and had a ' clear head.' He assisted Cranmer considerably by diligently reading the Fathers and gathering their teaching on controversial doctrinal questions. He was made prebendary of Canterbury and also Rector of All Hallows Church, Lombard Street. In 1554 he was obliged to return to Strasburg and was made a pastor there. He was, however, a difficult person to work with. In 1558 he was obliged to leave his post at Strasburg and he then returned to England, and recovered his prebendal stall at Canterbury, not before, however, he had caused dissension in the French Church in London. As a prebendary he probably had little chance of stirring up trouble !

Another of Cranmer's guests—Immanuel Tremellius— is interesting from the fact that he was an Italian Jew who had been converted through Cardinal Pole. He left Italy with Peter Martyr in 1542 and went with him to Strasburg, where he was given a prebendal stall in the Cathedral. He came to England with Martyr in 1547 and in 1550 he became a Reader in Hebrew at Cambridge University and later on a prebendary of Carlisle. He fled to the Continent in 1553 and in 1560 was made a professor at Heidelberg University. Later again, he paid a six months visit to his old friend, Archbishop Parker, in England.

We gather from the regular correspondence of John Burcher, an English merchant residing at this time in Strasburg, that Bucer and also Paul Fagius were at least sympathetic with Lutheran views. For Burcher writes to Bullinger on April 1, 1549, that " he trusts the Lord will preserve our England from both of them," and in recording their arrival a month later he adds, " I wish they may not pervert him (i.e., Cranmer) or make him worse." Burcher was evidently a violent partisan of Swiss Reformed theology, and he tells Henry Bullinger, Zwingli's successor at Zürich, that Bishop Hooper is " opposed to Lutherans and Bucerians." His remarks about Bucer furnish painful evidence of the bitter 'party' spirit evinced by the more extreme section of the Reformers (soon after to be designated ' Puritans '), and they also afford a glaring and sad example of the terrible lengths which the ' odium theologicum ' can carry otherwise earnest and sincere Christians. Thus Burcher informs Bullinger of Bucer's serious illness and of the small hope there was of his recovery, and he adds the most unchristian note of prospective exultation, " In case of his death England will be happy and more favoured than all other countries in having been delivered in the same year from two men of most pernicious talent viz., Paul Fagius and Bucer." This was written in April, 1550, but Fagius did not die until November 23, and Bucer lived until Feb. 28, 1551.

Again in June, 1550, Burcher describes Bucer as a ' hireling,' and declares that he is either ' childish ' or ' in his dotage '—" the usual result of a wandering and inconstant mind." But in recording Bucer's death he is bound to admit how greatly respected this celebrated foreign Reformed divine was " amongst the learned," although he cannot refrain from adding, " for my own part I desire one who may be more sincere and steady." But this wide esteem for Bucer was also abundantly shown by his funeral at St. Mary's Church, Cambridge, when " all the whole university with the whole town to the number of 3,000 persons " followed him to the grave, and his friend Dr. Parker preached the sermon. Sir John Cheke wrote at the time to the future Archbishop (Parker), telling him that it was impossible really to replace Bucer for " deepness of knowledge, earnestness in religion, fatherliness in life, and authority in knowledge," while Martyr wrote that Bucer's death was the " universal regret of all good men and to my incredible sorrow." Fortunately John Burcher, with his suspicious and censorious spirit and his uncharitable denunciation of all who were suspected of Lutheran teaching, seems at least at this time, to have been an exception. But unhappily, later, when Puritanism developed under Elizabeth, he had many followers in this attitude. He himself returned to England at that time and was ordained.

We get another striking illustration of the ardent desire which Cranmer had for the close association of prominent foreign Protestant divines with the English Reformation, in the most cordial invitation which was given to Wolfgang Musculus to come to England. Musculus was Minister of a Lutheran Church at Augsburg, but ended his days as professor of divinity at Berne. In 1548 Bernardino Ochinus, the celebrated Italian monk, who had come over with Peter Martyr in 1547 and was made a prebendary of Canterbury, wrote from London telling Musculus that the Archbishop of Canterbury was ' exceedingly desirous ' that he should come to England. He also informed him that as he had a large family, the Archbishop had asked a certain merchant to supply him with every necessary, and " he was sending a hundred crowns for his journey." He told Musculus that " a lectureship will be provided for you at Cambridge, and should not that situation meet your wishes, you might preach publicly in London, where a numerous auditory would not be wanting. For there are more than 5,000 Germans here, to whom you would doubtless be most acceptable." But Cranmer was not only on most intimate terms of friendship with all the leading foreign Reformers, he was also most anxious that a Conference or Synod of Reformed divines might meet in England and arrive at a complete unity of doctrine, especially on the thorny question of the Eucharist.

He felt that this achievement would act as a safeguard and as an answer to the promulgation and stereotyping of medieval doctrines, then being effected by the papalists at the Council of Trent. The evidence is clear that this project lay very near to the Archbishop's heart, and he made repeated efforts to accomplish it. Philip

Melanchthon, Luther's celebrated colleague, had been urgently solicited more than once to come to England for this object, and in July, 1548, Cranmer invited the Polish nobleman, John à Lasco, to co-operate in furthering it, so that by obtaining the opinions of the most learned of the Reformers, it might be possible " to do away with all doctrinal controversies and build up an entire system of true doctrine." A very beautiful ideal, but so long as freedom of thought is permitted, a scarcely attainable one. Martin Micronius records à Lasco's arrival in England in May, 1550, and says that " his coming was greatly to the delight of all godly persons." John à Lasco had a peculiarly varied and interesting career. The son of a Polish nobleman, he was born in 1499 and educated at Cracow. He was ordained in 1521, and travelled extensively in Italy, France, Germany, and Switzerland. He had influential friends, as his Uncle was Primate of Poland. À Lasco was soon appointed Dean of Gnesen and in 1524 he met and formed a close friendship with Erasmus, and Zwingli also influenced him to study the Scriptures. He returned to Cracow in 1525, largely imbued with Reforming views. He refused the bishopric of Cujavia in 1529, and frankly told King Sigismund of his change of convictions. He quitted Poland in 1538 and went to Antwerp and Louvain, where he married. He then went to East Friesland and was appointed Superintendent of all the Reformed Churches there in 1543, and he remained as minister of a Church at Emden till 1548, when, owing to the " Interim," to which he refused to submit, he was compelled to flee, and he accepted Cranmer's cordial invitation and arrived in London in September, 1548. He was entertained by the Archbishop for eight months, returning to Emden in 1549. But again in 1550 he was compelled to seek safety in England, and again he was welcomed by Cranmer as his guest. He was also appointed by Royal Charter Superintendent of the Stranger's Church, in London, which consisted of three separate congregations of Germans and French. These congregations à Lasco organised on a presbyterian model, with superintendents, ministers, elders, and deacons, and both liturgical and ' free ' prayers were allowed. On the accession of Mary he and his flock were compelled to leave England, and à Lasco found shelter at Danzig. Later, he went to Emden and Frankfort and then in 1557 returned to Cracow and was made Superintendent of the Polish Reformed Churches, and was one of the 18 divines concerned in translating the Scriptures into Polish. He died in 1560. He was described as " in science an Erasmian, in faith a Lutheran, in cultus a Zwinglian, in Church organisation a Calvinist, as a dogmatician loose and indefinite."

A very pressing and most cordial invitation was sent to Paul Fagius, Bucer's colleague at Strasburg, in March 1549. Peter Alexander was commissioned to write and inform him of the ' friendly feeling ' which Cranmer had " for the advancement of all the ministers of Christ " and in particular of his " exceeding goodwill and most favourable inclination towards you and your affairs." Alexander tells Fagius that Cranmer had heard of his dismissal by the Senate at Strasburg and that in consequence " he had taken a very lively interest in you and your affairs," and as the English churches were " in great want of learned men he desires to see you in England as soon as possible." " Come therefore," urges Alexander, " as soon as you possibly can and cheer the most reverend Archbishop, your attached friend, by your early arrival." " There is no doubt," he adds, " of your obtaining some honourable situation in this country, for I know for certain that you will be appointed to a most distinguished office in the University either at Oxford or Cambridge." We learn also from Miles Coverdale, in 1548, that Cranmer had even undertaken to educate in England Paul Fagius's son at his own expense.

Again, in March 1552, Cranmer reverts to this project for a close doctrinal unity amongst all the Reformed leaders. He writes to Henry Bullinger regarding the Council of Trent, where, as he says, " our adversaries are now holding their councils to confirm their errors," and he tells him that he has recommended Edward VI to allow in England a Synod to be convoked " of the most learned and excellent persons in which provision might be made for the purity of Ecclesiastical doctrine, and especially for an agreement upon the scaramentarian controversy." In a similar strain he writes at the same time to John Calvin, of the urgent necessity of " comparing their respective opinions " and especially " to leave no stone unturned " to guard against " the idolatry " of " the worship of the host " and " to come to an agreement upon the doctrine of the Sacrament." He also writes again to Melanchthon pointing out how desirable it was that the " members of the true Church should agree among themselves upon the chief heads of ecclesiastical doctrine " and " attest their agreements by some published document."

This burning desire for a clear statement of doctrinal concord amongst Protestant theologians was an outstanding feature in the aims of all the Reformers at this time, and we get many illustrations of it. There were undoubtedly important questions which divided the Lutherans from the Swiss Reformed, and the ' Conference of Marburg ' in 1530 registered an almost impassable gulf between Luther and Zwingli on the Eucharist. But since then, there had been a marked tendency for opponents to draw together, and secure a ' modus vivendi ' which would enable the Protestants to present a united front to their Romanist antagonists. The divisions on the Eucharist were of course the main obstacle, but already Calvin and Bullinger had found a formula of agreement in the ' Concensus Tigurinus ' of 1549, and prominent Lutherans, like Melanchthon, Bucer, and Fagius, were earnestly seeking for a similar rapprochement.

A conspicuous illustration of this desire to exmphasise the solidarity of all Reformers is furnished by a letter which Hooper wrote to Bucer from Zürich, in June, 1548. Hooper was a convinced Zwinglian and therefore a strong opponent of the Lutheran teaching of Consubstantiation, and so he entreats Bucer " not to burden the consciences of men with *Luther's* words on the holy Supper." Yet he adds, " I will readily acknowledge with thankfulness the gifts of God in him (Luther) who is now no more." And he tells Bucer that " all the ministers of this Church (Zürich) were grieved at his death, not as if they had lost an adversary or a detractor, but rather an ally and partner in their glorious work." In the same letter he makes it clear that although he dissented from Bucer's view of the Eucharist, he assures him that such differences " do not make any breach in Christian love " much less create any ' hostility ' and that he and others are anxious to aid him in his work by their prayers. A fine contrast and rebuke to the very different spirit which we have seen displayed by Burcher.

A careful study of the correspondence between the English divines and the foreign Reformers during Edward VI's reign leads us to the conclusion that the sympathies of our leading Reformers, including Cranmer, were with the Swiss rather than with the Lutheran divines on the question of the Eucharist, and this is confirmed by the sacramental teaching of the Forty-two Articles of 1553. Mr. C. H. Smyth, in his essay on ' Cranmer and the Reformation under Edward VI,' endeavours to establish the thesis that Cranmer so soon as he abandoned his belief in Transubstantiation, accepted ' Suvermerian ' views, which he describes as a sort of halfway-house between Lutheranism and Zwinglianism—the doctrine of spiritual eating—which he learned from the monk Ratramn or Bertram through Ridley. But the evidence which he adduces is not altogether convincing. It over-emphasises certain figurative and symbolical statements of Cranmer's Eucharistic teaching to the neglect of others which are far clearer and more definite. And as we have already seen (p. 28) it ignores the fact that Zwingli also believed in the ' spiritual eating ' of Christ in the Lord's Supper.

A review of Cranmer's teaching on the Lord's Supper leads us to the conclusion that his general position practically coincides with the ' receptionist ' view enunciated later by Richard Hooker, that " the real presence of Christ's blessed Body and Blood is not to be sought for in the Sacrament but in the worthy receiver of the

Sacrament "*.   Moreover to declare that Cranmer held ' Suvermerian ' views of the Eucharist would, in the opinion of Hooper, and apparently also of Bullinger, at once identify him as holding the Zwinglian or Swiss interpretation of the Sacrament.   For Hooper writing to Bullinger in March, 1549, reports to him a sermon delivered by Gasper Hedio, the Lutheran Professor of Theology, at Strasburg, in which he says that " he heard with pain " that Hedio " absurdly inveighed with great bitterness against the Suvermerians. May the Lord forgive him and bring him to a better mind." Hooper evidently regards ' Suvermerianism ' as equivalent to the Eucharistic views which he and Bullinger held in common, which were certainly not akin to Lutheran.   Moreover, in face of the very strong evidence we possess, it is rather difficult to question Cranmer's acceptance of practically Zwinglian views on the Lord's Supper.   Bartholomew Traheron, a layman, soon after appointed Dean of Chichester, reports to Bullinger in September, 1548, that " Latimer has come over to our opinion respecting the true doctrine of the Eucharist together with the Archbishop of Canterbury and the other bishops, who heretofore seemed to be Lutherans." Again, two months later, he records the result of the ' Three Days ' disputation on the Eucharist held in the House of Lords, about which he, as a Member of Parliament, would have the best opportunity of hearing. He declares to Bullinger that " the Archbishop of Canterbury, contrary to general expectation, most openly, firmly and learnedly maintained your opinion upon the subject . . . I perceive it is all over with Lutheranism now that those who were considered its principal and almost only supporters have altogether come over to our side."   Hooper, as we have already seen, also confirms this statement, for when writing in 1549, he declares that Cranmer holds " right views as to the nature of Christ's presence in the Supper."

*For a comparison of Cranmer's Eucharistic teaching with that of the Swiss divines, see the Author's ' Anglican Via Media,' pp. 51-4.

Later in June, 1550, he seems still a little doubtful of Cranmer's complete 'orthodoxy,' since he tells Bullinger "he is not so decided as I could wish and does not, I fear, assert his opinion in all respects." But Hooper was rather an 'extremist' and probably very critical of any slight variation from his own way of expounding controversial doctrines, since John ab Ulmis more than a year before this had assured Bullinger that Cranmer had delivered his opinion upon this subject (of the Eucharist) "learnedly, correctly, orderly, and clearly, and easily drew over all his hearers to *our* way of thinking." And we should remember that ab Ulmis himself was also a somewhat suspicious and careful critic, since he had not been satisfied, shortly before, with Peter Martyr's non-committal views, saying that he seemed "not to incline either to your opinion (i.e., Bullinger) or to that of Luther."

It is also in the nature of special pleading to discount, if not disregard, the many testimonies given by Edwardian divines and others to the practical identity of Anglican and Swiss doctrine at this time. Edward VI, in October 1549 wrote to the Senate of Zürich affirming that " there is a mutual agreement between us concerning the Christian religion and true godliness which ought to render this friendship of ours, by God's blessing, yet more intimate." The accuracy of this assertion is confirmed about six months later when Bishop Hooper tells Henry Bullinger that all lecturers and preachers have to subscribe certain Articles in order to get their licences 'to read and preach,' " one of which respecting the Eucharist is plainly the true one, and that which you maintain in Switzerland." And again in a letter a month later (March, 1550), Hooper emphasises this close accord in doctrine, as he writes " with the exception of the Church of Zürich and those who agree with it in religion, the Word is in no part of the world preached more purely than in England."

John ab Ulmis, the Swiss student, who was studying at Oxford as early as 1548, writes to Bullinger that Cox, who was Dean of Christ Church and Chancellor of the University, " entertains and expresses most excellent and correct notions respecting every article of the Christian Faith." This, of course, indicates Cox's practical agreement with the theology of Zürich. About 18 months later ab Ulmis is able to assure Bullinger that " a great number of the bishops now entertain right views respecting religion." Moreover, this testimony cannot be dismissed as that of an ignorant foreigner, because ab Ulmis had specially good opportunities of forming a correct judgment, since he mixed in the highest and most influential circles both at Court and at Oxford. In 1548 Cox had assured ab Ulmis of " the royal patronage and support " during his stay in England. He was also most intimate with the family of the Duke of Suffolk and received from that powerful nobleman a yearly allowance of thirty Crowns.

One of the best evidences that Swiss Reformed theology was generally professed by Anglican Protestants at this time is the high and almost reverent regard in which the celebrated Zürich Reformer Henry Bullinger was held. Bullinger seems in fact to have filled the role of spiritual Father and preceptor to the English Reformers. He was appealed to as a sort of protestant ' pope.' Cox tells him in 1550 that " not only the Queen Dowager, but likewise others of the more pious nobility of this kingdom regard their Bullinger with so much love and affection." The Duke of Suffolk and his accomplished and youthful daughter, Lady Jane Grey, write most gratefully of the help they received from Bullinger's letters and sermons—" O happy me," wrote Lady Jane, " to be possessed of such a friend and so wise a counsellor."

Hooper, who had stayed at Zürich, also had the highest opinion of Bullinger, and he tells him in August, 1551, that Cranmer was also " a great admirer of him." " No one," he says, " loves you in Christ more ardently than he does. I know of a truth that he loves you from his heart." John ab Ulmis, as early as 1548, had requested Bullinger to secure the good offices of the Archbishop on his behalf so that he might receive some pecuniary help, and he bases his request on the fact that Cranmer " has a great regard for you, in which you might commend me to him by some testimony of your approbation." Probably ab Ulmis does not exaggerate when, in January, 1551, he tells Bullinger that " the opinion of mankind respecting you is great, their praise of your learning great, the reputation of your writings great." John Stumphius, another Swiss studying at Oxford and befriended by Dr. Cox, also bears the same testimony. Speaking of the eminent and learned men of the University, he says to Bullinger, " these persons have a very high opinion of you, a great reverence for your learning and a perfect acquaintance with your writings."

Moreover, this respect for, and close intimacy with, the foreign Reformers, was demonstrated in a practical manner by the generous treatment accorded to the divines and students, who had taken refuge in or who came to England for educational purposes. Cranmer's hospitality seemed boundless, while the leading foreign Reformers, like Bucer, Martyr and Fagius, were given important and lucrative posts at the Universities. Students were also assisted financially and received as members of the different Colleges—a special concession which seems to have been withdrawn later on in the century. Cranmer, as we have seen, undertook the education of the son of Paul Fagius ; and Martin Micronius, the Minister of the Flemish Church in London, told Bullinger in 1550 that " the Archbishop of Canterbury is the especial patron of the foreigners " and had been "the chief support and promoter of our Church." The Duke of Suffolk was also regarded as the refuge of the foreign students and he sponsored John ab Ulmis. Bishop Hooper, in 1551, speaks of " Germans who flock over to us for the sake of study," and it was not surprising that they wished to take advantage of the generous hsopitality which was offered them. For Hooper offered to defray part of the education of Rudolph Gualter's son, and he promised Bullinger that " if the young men of Zürich who come over here for the sake of study, should stand in need of my assistance, I will aid them as far as my slender means will allow."

The considerable amount of friendly correspondence

between the English and foreign Reformers at this time which has been preserved is most interesting and instructive in affording us incidentally a fairly clear picture of contemporary and social conditions. We are able to form a fairly correct idea of the dangers, and difficulties, and serious deprivations which were endured under the civilisation of those days. The ease, comfort and luxury of the modern travel was of course unknown then, and a journey to the Continent must always have been a serious and formidable, and often a lengthy and tedious undertaking. A great deal, for instance, depended on a favourable ' wind and tide '; so that we find John à Lasco crossing from Calais to London in the short space of two days. On the other hand, Hooper speaks of his long and dangerous journey to England when " I suffered many things by land, twice I suffered bonds and imprisonments. I was wretchedly harassed by sea for three months both by enemies and storms." Christopher Hales was nearly captured by a French pirate on his way to England in 1550. He lost his trunk, and his little dog refused to follow him " across the open plain of Brabant." Yet in spite of these dangers and privations numbers seemed to have travelled frequently and regularly on the Continent.

We get also many friendly and domestic touches which reveal that underneath a rigid and stern and severe demeanour human nature asserts itself in all ages and circumstances. For instance, one grave and learned divine evidently possessed a ' sweet tooth,' for he troubled to write from London to the great Swiss Reformer, Bullinger, asking him to forward to him by way of the Frankfort fair, a ' spiced cake,' of the same kind which he had tasted two years previously at Zürich ! This cake had apparently made a lasting impression on his palate. But this somewhat trivial request was evidently overlooked by the much occupied Zürich theologian, so that *two years later* the same correspondent again reminds Bullinger of his great wish that a ' large cake,' similar to the one of such a ' happy memory ' four years ago, should be sent him !

Christopher Hales sends to Rudolph Gualter at Zürich

" six large dishes, six small and 12 large plates and saucers " for the cost of 26s/7, and apologises that it is " twice as dear as usual." He also sends Mrs. Gualter, as a present, ' two candlesticks,' and ' twenty dishes.' Mrs. Richard Hilles asks for Bullinger's prayers for her approaching confinement, and thanks him for the present of some shoes for her small boy of two years.

Thomas Knight, an English bookseller in Venice, does not scruple to use the celebrated Bullinger as a sort of ' clearing house,' and forwards him a ' cask ' marked ' R.H.', requesting him to send it on to Richard Hilles, an English Protestant merchant, and also a disciple of the Zürich Reformer, "by means of some of your friends." He adds " you will not receive the jar of figs at the present time because there was not room for it in the carriers' chest." One wonders whether the ' figs ' were a sort of ' commission ' for Bullinger ?

Christopher Hales asks Gualter to get six portraits of the leading foreign Reformers painted for him to adorn the walls of his library, but much to his disgust, through the influence of Burcher's ' Puritan ' scruples, his request is refused for fear of opening ' a door to idolatry.' We learn also that board for an Oxford term cost five crowns and that 30 crowns covered a whole year's expenses at the University. But this amount would probably differ, as it would to-day, on the careful or expensive ' habits ' of the student ! Moreover, we should probably have to multiply these figures by about 15 to arrive at the equivalent cost of living today ; but even so, £90 a year would not go far now towards a students' annual expenses at Oxford or Cambridge. Evidently, however, it was an age of plain and simple ' living ' and of high and strenuous ' thinking.' Thomas Lever, Master of St. John's College, Cambridge, in 1551, in a sermon in 1550, gives us an insight into the daily routine and the ' sumptuous ' fare of the student of those days. " There be divers there, i.e., at Cambridge, which rise daily betwixt four and five of the clock in the morning and from five until six of the clock use Common prayer, with an exhortation of God's Word in a common chapel, and from six unto ten of the clock use either private study or common lectures. At ten of the clock they go to dinner, whereas they be content with a penny piece of beef amongst four, having a few porage made of the broth of the same beef with salt and oatmeal and nothing else. After this slender dinner they be either teaching or learning until five of the clock in the evening, when as they have a supper not much better than their dinner. Immediately after which they go either to nine or ten of the clock, and their being without fire are fain to walk or run up and down half-an-hour to get a heat on their feet when they go to bed " (3). There are few students today who could endure such a strenuous day of study on two such slender meals, even though they had only a half-hour's physical exercise !

The close alliance and the doctrinal unity of the English and foreign Reformers was not confined to personal friendship or practical agreement in their writings and teaching on the Sacraments. It was reflected very clearly in the doctrinal and liturgical formularies which the Edwardian Reformers put forth at this time, for the English Church. The Forty-Two Articles of Religion which were finally issued in May, 1553, to be publicly subscribed, by clergy and school-masters, were in all probability similar, if not identical, with those referred to by Bishop Hooper in February, 1549, as necessary for licensed preachers to sign (see p. 49). Although about 30 of these Articles were compiled by the English Reformers themselves, the doctrine they set forth was closely in accord with that held at the time by the foreign Reformed Churches. This was demonstrated some 50 years later when Thomas Rogers in his ' Catholic Doctrine of the Church of England,' examined and compared each single Article and quoted parallel statements in the foreign Reformed Confessions of Faith. Moreover, not less than eleven of these Forty-Two Articles were either based on, or drawn from, Lutheran Confessions of Faith, although on the question of the Eucharist Lutheran teaching was definitely rejected in favour of ' Reformed ' views. For instance, the language used in Articles I, II, XI, XIX, and XXV, is very close to that employed in the Augsburg Confession on these subjects.

The First Prayer Book of 1549 had been drawn up mainly by Cranmer, before the arrival of Bucer and other prominent foreign Reformers, but even so the compilers borrowed considerably from Lutheran and other Protestant sources. As Dr. Jacobs points out, the services for Matins and Evensong follow most closely the parallel Lutheran services of 1542, while the Baptismal service is largely Lutheran. It is based on the baptismal Service which Bucer compiled at the request of Archbishop Hermann for his ' Consultatio ' which was published at Cologne in 1543. In the Communion office also much was borrowed from Archbishop Hermann's ' Consultatio '—the Confession, Absolution and ' Comfortable Words '—while part of the words for the distribution of the elements—" the body of our Lord Jesus Christ, *which was given for thee* " . . . " which was shed for thee " were drawn from the ' Nurnberg formula.' Similar German influence is traceable in the Marriage Service. In fact, as Cardwell declares, " The new Liturgy was greatly indebted, wherever it deviated from the ancient breviaries, to the progress made upon the Continent in religious worship " ([4]). But this indebtedness was indirect, and was not due to the direct influence of the foreign Reformers themselves. Bucer makes this point quite clear when, in writing to a friend in Cambridge on January 12, 1551, he distinctly says in reference to the first Prayer Book, " what you admonish concerning the purity of the rites, know that here *no fereigner was asked concerning them* " ([5]).

But with the learned foreign divines actually residing in England and filling important posts at the Universities the case was different concerning the revision of this 1549 Prayer Book. A Committee was appointed for this purpose in the autumn of 1550 and Strype declares that Cranmer, through the medium of the Master of Christ's College, desired Bucer impartially to review the whole book, which he had translated into Latin for him to understand, in order to see if anything in it might be explained more agreeably with God's Word.

55

Cranmer, he says, also sought the opinion of Peter Martyr, and asked him to set down in writing what he thought needed correction. Strype adds that such deference was given to the judgment of these learned foreign divines that most of the things which Bucer took exception to " were corrected accordingly " [6]. Bucer had previously paid a visit to Bishop Goodrich at Ely, in July, 1550, and it is quite possible that on this occasion Goodrich, either on his own behalf or at the instance of Cranmer, asked Bucer to write his ' Censura ' or opinion of the First Prayer Book as a guide for the forthcoming revision. In any case, Martyr writes to Bucer in January, 1551, rejoicing at the opportunity thus afforded them of advising or ' admonishing ' the bishops on this important matter, and telling him that Cranmer had already informed him that " many things should be changed." Bucer had given in his ' Censura ' to Bishop Goodrich on January 5, and apparently it was addressed to the Bishop of Ely and not to the Archbishop himself. It contained in detail many suggested changes, although Bucer paid a warm general tribute of appreciation of the 1549 Book as a " service so pure and ordered so religiously according to the Word of God." He wished, however, that the old vestments or ' habits ' might be discarded because " many used them superstitiously " and they caused much contention. He desired more frequent lay communion and he wished the sacrament to be delivered into the hands and not put into the mouth of the communicant. He condemned prayer for the dead as non-Scriptural, and he thought the prayer of Consecration—that the elements might be unto us the body of Christ—savoured of transubstantiation. He wished for the baptism of infants to be publicly performed in Church, but he disliked the hallowing of the water and the use of the chrism and the bestowal of the chrisom and the exorcism of the devil. Confirmation should be delayed till the candidates really desired to renew the baptismal vow and catechising should be held every holy Day. On the publication of the 1552 Book it was evident that most of these suggestions had been adopted,

56

but as the bishops had themselves previously determined on ' many changes ' it must not be concluded that all the alterations were due to Bucer's criticisms even where they may have coincided with them. Yet there is no doubt that these celebrated foreign divines did exert a considerable influence on the revision of the Prayer Book, and that the general aim and desire of Cranmer and the leading English Reformers were to establish a Scriptural form of worship which would be acceptable and in harmony with the views and teaching of their Continental brethren. That they had succeeded in this aim was evident from the fact that Cranmer confidently associated the name of Peter Martyr with his own in his rash offer, at the beginning of Mary's reign, to defend publicly " the whole doctrine and order of religion " lately set forth " as more pure and agreeable to the Word of God than any sort of religion that hath been used in England these thousand years " (7).

CHAPTER IV

THE MARIAN EXILES

A S we have already seen there had been a considerable intimacy and intercourse, even in the reign of Henry VIII, between English Churchmen inclined to Reforming views and the German Reformers. Cranmer had visited Germany and had become intimate with the leading Reformed divines, and Coverdale resided and taught and preached in Germany for about eight years prior to the accession of Edward VI. The passing of the Act of Six Articles in 1540 was the signal for a large exodus of 'gospellers' to the Continent. It was the first really religious emigration and very many in different ranks of life, and particularly young men, of promise and ability, fled from their native land to escape the harsh penalties of the 'whip with six strings.' They found places of refuge in the towns of both Germany and Switzerland which had welcomed the doctrinal Reformation. Zürich, Basle and Strasburg were especially popular centres for these refugees. In this way, not only tradesmen, and merchants like John Burcher and Richard Hilles, but also zealous and prominent Reformers, such as Bartholomew Traheron and Hooper, came in close personal contact with the leaders of the Continental Reformation. Hooper had escaped to Paris but soon discovered that this strong papalist city was no safe harbour, and so with much difficulty and danger he managed to reach the higher parts of Germany and sojourned at Strasburg for a time, and in 1546 married Ann de Tserclas, a Flemish lady of noble birth. From 1547-9 he was in

Zürich attending the lectures of the learned Swiss divine, Henry Bullinger, and cementing an affectionate friendship with him which was only severed by his own martyrdom. Hooper gratefully regarded Bullinger as his " master," and was not slow to acknowledge his indebtedness to his spiritual teaching. Soon after his return to England he writes beseeching that Bullinger will preserve his annotations, especially on Isaiah, and have them copied out and sent to him with the greatest care. " I will," he says, " pay every expense, you know not how wonderfully they promote the glory of God." He adds that he owes all he can accomplish for the " Church of Christ " " to yourself and my masters and brethren at Zürich " ([1]).

With the sudden and violent overthrow of the Protestant Reformation in England on the accession of Mary, it was only natural that the English Reformers should hasten to escape from imminent peril and persecution by flight to the Continent, where they could find safe havens with their former friends and brethren. Several of the leading English Churchmen had been arrested and imprisoned and thus compelled to face the impending storm. Amongst these was Bishop Hooper, who from his ' filthy ' prison wrote in May, 1554, to his old friend, Bullinger, to beg him and the Church at Zürich, " to show yourselves kindly affectioned and merciful to those wretched and unfortunate individuals who have fled from hence for the sake of the Christian religion " ([1]).

Certainly this earnest and pathetic appeal did not fall on deaf ears as regards the foreign Reformed in general and Bullinger in particular. Two years later (April, 1556) John (afterwards Bishop) Ponet, writes from Strasburg a special letter of gratitude to Bullinger, declaring that " many thanks are due from us to our Lord God for having placed over His Church in this calamitous age such a teacher as yourself. . . How greatly your kind offices towards them have bound the rest of the English to you I had rather imagine than express . . . lest I should seem to obscure their greatness by recounting them." He then recounts his own special personal indebtedness, since he had been deprived of all his "ample" means of livelihood. But he praises God who, in place of this severe trial, had "afforded him for his comforters, Bullinger, Melanchthon, Martyr and other shining lights of His Church " ([1]).

Peter Martyr Vermigli, the Florentine ex-Abbot, whose father had been a disciple of Savonarola, had with some difficulty been able to leave England on Mary's accession and return to Strasburg, where he resumed his post of Professor of Theology. England and Oxford had treated him well for the past five years and he was not slow to acknowledge the debt. In 1555 he entertained John Jewel who had escaped to the Continent and when Martyr accepted the Chair of Hebrew at Zürich in 1556, he took with him Jewel, Sandys and Grindal.

In Zürich these refugees for conscience' sake were received with special kindness. Bullinger himself received many into his own house and the magistrates supplied enough food to sustain 13 or 14 families. But the exiles, wherever possible, refused charity and insisted on paying their way. Edmund Grindal, the future Archbishop of Canterbury, escaped to Strasburg, and Strype tells us that the magistrates there "did freely and christianly give harbour to divers English Protestants of the best rank, both of the laity and the clergy, and allowed them a church for the exercise of their religion, according as they professed it in England." The laity included Sir A. Cook, Sir R. Morison, Sir John Cheke, and Sir T. Wroth, "all persons of great learning and extraordinary worth and goodness." But besides these prominent laymen Strasburg hospitably sheltered many promising English divinity students, for Martyr wrote to Bullinger in February, 1554, telling him that

English youths have come over to us in great numbers, partly from Oxford and partly from Cambridge, whom many godly merchants are bringing up to learning, so that if religion is reformed to its former state in England they may be of some benefit to the Church of England ([2]).

The general adherence of the English exiles to Zwinglian or Calvinistic views on the Eucharist caused them often to be received with a certain coolness, and even at times with open hostility, by many Lutherans. Strype makes a sweeping statement which is scarcely borne out by the recorded facts, when he says that the exiles—

found little hospitality in Saxony and other places in Germany where Lutheranism was professed. But on the contrary the exile English were much hated by those of that profession because they looked upon them as Sacramentaries and holding as Calvin and Peter Martyr did in the doctrine of the Sacrament. Therefore when any English came among them for shelter they expelled them out of their cities ([3]).

He says that books on Ubiquitarian teaching were published and attempts were made to inflame magistrates against the English exiles, and the Saxon divines called them 'heretics' false prophets and Suvermerians. While this may be true of certain extreme Lutherans, other evidence proves that the most part showed a more tolerant spirit and recognised the exiles as persecuted brethren suffering in a common cause. They subordinated their difference on Eucharistic teaching to their whole-hearted agreement on the main principles of the Reformation. At Wesel Philip Melanchthon specially interceded with the Senate to befriend the English refugees—" they should," he urged, " be retained and helped and not afflicted and vexed with any rough sentence." He wrote in a similar strain to the authorities at Frankfort—" The English," he said, " were not to be oppressed, but to be cherished, considering their sentiments were sound in the main Articles of the Christian Confession and that whereas they differed in some points they were to be instructed and not to be rudely thrown out from among them by force and violence " ([4]). Certainly this appeal did not lack response, for the magistrates at Frankfort showed conspicuous hospitality and much forbearance to the English exiles there, who as we shall see, gave them no little trouble by their unseemly and unbrotherly contentions. But Bishop Grindal singles out Frankfort for special commendation when writing to the authorities there in 1561. " No time," he told them, " could ever

root out of their minds " the benefits of the " charitable
and christian harbour afforded them " in their exile.
The fact—

that England had so many bishops, and other ministers of God's
Word, which at that day preached the pure doctrine of the
Gospel, was owing to Strasburg, Zurich, Basel, Worms, but
above all the rest to Frankfort. " You received our people to
harbour, and having received, embraced them with the highest
humanity and defended them with your authority. And if we
should not acknowledge and speak of this piety of yours with
thankful minds, we were of all mankind the most ungrateful " (5)

One prominent Lutheran earned the special gratitude
of Grindal for his hospitable and friendly treatment of
the English exiles. The Duke of Wurtemburg con-
tributed as much as 400 or 500 dollars to those at
Strasburg, besides giving even more to the Frankfort
exiles. When the Duke visited England in Elizabeth's
reign, Grindal showed him great respect and entertained
him at his own house and enjoyed friendly conferences
with him even on the contentious question of the
Lutheran theory of consubstantiation. And although
he did not agree with the Duke on this point, apparently
the discussion was both frank and amicable, as Strype
tells us that " they were contented to hear one another's
arguments and each to suffer other to abound in his
own sense." Seeing that Grindal was definitely a strong
Calvinist, such display of tolerance, in that age, for
condemned Lutheran Eucharistic teaching, is surprising
and it exhibits Grindal in an unexpectedly favourable
light.

We also get from Grindal direct first-hand knowledge
as to the places of refuge of many of the exiles. For
while he, himself, was at Frankfort, he wrote a letter
(6 May, 1555) to Bishop Ridley, then in prison awaiting
martyrdom, telling him—

we be here dispersed in divers and several places. Certain be
at Tigurye, good students of either University a number, very
well entreated of Master Bullinger, of the other ministers, and
of the whole city. Another number of us remain at Argentine
and take the commodity of Master Martyr's lessons, who is a
very notable father. Maister Scory and certain other with him,
be in Friesland and have an English church there, but not very

frequent. The greatest number is at Frankfort where I was at this present by occasion, a very fair city, the magistrates favourable to our people, with so many other commodities as exiles can well look for. Here is also a church now well quieted by the prudency of Maister Coxe, and other which met here for that purpose. So that now we trust God hath provided for such as will flye forth of Babylon, a resting place where they may truly serve Him, and hear the voice of their true Pastor. I suppose in one place and other dispersed, there be well nigh an hundred students and ministers on this side the seas (⁶).

But although the hospitality provided was so general and widespread amongst both Lutheran and Reformed, yet the privations of the exiles were often great and the difficulty of obtaining employment very real. Very many of the divinity students and clergy who knew no trade, depended for their subsistence on the financial supplies sent secretly by their friends and sympathisers in England. This source of help was soon discovered by the English papists, and the ecclesiastical authorities used every effort to stop it. Thus James Haddon, Dean of Exeter, writing from Strasburg in January, 1555, to Bullinger, says—

"I have been entirely stripped of all my property," but he adds that there was now "some hope from other quarters." He was probably referring to the liberality of his hosts. In the previous month John Banks wrote to Bullinger from Strasburg telling him that "Our adversaries are endeavouring to exclude us from the liberality of those from whom we were expecting the necessary means of subsistence. Nothing indeed now seems to be left for us, but either that we English, who are in exile from our country for the sake of God's Word, must support ourselves by the labour of our hands or else implore the assistance of godly individuals to enable us to continue our studies " (⁷).

He adds that

the godly men by whom we have hitherto been aided and supported are either all of them cast into prison on *our account* or if any are still at liberty, they are so carefully watched by the papists, that they can afford us no assistance without the greatest danger. Whence it is that we are at this time placed in great difficulty and it is come to this, that each individual must look out how he can best provide for himself. For my own part I have no hope of being able to continue in the course of studies I had determined to pursue, for he who has maintained me hitherto is now reduced to like straits as the rest of the English, being spoiled of all his property without any hope.

Banks here refers to his patron—James Haddon—who was at this very time (apparently unknown to him) soliciting Bullinger's help to secure Banks a post as a reviser and corrector of proofs with some pious printer at Basle. A month later Banks wrote a letter of profound gratitude to Bullinger for his interest in obtaining him this employment.

Bullinger evidently spared no effort to befriend the English refugees and in September, 1557, a number of exiles at Frankfort wrote a special letter to him thanking him most warmly ' as a messenger of God ' for all his efforts and self-sacrifice for the " miserable and afflicted churches of the exiles " " from whom no human support or worldly advantage can be expected." " You," they tell him, " have not sought for any benefit to yourself, but the comfort of the churches groaning under the Cross, placing your hand as it were under the burden and partaking and sympathising in our calamities." This tribute was well deserved. For as early as March, 1554, we find Bullinger appealing to Calvin for hospitality to two English exiles, in language with a truly Apostolic ring. He describes them as

"learned and very godly " and says he has entertained them for a fortnight and as they wish to remain at Geneva for some time he hopes that Calvin will act as host to them and " whatever kindness you may show them I shall consider as conferred on myself, nay rather you will confer it upon Christ " (8).

Apparently many of the exiles maintained themselves by teaching in schools, or by writing books, while many were engaged with Calvin and Theodore Beza in preparing for the ' Geneva Bible.' A good many settled at Basle as the people there were specially kind and courteous, and a good few were able to gain employment in the printing works, which were famous, and the English were noted for their carefulness and diligence in this art. John Scory, Bishop of Chichester, was preacher to the Exiles at Emden and from here and from Wesel many Protestant books were sent to England to encourage sympathisers there to stand firm in their faith. John Jewel, at Strasburg, assisted Peter Martyr in writing his Commentaries on Judges, and he was reader in divinity there, and had for a time prominent men in his audience, like Grindal, Sandys, Sir J. Cheke, and Sir A. Cooke. John Foxe went to Basle and was occupied in getting together his material for his famous ' Acts and Monuments,' and Thomas Lever was the preacher to the small English congregation at Arrau.

The more extreme, or as they were soon styled, ' Puritan ' exiles, migrated to Geneva and the fellowship there included John Knox, Goodman, Whittinghame, Gilby, Sampson, Laurence Humphrey, John Pilkington and Bishop Coverdale. Here they inaugurated a Church on a presbyterian basis and their familiarity with the Genevan presbyterian discipline led most of them to give much trouble concerning ' non-conformity ' later on under Elizabeth. In this way, at least from association, the Swiss Reformers exerted a disquieting influence on the Elizabethan Settlement of religion, as this ' puritan party ' on their return to England tenaciously advocated their Genevan forms of discipline and worship for the Anglican Church.

The seeds of this future discord had, however, been sown in the early days of the Exile in the dissension which arose amongst the English refugees at Frankfort. It is necessary to refer to this unedifying dispute, which reflected no credit on either party, because, bitter and acute as it was, it did not interfere with or interrupt the close fellowship which existed, and continued to exist, between the Anglican Reformers and their Continental brethren. Although each side sought to win the support of Calvin, the quarrel ended, as it began, as a solely domestic concern of exiled English Churchmen. It was in April, 1554, that a party of French Protestants arrived from London at Frankfort and they soon secured from the Senate the use of a church for worship and were ministered to by Valerandus Pollanus who had been superintendent of a French Church at Glastonbury. Two months later, a small party of English exiles, including William Whittinghame, arrived at Frankfort, and the magistrates were persuaded to grant them the use on alternate days of the French Church for their worship, provided that they agreed in doctrine and in

65

ceremonies with the French Church. They were to subscribe a common Confession of Faith with the French, and their worship, if not identical, must be such as the French fully approved of.

The English chose the 1552 Prayer Book as their model, but they made considerable alterations in it. In particular they gave up the use of the surplice, the Litany and the English Confession, and altered much in the Sacramental services which they considered both superfluous and superstitious. They then invited their fellow exiles in Strasburg, Zürich, Duisburg, and Emden, to join in their Church. These other exiles replied that they must require as a basic condition of their joining into ' one Congregation ' the agreement of their worship with the Order set forth in England in 1552. They argued very forcibly that any serious alterations of this Service would " seem to condemn the chief Authors thereof " who were now confirming their belief in that Service " with the price of their blood." It would give occasion they affirmed, " to their adversaries to accuse our doctrine of imperfection and us of mutability." It would also cause " the godly to doubt the Truth wherein they were before persuaded." This definite position was maintained by men destined to become prominent in the Elizabethan Church, such as Robert Horne, Thomas Lever, John Parkhurst, Laurence Humphrey, James Haddon, Edmund Grindal, and Edwin Sandys. Meanwhile the Frankfort congregation invited John Knox, from Geneva, to accept the pastorate of their church, and they then refused to agree to the use of the 1552 Prayer Book, since they declared it to contain " many unprofitable ceremonies." Whittinghame and Knox then sought the opinion of Calvin on the Second Prayer Book of Edward VI, sending him a Latin translation of it. Calvin in his reply admitted that there was " no manifest impiety " in the English Liturgy, although he considered that it contained " many tolerable foolish things," or rather that " there was not in it that purity which was to be desired." And he considered that " it behoved the learned grave and godly Ministers of Christ to enterprise further, and to set forth something more filed from rust and purer."

In March, 1555, another party of English exiles led by Dr. R. Cox, lately Chancellor of Oxford University, arrived at Frankfort, and they were most insistent on the full use of the English liturgy. Moreover, they refused to sign the Discipline drawn up for the Church and they were at length only admitted to membership on the special intreaty of John Knox. The result of the inclusion of this new body of exiles in the church was that they outvoted the original and 'puritan' party and dismissed Knox from his office of Minister. This action seems strangely ungrateful and high handed, but it should be explained that these exiles were fresh from England where their brethren were being grievously persecuted for their defence of the 1552 Prayer Book. They had therefore been greatly provoked by a sermon of John Knox's, in which he had denounced this Book as containing in it things " both superstitious, impure and unperfect." The ' Knox ' party then complained to the Magistrates, who ordered the newcomers to conform to the discipline of the French Church. By way of retaliation the Prayer Book party reported to the Magistrates some violent and treasonable language used by Knox against Queen Mary and the Emperor Philip, which they declared endangered their whole position. The Magistrates, in alarm, ordered Knox to depart, and he was accompanied by John Foxe and William Whittinghame. The triumphant party soon secured the Magistrates' consent to use the English liturgy.

What is of interest for us to notice in this disgraceful dispute, is the nervous anxiety of Cox and the Frankfort Church to justify their action in the eyes of Calvin and to correct the partial account which he had been given by their opponents. The letter written in April, 1555, and signed by Cox, Sandys, Grindal, and others, is further evidence of the warm regard and great respect which these future leaders of the Anglican Church displayed towards this outstanding champion of the Continental Reformation. It is quite evident that they regard Calvin as an acknowledged leader and guardian

67

of the common Protestant Faith. They commence by saying that " they considered it a mark of our duty and regard to you to inform you, as early as possible of all that has been done and with what design." They are at pains to explain the reason of their delay to write to him sooner—before the quarrel was ended—was not in any sense " to undervalue your authority which is and ought to be most highly esteemed and regarded, not only by ourselves, but by the world at large." Their excuse was that as he was at such a great distance from them, they were " unwilling to disturb your most important meditations by our trifling domestic concerns." They then inform him of the concessions which they made in order to placate, if possible, the scruples of those they describe as wilfully factious brethren—" We gave up," they say, " Private Baptisms, Confirmation of Children, Saints' Days, Kneeling at Holy Communion, the Linen Surplice of the Ministers, and other things of like character, not as being impure and papistical but because they were in their own nature indifferent and we chose to lay them aside rather than to offend the minds or alienate the affections of the brethren."

In a later and much fuller letter, written in September, 1555, they again declare to Calvin—" we regard you with entire veneration and love, both by reason of your singular godliness, and also of your especial pre-eminence in the most valuable attainments. . . Your name ought deservedly to have influence both with us and with all godly persons." They tell Calvin that he had been most scandalously deceived by false reports concerning their services and ceremonies, and that they were ready to give him a true account of them whenever he pleases. They add that it was not surprising that their ceremonies seemed " burdensome to those persons who exclaim against the public reading of the Word of God as an irksome and unprofitable form."

The controversy resulted, for a time at least, in a virtual schism between the Prayer Book and the ' Puritan ' parties, but it did not create any breach in the close friendship between Calvin and the other leading foreign Reformers and the ' Anglican ' party. Calvin was " very glad " that they had " stilled the matter with quietness " and he exhorted both sides to " keep the holy band of amity." Moreover, there was evidently a diversity of view amongst the Continental Reformers as amongst the English, on the disputed question of worship and ceremonies. That the Swiss Reformed did not all side with the ' Puritan ' element on the question is plain from the readiness of Peter Martyr to defend publicly with Cranmer the 1552 Service Book " as more pure and agreeable to the Word of God than any sort of religion that hath been used in England these thousand years." Yet John Knox declared of this same Book " that there were things in it placed only by man's authority and no ground in God's Word for the same, and had also a long time very superstitiously in the Mass been wickedly abused " (9).

There seems, however, little doubt that, as regards worship and ceremonies, the sympathies of the Swiss Reformers lay more on the side of the ' Puritan ' principle—that nothing should be allowed unless it was expressly commanded in Scripture, rather than the mere exclusion of everything which was not in accord with the teaching or usage of the New Testament ; though, as we shall see later, they were not prepared to insist on the exclusive adherence to this Puritan ' principle ' at all costs. Bullinger, however, definitely disliked the surplice, the ring in marriage and the Churching of Women, and probably a large party desired a distinct break with the liturgies and ceremonies of the Medieval Church, and the use of simpler forms and rites more entirely drawn from Scripture. But as we shall see later, it would be dangerous to make any precise generalisation on this point.

CHAPTER V

THE ENGLISH REFORMATION SETTLEMENT UNDER ELIZABETH

THE position of England in 1558 on the death of Mary was anything but bright. Her successor, Elizabeth, was at the head of a Nation which was beset by enemies, and she possessed only a questionable title to the throne, since the Papalists regarded the daughter of Anne Boleyn as an illegitimate heretic. Many of them wished to press the superior claims of Mary Queen of Scots to the English throne, a policy which was at this time actively encouraged by France. The danger from this quarter grew even more serious a few months later when Mary Queen of Scots became also Queen of France on the accession of Francis II in 1559.

Philip of Spain, who had now lost his hold on England, was irritated because Elizabeth refused to allow him to transfer his affections to her. He was also seriously alienated by the defection of England into ' heresy.'

Although careful and diplomatic, Philip was really a fanatical Romanist, and had all the wealth of the New World at his disposal, while the Roman Church was at this time specially powerful and actively aggressive owing to the zeal of the newly-formed " Society of Jesus," and to the reforms effected through the Council of Trent. Moreover, the defences of England were in a feeble condition. There was only a small antiquated and badly equipped military force, the Treasury was depleted and the coinage debased. Calais—the ' gate of

France '—had just been lost, and pestilence and famine were devastating the land. Elizabeth was also faced with a serious religious problem, especially as the English Reformers had no outstanding religious leader, like Calvin or Cranmer, and they had been engaging while in exile, in unseemly, unprofitable squabbles about what were really trifling non-essential differences.

Had Elizabeth chosen to maintain the religious position of her sister, her prospects would have seemed far more promising and more secure from outside interference. Certainly the espousal of the Reformed cause was a most courageous experiment, apart altogether from the then unsolved problem of her own personal convictions. There is much, however, in her subsequent actions to show that Elizabeth was a convinced Protestant, and it is scarcely fair to attribute them all merely to astute political diplomacy, even though there may be much in her official policy to lend colour to Bishop Creighton's extreme assertion that " there was no truth or honesty in anything she said ([1])." For instance, she deliberately left the church during a service rather than countenance the elevation of the host, a ceremony which she expressly forbade Bishop Oglethorp to perform at the Coronation Mass Service. The following Easter she received the Communion in both kinds. Some eighteen years later Bishop Horn declares that the Queen was " solely intent on advancing the truth of the Gospel with full sails, both at home and abroad." And he adds that " she has always abominated popery from her infancy ([2]) ".

It is also difficult to discover, apart from her own personal preference, what could have induced Elizabeth at such a juncture to espouse the Protestant cause. For it was a pathway at once beset with complications, difficulties and dangers. The immediate outcome of the Treaty of Château Cambrésis was the marriage arrangement between Philip of Spain and Elizabeth, daughter of Henry II of France, an alliance which pointed very clearly to an attempted or designed extirpation of Protestantism by these two formidable European powers. In fact the desire of these Sovereigns to crush ' heresy ' in Europe was the underlying aim of that

71

Treaty. Such a prospect alone, made it necessary for Elizabeth to walk most warily so as not by any too openly aggressive action to alienate either France or Spain.

She therefore commenced her reign with the definite announcement of a moderate religious policy. She carefully instructed Lord Keeper Bacon to warn the Parliament " that no party language was to be kept up in this kingdom, that the names heretic, schismatic, papist and such like were to be laid aside and forgotten " (³). But the passing of the Act of Uniformity in April, 1559, restoring the 1552 Prayer Book, was a clear indication that Elizabeth had determined to cast in her lot on the Reformed side, while 4 years later the Convocation confirmed and stereotyped the Protestant character of the Church by the authorisation of the Thirty-Nine Articles of Religion as its standard of doctrine. Their purpose was clearly stated to be "for the Avoiding of Diversities of Opinion, and for the establishing of Consent touching true Religion," and not, as is sometimes asserted, " as formularies which men of differing views might accept, because their language admitted of various interpretations " (cf. *Times Literary Supplement*, April 20, 1933).

The news of the accession of Elizabeth was naturally the occasion of much relief and joy to the exiles on the Continent. They at once called a truce to their fratricidal quarrels, and the English Church at Geneva, consisting mainly of the more extreme or ' puritan ' section issued an urgent call to unity to their fellow exiles in the different havens of refuge where they had settled. They recognised the necessity of an " unfeigned reconcilation," " so that no Papist should take advantage of a further dissension in their own country." " The greatness of this marvellous benefit," they declare, " overcometh our judgments and thoughts," and they seek for " godly counsel and brotherly conference," so that " together we may reach and practice the true knowledge of God's Word, which we have learned in this our banishment, and by God's merciful providence seen in the best Reformed Churches." This wording of the desired ' goal,' was no doubt significant, suggesting that although they were ready ' freely ' to " remit all offences" and ' embrace ' their brethren, this happy reunion was to be on their own terms. For they had apparently only ' learned ' " the true knowledge of God's Word," in " this our banishment." This was an assertion which certainly might be interpreted as a reflection on the purity or perfection of the religion authorised in England under Edward VI ! The Frankfort Congregation therefore return a very friendly but also a very guarded reply. They tell the Geneva Church that it will be little use to have further contention about ceremonies since the decision on these questions " will not lie either in your hands or ours," but in the " common consent of Parliament." They trust, however, " that we shall not be burdened with unprofitable ceremonies." But in any case they inform the Geneva brethren that they " purpose to submit themselves to such Orders as shall be established by authority, being not of themselves wicked, so we would wish you willingly to do the same." Further they emphasise the comparatively unimportant nature of such questions when they add " For whereas all the Reformed Churches differ among themselves in divers Ceremonies, and yet agree in *the unity of Doctrine*, we see no inconvenience, if we use some Ceremonies diverse from them, so that we agree in the chief points of our Religion " [4]. This clear statement of " in essentials unity and in non-essentials liberty " was the foundation principle of the Anglican Reformers, and it largely explains their later attitude and relationship with the foreign Protestant Churches.

There was very clear evidence of this general unity amongst all those of the Reformed Faith " on the chief points of our Religion " at this time. In December, 1558, just as Elizabeth was commencing her reign, Peter Martyr wrote to her from Zürich, a long letter of advice exhorting her to restore the purity of the Christian Faith in England. The whole purport of this earnest appeal was evidence of the practical unity and solidarity in aim and purpose of all the Reformed. " I feel confident," he writes, " that your Majesty has a ready mind

73

and will for re-establishing Evangelical Religion."
" Wherefore," he concludes, " gird thyself with courage
to the sacred work which all good men look for from
thee " ([5]).

A similar example of this practical unity of interests
is afforded in the letter which Hierome Zanchius wrote to
John à Lasco in January, 1559. Zanchius was the
Public Reader in Divinity at Strasburg, and although he
could not accept the orthodox Lutheran view of the
Eucharist, he was able, after putting his own interpretation on it, to subscribe the Augsburg Confession—" I
cannot by any means admit that the body of Christ is
present with our bodies in the Supper. But that the
same true and substantial body of Christ is present
with my mind in the Supper, where it is most efficacious,
I cannot deny " ([6]). Zanchius writing from Strasburg,
tells à Lasco that almost all the English who have been
exiles here for five years more or less, on account of
religion, have returned to their country. I do not doubt
that the Lord will make use of the services of many of
them for the restoration of the Reformed Faith in
England as a real support and strength to all other
branches of it in Europe." " We feel persuaded,"
he says, " that the happy introduction of the kingdom of
Christ into the kingdom of England, would be no small
help to *all other Churches* dispersed through Germany,
Poland and other regions " ([7]). Yet although he men-
toins Lutheran countries, he must have been well aware
that the ' Elizabethan Settlement ' was not conducted
on Lutheran lines. Bullinger makes this point quite
clear when writing to Utenhovius in August, 1559, " I
see," he says, " there will be no little disturbance in
England if the Augsburg Confession be received, which
some persons wish, a most undesirable thing on many
accounts. . . The Reformation in England satisfies the
pious, this is much better than the Augustan Confession " ([8]).

There were certainly minor differences on doctrine
and practices between the Lutherans and the Helvetians,
but these did not prevent the Anglicans from stretching
out the right hand of friendship and fellowship to both,

even though they shared the Sacramental teaching of the Swiss rather than of the Germans. Bishop Jewel, when referring to the spiritual darkness of the pre· Reformation days, speaks of the conversions of Martin Luther and Hulderic Zwingli, whom he describes as " most excellent men, even sent of God to give light to the whole world " (⁹). Referring again to the differences between the Lutherans and the Zwinglians, Jewel says, " in very deed they of both sides be Christians, good friends and brethren. They vary not betwixt themselves upon the principles and foundations of our religion, nor as touching God nor Christ, nor the Holy Ghost, nor of the means to justification, nor yet everlasting life, but upon one only question, which is *neither weighty* nor *great*; neither mistrust we, or make doubt at all, but they will shortly be agreed " (⁹). Jewel of course referred to the difference on the doctrine of the Eucharist.

But the unity of the foreign Reformers, which Jewel emphasises, " upon the principles and foundations of our religion," primarily implied the agreement of Lutherans and Zwinglians on the main articles of the Catholic Faith as expressed in the early Creeds of the Church—the Apostles' and Nicene. As early as A.D. 431 the First Council of Ephesus had accepted the profession of the Nicene Faith as a sufficient test for orthodox or Catholic belief, so that in this historical and primitive sense the foreign Protestants were true Catholics. Moreover they were not slow to claim this title. The ' Second Helvetic Confession ' disclaims any thought of rashly " breeding or nourishing schisms in the Church." The truth and unity of the Church, it declares, consists " in the truth and unity of the Catholic Faith," and it adds, " This Catholic faith is not taught us by the ordinances and laws of man, but by the holy Scripture, a compendious and short sum whereof is the Apostles' Creed."

But it is necessary for the present purpose to study in detail the Anglican Settlement under Elizabeth and see or enquire how far it was in agreement, on those " principles and foundations " of religion, with the unity already attained amongst the Continental Protestants.

(A) THE CHURCH AND MINISTRY

We will first deal with the doctrine of the ' Church.' The Anglican Reformers had, even in Henry VIII's reign, emphasised the distinction between the ' invisible ' and the ' visible ' aspects of the Church.   The *Institution of the Christian Man* (1537) had described the ' Invisible ' Church as the ' very mystical Body of Christ " as a " Company of elect and faithful people of God," both here and in heaven ' ordained to everlasting life ' (¹⁰).

The Elizabethan Churchmen enunciated still more clearly this distinction. The Convocation of 1562 authorised Dean Nowell's Catechism, in which the nature of the Catholic Church is treated at some length. The Church is defined in its invisible aspect as " the universal number and fellowship of all the faithful, whom God through Christ hath before all beginning of time appointed to everlasting life." " Although they be severed by divers and far distant times and places . . . they are members of the one self-same body whereof Christ is the head. . . . But this communion of Saints cannot be perceived by our senses . . . since it is the congregation of those whom God hath by His secret election adopted to Himself through Christ, which Church can neither be seen with eyes, nor can continually be known by signs."   Yet Nowell adds, " there is a Church of God visible, or that may be seen, the tokens or marks whereof He doth shew and open to us." Richard Hooker also declares that the serious ' oversights,' that have been made because men failed to observe the clear difference " first between the Church of God mystical and visible, then between visible, sound and corrupted," " were neither few nor light " (¹¹). It was this confused connotation of the ' Church,' which was so conspicuous a feature and fraught with such melancholy and disastrous results at this time. For instance, Sir T. More, in declaring that " Christ's Church can be but one, and that it must needs follow that there can none go out of it to begin any new Church of Christ," and that " those that go out thereof must needs be churches of heretics ; " * is confusing the 'mystical' and the 'visible' Church of God, and attributing to the latter a perfect spiritual unity which is only applicable to the 'Mystical Body of Christ.'

The XIXth Article of 1562 also speaks of the 'Visible' Church of Christ, while the Prayer Book certainly implies the invisible aspect of the Catholic Church when it speaks of "the mystical body of Thy Son, which is the blessed company of all faithful people " [12].

The same distinction is made in the foreign Reformed Confessions of Faith. The Augsburg Confession, although avoiding the use of the term, 'Invisible Church,' defines the Church as ideally or 'properly' 'the congregation of saints and true believers,' and then it adds " in this life many hypocrites and evil persons are mingled with it " [13]. Similarly the Second Helvetic Confession (1566) defines the Church as " a company of the faithful . . . a communion of all saints, that is of them who do truly know and rightly worship and serve the true God in Jesus Christ the Saviour . . . one church which we call Catholic, spread abroad through all the parts and quarters of the world." And it explains that this Church " may be termed invisible " . . . because its true members " being hidden from our sight and known only unto God, cannot be discerned by the judgment of man." In its visible aspect it declares " not all that are reckoned in the number of the Church are saints and lively and true members of the Church " [14].

Again the Scotch Confession of 1560 describes the one Catholic Church as " the elect of all ages, of all realms, nations and tongues, one company and multitude of men chosen of God—out of which Church there is neither life nor eternal felicity." But it adds, " this Church is invisible, known only to God " (Art. XVI).

In 1566 Thomas Rogers published a Commentary on the Thirty Nine Articles, which he entitled the 'Catholic Doctrine of the Church of England.' He was what would be called today, a 'Central Churchman,' strong in his opposition to the Romanists on the one hand and

---

* More's "English Works" (1557), p. 628.

to the presbyterian Puritans, of the Cartwright type, on the other. He was the first to expose the extravagant Sabbatarian tenets propounded by Dr. Bound (an advocate of the extreme Puritan ' Brethren ') in his book ' Sabbath Doctrine ' (published in 1595). According to the teaching of these ' Brethren,' it was as great a sin to throw a bowl, or to ring more bells than one on the Lord's Day, as to commit murder. Rogers was the means of bringing these " sabbatarian errors and impieties " to the notice of the authorities, and so of getting their books called in. This thoroughly representative Anglican became Chaplain to Archbishop Bancroft, and in 1607 he dedicated a fresh edition of his exposition on the Articles to the Archbishop, who thought so highly of it that he caused it to be circulated throughout his Province. Rogers reminds Bancroft in his ' Preface ' that " the purpose of our Church is best known by the doctrine which she doth profess ; the doctrine by the Thirty Nine Articles . . . the Articles by the words whereby they are expressed . . . other doctrines than in the said Articles is contained, our Church neither hath nor holdeth." This is a very unequivocal statement, which probably would not pass without some challenge even by ' Central Churchmen ' today.

The purpose of Rogers' Commentary was, as he expressed it, to prove to all that the Church of England was " at unity . . . with the neighbour Churches abroad—Christianly reformed—in all matters of chiefest importance and fundamental points of religion."

As an illustration of this assertion, Rogers, in dealing with Article XIX, defines the ' Church of Christ ' as ' to man partly visible and invisible partly.' " The ' invisible ' being the elect either triumphing in heaven or fighting on earth "—" these as members of the Church are said to be invisible, not because the men be not seen, but for that their faith and conscience to Godward is not perfectly known unto us." He then defines the ' members ' of the Visible Church " as being some for God and some against God," " but all notwithstanding deemed parts of the Church and accounted faithful, so long as they make no manifest and open rebellion against the Gospel of Christ." And he cites passages from the 'Confessions' of the foreign Reformed Churches to prove that this was the doctrine held by them all.

A similar harmony or unanimity is evident with regard to the necessary 'notes' of the Visible Church of Christ. The Anglican Article mentions these as the 'preaching of the pure Word of God' and the 'due ministration of the Sacraments'— a definition which is based on the almost identical language of Article VII, of the Augsburg Confession. The great Elizabethan churchman Richard Hooker, in dealing with this subject declares "the unity of the body (the Church) consists in these three things. Its members own one Lord, profess one faith, and are initiated by one baptism. In whomsoever these things are, the Church doth acknowledge them for her children, them only she holdeth for aliens and strangers in whom they are not found " ([15]). The French Confession of Faith of 1559 further declares that "there can be no Church where the Word of God is not received, nor profession made of subjection to it, nor use of the Sacraments " (Art. XXVII).

The Second Helvetic Confession enunciates the same two 'Notes,' of sincere preaching and ministration of the Sacraments ordained by Christ; while the Scotch Confession of 1560 states clearly "the notes of the true Kirk of God we avow to be first, the true preaching of the Word of God. . . Secondly the right administration of the Sacraments . . . and lastly, Ecclesiastical discipline uprightly ministered as God's Word prescribes " (Art. XVIII).

But if we turn to the 'notes' of the Church, as enunciated by the Græco-Russian Church, we see at once the sharp distinction and division between the position adopted by the Reformed and the unreformed Churches. The 'Full Catechism' of Philaret, 1840 (Philaret was Metropolitan of Moscow for 50 years), was approved by all the Eastern Patriarchs and by the Russian Holy Synod. It therefore can be regarded practically as the official teaching of the Orthodox Church. In this Catechism, the Church is defined as "a divinely instituted Community of men, united by the Orthodox

79

Faith, the law of God, the hierarchy, the Sacraments."
Thus, instead of the Reformed teaching that the 'church'
is a " Congregation of faithful men," we have it described
as a " divinely instituted community of men." And
instead of the two definite Evangelical Notes of the
" preaching of the Word of God and the ministration of
the Sacraments," we get the exclusive ' Notes ' of
' The Orthodox faith,' ' the hierarchy and the Sacraments.' This insistence on the ' hierarchy,' that is on
the possession of a certain type of polity or organisation
as necessary for the mark of a true Church, at once
introduces a medieval and unevangelical conception of
priesthood and ministry, which can best be summed up
in the slogan, ' No bishop, no Church.' It represents a
view which, since the Tractarian Movement, has been
assiduously taught in the Church of England by many—
that it is episcopal polity alone which makes a Church,
and that non-episcopal communities are only organised
religious ' bodies.' In accordance with this medieval
and Tractarian view of ' Catholicity,' it is assumed that
Continental Reformed Churches were only first ' formed '
at the Reformation after they had, like the Anglican,
repudiated as unscriptural much of the current Roman
teaching, as stereotyped by the Council of Trent. But
since the ' Church ' is ' a congregation ' of professing
believers and not a community governed by a certain
necessary type of hierarchy, these ' congregations of
faithful men ' in Germany and other Countries, at the
time of Luther, had continued as parts of the one
Catholic Church. They were not dissolved, nor was
their continuity broken, because owing to unscriptural
and unfaithful teaching and practice, they were compelled to dispense with one of their orders of governing
officials, and substitute another in its place. Luther
clearly recognised this fact. He asserted that the
Reformed German Evangelical Church " was a member
of the old true Church, inasmuch as it possessed the
Sacraments of Baptism and the Lord's Supper, the
power of the Keys, the Word and preaching, without any
addition of man, the ancient faith as contained in the
Apostles' Creed " (16).

80

For we must carefully bear in mind that it is not a special outward organisation that mars or makes the Church of Christ, since the living members who are in vital touch with the Risen Head of the Church, can adapt or alter their particular outward organisation as emergency or changing necessities require. This is a natural consequence and application of the New Testament doctrine of the priesthood of all believers. This, at least, was the view of the Church and its Ministry which was held by the Elizabethan and foreign Reformers. Certainly the teaching of the Greek Church of ' no bishop, no Church, no Sacraments', had no support from any Anglicans at this date, and the Bishop of Gloucester has recenly declared that even to day only " a small knot of English Churchmen " maintain a similar position, and that they " have against them the whole body of competent historical scholars " [17].

But this is unquestionably the exclusive position still maintained by the Eastern Orthodox Church. In the ' Declaration ' which it put forth in August, 1927, at the ' World Conference on Faith and Order,' the Eastern delegates stated clearly that they could come to no agreement with those who did not hold that the Ministry " was instituted by Christ Himself in its three degrees of bishop, priest and deacon " [18] ; while the Patriarch of Alexandria in the Conference between Anglican and Eastern Church representatives in July, 1930, declared that " the Church has no power to recognise Ordinations in Churches where the Apostolic Succession has been broken " [19]. But as regards the ' Apostolic Succession ' through Bishops, as the exclusive officers for Ordination, this is a statement which the Anglican Church under the ' Elizabethan Settlement,' by its official actions, definitely challenged.

The Anglican Reformers were fortunate both in Edward VI's reign and also under Elizabeth in being able to retain the historic episcopal government and ministry for the Church of England, owing to the fact that a large number of the existing bishops led by Archbishop Cranmer, espoused the Reformed Faith. But there is abundant evidence to prove that they did not regard episcopacy as a necessary 'note' of the Church, but only as an ancient, scriptural and desirable form of Church organisation which the Anglican Church had decided to maintain. Cranmer had declared " that in the beginning of Christ's religion bishops and priests were no two things but both one office. In the New Testament, he that is appointed to be a bishop or priest, needeth no consecration by the Scriptures, for election and appointing thereto is sufficient " [20]. In 1540 he had officially stated that " there is no more promise of God that grace is given in the committing of the ecclesiastical office than it is in the committing of the civil office." Bishops Barlow and Cox also concurred in this view, while Prebendary John Bradford, the martyr and close friend of Bucer, Cranmer and Ridley, declared that " the true Church was not tied by any succession, but the Word of God... You shall not find in all the Scripture that your essential point of succession of bishops . . . Tell me whether the Scriptures know any difference between bishops and ministers, which you call priests ? " [21]. The retention of the historic Catholic polity did not therefore in any way interfere with the fellowship and unity of spirit and interest shown by the early Anglican Reformers to their Continental Reformed brethren, most of whom were compelled to adopt a presbyterian form of government, for which they could claim ancient and primitive authority.

It should be remembered that it was usually only the force of adverse circumstances which occasioned the abandonment of episcopal government by the Continental Reformed Churches. Melanchthon, in Article VII of the 'Apology' of the Confession of Augsburg, makes this fact quite clear when he says, " The severity of the bishops is the cause whereby that canonical polity is dissolved anywhere *which we very greatly desire to preserve.*" Again, in the 'Wittenberg Reformation,' drawn up in 1545 by Luther, Melanchthon and other theologians, as a limit of their concessions to the Romanists, the Lutherans state that they are prepared to accept the episcopal polity and ordination, if the bishops will maintain true doctrine and right use of the Sacraments, renouncing the sacrificial conception of the Ministry and the sacrificial character of the Lord's Supper, with the abolition of private masses " ([22]).

Calvin also, had no objection to Episcopacy on Scriptural grounds, and he definitely asserted that " the ancient bishops had no wish to frame a form of Church government different from that which God has prescribed in His Word " ([23]). At the time when Cranmer was seeking to secure a Synod of all the Reformed divines to set forth a unified statement of doctrine as against the decrees of the Council of Trent, then being formulated, Calvin joined with Bullinger and others in writing to Edward VI, and offering to have bishops in their churches and to constitute him their Defender, as an effective means of illustrating the organic unity amongst all the Reformed ([24]).

The Elizabethan Settlement did nothing to change the attitude of the Anglican clergy on this subject. While the Church leaders reaffirmed their intention of ' continuing and reverently esteeming the Orders of bishops, priests and deacons which had existed ' from the Apostles' time,' they also recognised fully and practically the validity of the Ministry and Sacraments of the Continental non-episcopal Churches. It is true that the rigid enforcement of the popular principle of ' national ' or ' regional ' religions, presented at times certain legal obstacles in the exercise of such non-episcopal ministries in the episcopally governed National English Church. But the Act of 1571 (xiii Eliz. cap. xii) was interpreted as permitting foreign presbyterian ministers to exercise their ministry and receive cures of souls in England, and several availed themselves of this privilege. The teaching of the leading Elizabethan Churchmen leaves us in no doubt about their view of episcopacy. Bishop Jewel the outstanding theologian and exponent of Reformed Catholicism, states his definite belief in the one Catholic Church of Christ and of the need of a regular and properly organised ministry for its visible branches. His language implies the ideal and mystical aspect of the Church. " We believe," he says, " that there is one Church of God and that the same is not shut up in one corner or kingdom, but that it is catholic or universal, and dispersed throughout the whole world ; so that there is now no nation which can truly complain that they be shut forth, and may not be one of the church and people of God, and that this church is the kingdom the body and the spouse of Christ, and that Christ alone is the prince of this kingdom, that Christ alone is the bridegroom of this spouse." Here Jewel is evidently referring to the spiritual government of the Church. As regards its external government, he says, " Furthermore that there be divers degrees of ministers in the Church, whereof some be deacons, some priests, some bishops, to whom is committed the office to instruct the people, and the whole charge and setting forth of religion." But Jewel follows the example of Article XXIII and is silent as to the particular persons who are deputed and authorised to " call and send ministers into the Lord's vineyard," although he emphasises, as that Article does, the point that " no man hath power to wrest himself into the holy ministry at his own pleasure and list " ([25]). Clearly he refuses to limit the " grace of Orders " to any special form of organisation, since he asserts that " God's grace is promised to one who feareth God and not to sees and successions." The " succession of doctrine " was, he declared, "the chief way to avoid anti Christ."

The very carefully expressed language of Article XXIII on the Ministry, is weighty evidence of the position taken on the question of the value of episcopal government by the Elizabethan divines. These Articles were carefully revised and reissued in 1571 just at the time when a new party of avowedly presbyterian Puritans was arising, led by Thomas Cartwright, which boldly denied the Scripturalness of episcopal government. Had the Elizabethan bishops believed in the doctrine of ' No bishop, no Church,' this was the precise moment in which to set this theory clearly forth in their ' Articles of Religion,' in order to refute effectually these intolerant presbyterian claims.

It is significant therefore that they left the indefinite wording of Article XXIII severely alone, although Dr.

84

Whitgift, afterwards Archbishop of Canterbury, was commissioned by Archbishop Parker to write an Answer to Cartwright's 'Admonition to Parliament.' This 'Answer' was specially reviewed and approved by Parker. In it Whitgift, instead of asserting the exclusive claims of episcopacy, defends its use in the English Church on the sole grounds of policy and expediency as an indifferent matter of external government. He tells Cartwright that it was not a question of what might " fitly be used in the Apostles' time, or may now be well used in some places, or be conveniently used in sundry reformed churches at this day." For he adds, " we *do not take upon us either to blame* or *to condemn other churches*, for such orders as they have received *most fit for their estates*." " As no certain manner or form of electing ministers is prescribed in Scripture," " every church," Whitgift declares " may do therein as it shall seem most expedient." And he adds, " In the Apostles ' time there were divers manners of ordaining and electing ministers " and the " ordering of ministers doth not appertain only to bishops . . . and it doth not therefore follow that there must always be one kind and form of government " ([26]). This was evidently the recognised Church teaching on the subject. We find, for instance, that Dr. Hammond, the Chancellor of London diocese in 1588, advanced the view that " episcopus being no name of distinction in office from the elder, could not import superiority over elders," and he added that since the Queen was supreme in ecclesiastical as well as civil matters, " if it had pleased her Majesty to have used no bishops at all we could not have complained of any defect in our Church " ([27]). This was an extremely bald Erastian claim, but it undoubtedly represented the accepted view of most churchmen of that period. It is also evidence of the current view of episcopacy which is confirmed by other definite official actions. For in 1582 Archbishop Grindal officially declared that a Scotch presbyterian divine, Morrison, had been ordained according " to the laudable form and rite of the Reformed Church of Scotland." He therefore licensed him " to celebrate the divine offices and minister the Sacraments throughout the whole Province of Canterbury " ([28]).

Moreover, as Strype declares, the Act of 1571 " was intended to comprehend cases of those who had received their orders in some of the Reformed Churches when they were in exile under Queen Mary " ([29]). Again, in the middle of the next century, Bishop Cosin declared that he himself had known men ordained in the French Reformed (presbyterian) Church " who had received cures of souls among us in the Church of England," and that the bishops " did not re-ordain them before admitting them to their charges," and that the laws only required them to consent to the established religion and subscribe the Articles ([30]).

Although such and similar testimony is well established, it has been urged that there are three or four specific cases during this reign which seem to favour the theory that the validity of foreign presbyterian Orders was questioned, if not denied, by Elizabethan Churchmen in authority. The names usually brought forward to prove this contention are those of Dean Whittinghame of Durham, Walter Travers, Reader at the Temple Church, Adrian Saravia and Robert Wright. It will be sufficient to say here* that with Whittinghame the contention really was whether he had been ordained ' presbyterianly ' at Geneva, since Archbishop Sandys expressly disclaimed any intention to " discredit the Church of Geneva." With regard to Travers, Archbishop Whitgift clearly pointed out that it was his " contempt for the (episcopal) Ministry of his own Church " and " the condemning of the kind of Ordering of Ministers " in England, by sneaking across to Antwerp to receive presbyterian Orders, which led his position and ministry to be questioned, at least as to its *legality*. He had openly defied the established " laws of Church and realm " concerning Ordination. There is no evidence to show that Saravia, a minister of the Dutch Reformed Church, who expressly taught that when

---

* I have dealt with these cases more fully in my ' Anglican Via Media,' p. 95.

" bishops fell away into idolatry," presbyters may ordain, was ever re-ordained in England by a bishop.

THE CASE OF ROBERT WRIGHT

The case of Robert Wright is a singular one and decidedly complicated. It is well, therefore, to examine it in some detail.

We should, however, carefully bear in mind that all attempts, at this time, of *Englishmen* to secure presbyterian ordination abroad and then try to exercise this ministry in England, were direct acts of rebellion against the law ' of Church and realm ' concerning ordination in the English Church. It was an attempt to thwart the National rule for episcopal ordination as one best suited for England. Consequently all *Englishmen* trying to exercise such non-episcopal ministries could at once have been refused as not being legally qualified, and as virtual rebels against the laws of the realm. Furthermore, a bishop who, like Whitgift, fully acknowledged the spiritual validity of presbyterian ordination, might still have described a disloyal Englishman who had clandestinely secured such Orders abroad, as *legally* in England ' no minister.' This, in fact, was the line which Whitgift was ultimately forced to take with Travers. He himself had previously elected Travers as a Fellow of Trinity College, Cambridge, but he soon discovered his great hostility to the established Church discipline, and declared that he " never found any who showed less submission and humility."

Consequently when Lord Burleigh petitioned the Queen to appoint Travers to the Mastership of the Temple instead of Hooker (in 1583), Whitgift warned her against him as " likely to do very much harm." He told Elizabeth that " Travers hath been and is one of the chief and principal authors of dissension in this Church, a contemner of the Book of Prayers, an earnest seeker of innovation, and either is of no degree of ministry at all, or else ordered beyond the seas, *not according to the form in this Church of England used*."

It is well to notice here that Whitgift does not deny

the validity of this foreign presbyterian ' ordering ' or call it " of no degree of ministry at all " ; but simply states that it is not *legally* regular or valid for an *Englishman.* All the same, a little later, Whitgift tells Burleigh that if " time and years have altered " Travers ' disposition ' and attitude (which he doubts), he " will be ready to do him good as any friend he hath." But as the Archbishop found that Travers by his writings and actions was just as obstinate and mischievous as ever, he determined, before he would consent to his appointment to the Mastership, or any other post, to make him prove that " he is a minister ordered according to the *laws* of the Church of England." This was a most natural and sensible way of excluding men of this troublesome type. The wisdom of this policy was at once apparent, since Travers, who was then Reader at the Temple, soon made Hooker's life miserable by continually and publicly from the pulpit controverting his teaching, until at length he was suspended.* In normal practice, however, this strictly legal policy does not seem to have been pursued, probably because the Elizabethan bishops had such a tender affection towards their former friends and benefactors of the foreign Reformed Churches that they were reluctant in any way to seem to reflect on their ministry.

But when these ' disloyal ' English Puritan ministers, in addition to obtaining their Orders in this illegal way, also stirred up faction and schism by reviling the Anglican Liturgy and discrediting its clergy, it is small wonder that the Bishops questioned very narrowly their professed foreign credentials for ministering in the Church. Robert Wright was apparently a man of this troublesome type. He was born in 1550 and went to Cambridge in 1565 and took his M.A. in 1572. After that he commenced preaching and was allowed to do so as an M.A. " by order of Her Majesty's Injunctions." He says that he did this with ' approbation,' and that therefore he did not even then regard himself " altogether in the common degree of laymen," especially because it

---

*Hooker's Works, I, 22-4 (1850).

was his "full purpose of serving in the Ministry when God should call him thereto." He was in fact what we should call to-day a 'Lay Reader.' From his own account we learn that he remained on in the University until quite the end of 1578. But from the statements or 'Charges' made against him at his different hearings and trials, it is evident that he was a very stiff and mischievous Puritan, noted for his 'nonconformities,' and for his uncharitable and sweeping criticisms of non-puritan clergy and dignitaries as 'dumb dogs' and 'clogs of Anti-Christ.'

After, if not before leaving Cambridge, he was welcomed into the family of the strongly Puritan Lord Rich of Rochford Hall in Essex. Evidently, Rich held the 'Anabaptist' view that a 'call' by the 'flock' was equivalent to ordination. Consequently in Wright's absence, he called his household together and asked if all were agreed to accept Wright as their spiritual teacher, and on their consent he appointed him to the post of private Chaplain to his household and 'esteemed him as his pastor.' At the same time, apparently, from Wright's statement, Lord Rich informed Aylmer, Bishop of London, that Wright was acting in this capacity (for which duties in a peer's house he needed no Bishop's licence), and also appealed to him to grant Wright a Public Preacher's Licence. But Aylmer refused this request, "when he understood I was no minister." This appointment and appeal must have been made in 1579, the evidence is not sufficient to decide the exact month. But *after* this refusal of a public licence, Wright adds, "But I continued without his (Aylmer's) check from Christmas was Two years till last Michaelmas." Wright wrote this in May, 1582, so that he must have continued his duties as private Chaplain at least from Christmas, 1579, to Michaelmas, 1581. Wright, however, declares that "he took not himself to be any other than a private man to do them some good till they might have a sufficient Pastor." Then he adds, writing in May, 1582, that—

It is true, that of the house of this Lord Rich, he said he took them for his Flock, not by virtue of the former Choice,

89

but having been called since the death of the old lord, unto the Ministry. And this (present) Lord being desirous to use his Ministry, with promise that he would labour to have it public, and my Lord of London not utterly denying Licence, but saying he would first see some testimony, that the said Minister was ordained Minister ([31]).

While this investigation as to Wright's credentials was being made, Wright tells us that he only continued to act as private Chaplain and "neither preached publicly nor ministered any Sacrament." He would, of course, have committed a distinct breach of the law if he had presumed to preach *publicly* or administer the Sacrament without a bishop's licence.

There is, in the absence of any absolutely conclusive evidence, a certain ambiguity in interpreting the language used by Strype in the account quoted above which he has taken from the Landsdowne MSS. Wright wrote it in May, 1582, and at that date the third Lord Rich, a young man, was ruling at Rochford Hall. Wright, in describing his ' puritan ' call to the chaplaincy some time in 1579, refers to the action of the second Lord Rich, who died in February, 1581. Consequently when he says in 1582, " It is true in the house of this Lord Rich," it is natural to suppose he is speaking not of the second, but of the third Lord Rich, and Strype evidently interprets his language in this sense, as he adds in brackets in the next sentence " And this (present) Lord being desirous to use his Ministry &c.". On this interpretation the meaning seems clear that when Wright says " in the House of this Lord Rich he took them for his flock, not by virtue of the former choice " ; he means the puritan ' call ' of the second Lord Rich in 1579 ; and when he adds " But having been called since the death of the old Lord Rich unto the Ministry," he means since the death of the second Lord Rich in February, 1581. This of course would mean that he secured ordination after February, 1581. Strype's interpretation has, however, been seriously challenged, and it has been contended* that the

* In an Article by Canon Maynard Smith in the ' Quarterly Review ' for April, 1931.

' Lord Rich ' referred to in Strype as " this (present) Lord," is the *second* Lord Rich, and that the ' old Lord Rich ' refers to the first Lord Rich who died in 1567, when Wright was only seventeen.   But Wright tells us that at the end of his seven years' preaching in the University, i.e., about the end of 1578, he was then " of full purpose of serving in the Ministry *when God should call him thereto*."   Obviously he was not *then* ordained. It seems extraordinary therefore that he should date his ordination, which thus could not have been *before* 1579, as " since the death of the ' old ' or first Lord Rich," who died as far back as 1567 ! He might almost as appropriately have said " since the death of Edward VI " !

But apart from the question of the precise date (1579 or 1581) of his ordination, Wright describes its place and occasion in the same account.   He says it was at Antwerp—" not that he went over for that end, but being at Antwerp, whither he went to see the Churches from whence *idolatry had been lately driven*, and English Merchants desiring him to assist in the Ministry, he was religiously ordained thereunto and there did execute it.   As also at Vilfort, where was also a Garrison of 600 Scots, by the earnest suit of their Band . . . and with consent of the Ministers of the three several languages in Antwerp." At his trial in November, 1581, he had declared that Villiers, the Minister for a time of the Reformed Church in Antwerp, had ordained him.

The reference to " the Churches from whence idolatry had been lately driven," narrows down the possible dates for Wright's clandestine ordination. This statement might possibly refer to the Protestant riots and destruction of images in the Romanist churches, which occurred in Ghent (not Antwerp), in 1578, owing to a wild popular outbreak which was sternly condemned by the Prince of Orange—the Protestant Leader. But it seems far more natural to construe it of the complete suspension by definite Edicts of the Romish worship which was carried out in July, 1581, in *Antwerp* itself, and Utrecht and other cities in Holland. There does not appear to have been any iconoclastic outbreak in Antwerp itself in 1578, so that Wright's statement about the churches being freed from idolatry *there* in 1578 would be scarely accurate ; whereas it fits exactly the position there in August, 1581, just after the Edicts of suspension of the Romish religion had been promulgated. Moreover, in his second letter to Lord Burleigh, in which Wright replies *seriatim* to the ' Notes of Matters proved against him by Sworn Witnesses ' (who were sent to examine him in prison early in 1582), we get further information which seems to fix the approximate date of his Ordination as not *before* May, 1581. These ' Witnesses ' had established the fact against Wright that he had drawn people away from their parish church by tolling a bell inviting them to a sermon which he preached in Rochford Hall. He was then asked by " What authority he preached," and these ' Witnesses ' reported that he answered that " he was called by the Reformed Church." Wright, in his explanatory letter to Burleigh, declared " No magistrate examined me, by what authority I preached unto whom I might give any such answer. Neither is it set down when or where I spake the words. If I said any such thing in private speech within this year (which I remember not) I might justly say it, though I took not upon me to do any public duty." (This cautious abstention from public duty was because he had not yet received the Bishop's licence.) As Wright wrote this in May, 1582, this would appear to settle the date of his ordination ' by the Reformed Church '—by which he meant the Reformed Church of the Netherlands—as within the year, i.e., not before May, 1581. Wright had previously confessed at his trial in November, 1581, that " he had received Orders of Villiers and other Ministers, at Antwerp," and as we know at the request of " the English Merchants desiring him to assist in the Ministry." This church of the English Merchant Adventurers was founded on a presbyterian basis on May, 1578, and Walter Travers (Hooker's colleague at the Temple) was ordained on that day as its first Minister by Villiers and two other presbyterian Ministers ([32]). Villiers was apparently the head

of the Reformed Church at Antwerp and a close friend
and adviser of this newly-founded English Merchants'
church. Two years later, when Thomas Cartwright had
succeeded Travers as Minister of this Church, he was
offered a professorship at Leyden University with the
request of an immediate answer. Cartwright wrote at
once regretting that there was not time given him to
consult the Antwerp Ministers and in particular his
friendly counsellor—Villiers—about the matter ([33]). This
would point to the fact that Villiers was still in Antwerp
in 1580 and so probably was there the next year, and
could then have assisted in the ordination of Wright in
August of that year. It has been objected that there is
not sufficient time to allow Wright to have heard of the
suspension of the Romish religion in Antwerp in July
and then to have travelled there from Essex, and received ordination and execute his ministry there and at
Vilfort, and yet have returned to England by the
month of October, when he was arrested (with the
bastard uncle of Lord Rich) and examined before the
Ecclesiastical Commissioners.

Certainly it must be admitted that a period of
ten weeks is not overlong for all these incidents,
but we must remember that there was close and
frequent intercourse then between England and the
Low Countries, and as we have seen, the celebrated
Polish nobleman—John à Lasco—thirty years before,
crossed from Calais to London in two days, and the
journey from Essex to Antwerp need not, with favourable weather, have taken any longer time. À Lasco
made a much longer journey from London to Emden in
March, 1549, in only three days. Moreover, Wright
had already travelled on the Continent, as we find a
record of him as being enrolled as a student at Heidelberg University on January 31, 1575 ([34]). He must
have paid visits to the Continent during his period of
residence at Cambridge University. He was therefore
probably, as a prominent Puritan, well known to the
English Merchants at Antwerp as an acceptable preacher.
They would naturally at once urge his ordination so
that they might have the benefit of his ministry. And he

could at the same time preach by special request at Vilfort. But even if the far more unlikely date of 1579 be the correct one for his ordination, it would not then prove that Aylmer declared he " was no minister " *after* this ordination—thus apparently challenging the spiritual reality of presbyterian Orders. For it was on the appeal for a licence by " my lord Rich that dead is," i.e., the second Lord Rich—that Aylmer refused this licence because, as Wright says, " he understood I was no minister." As we have seen, this appeal must have been sometime in 1579 and could well have been made before Wright had visited Antwerp and been ordained there later in 1579. The next appeal for a licence was made by the third Lord Rich who, together with his bastard uncle, visited Aylmer at Fulham, as we learn from Strype, in September, 1581. Aylmer asked Burleigh to inform the Queen of this visit, saying, that " now lately the present Lord Rich and his bastard Uncle came unto his house . . . to solicit him to licence the aforesaid Wright to preach in his diocese, but this the bishop utterly denied to do unless he would subscribe to the orders of the Church."

We should notice that the bishop's refusal is not based on the question of his foreign Orders, although it was almost certainly on this occasion that Lord Rich informed Aylmer of Wright's foreign Ordination and elicited the cautious reply from the Bishop that " he must first see some testimony that the said Minister was ordained Minister." It would seem that Lord Rich had not been careful to secure any convincing or documentary evidence of Wright's ordination at Antwerp to show Aylmer. Travers had received formal ' Letters of Orders ' from the Antwerp Church (a copy of which Fuller transcribes), but Aylmer reports from this interview with Lord Rich, that, as far as Wright's claim went, " he could not tell how or where " he was ' ordered ' [35]. It was at this interview that the Uncle grossly abused the Bishop for this refusal of a licence. Aylmer had for long tried to arrest Wright as a troublesome Puritan, but without success. The Queen was irritated at the inability to punish this determined nonconformist, but shortly after this stormy interview, Aylmer contrived to bring both Mr. Rich and Wright before the Commissioners in October, 1581. In the following month they were again accused of definite offences before the Bishop and the Commissioners. The most serious was " concerning a speech of theirs about solemnising the Queen's (Accession) Day, viz., November 17, and against Wright, for asking if they would make it a holy day." " For this cause and for rejecting the book and many other disorders, the bishop with the rest of the Commissioners sitting the 7th of November, committed them both to prison."

Here again there is no specific charge against Wright's foreign Orders, although it was probably at this trial that Wright declared " the manner of his admitting " to the Ministry. Had there been any definite official repudiation of his foreign presbyterian ministry, this stiff Puritan divine would have been the first to expose and denounce such a glaringly unfriendly act towards the foreign Protestants, instead of quietly writing to Burleigh, " I hope this Church will no more disallow the Ministers of other Reformed Churches than they disallow ours." But such a query was really beside the point, because even if Wright had been refused a licence on the ground of his foreign Orders, this would not have in any way " disallowed the Orders of the Ministers of other Reformed Churches." It would have been only a strict enforcement of the law of the Land concerning Ordination for *Englishmen*, and this was clearly episcopal. He would have been refused permission to exercise his foreign Orders in England, not because they were *spiritually* invalid or doubtful, but because they were *illegal* according to the laws of the Land. It is certain, however, that Wright, who expressly declared that he had been ordained by the Reformed Church, would not have quietly acquiesced in Aylmer's statement made in 1579, " that he understood I was no minister," if *then* he had already " been called by the Reformed Church to the Ministry."

In the end, Wright, after some 10 months in prison, was inclined to sign two articles allowing the ministry of the Church of England and the Book of Common Prayer, and Aylmer also required him to be bound over "in a good round sum" that from henceforth he should "neither commit in act nor preach anything contrary to the same." On this assurance "the Bishop did not mislike that he should have further favour." Evidently, this 'further favour' gave him liberty to preach, as we find Wright attending a 'presbyterian' General Conference as an Essex deputy, while in 1589 he was instituted by Bishop Scambler to the benefice of Dennington, in Suffolk.

Thus a careful survey of this case reveals no evidence that Aylmer ever declared that Wright was 'no minister' *after* his Ordination at Antwerp. Neither were his foreign Orders, although inquired into, ever made a definite charge against him at his trials, although they well might have been as contravening the law of the land concerning English Ordination. Certain modern historians, like Bishop Frere, have been led astray on this point by the definitely misleading statement of the Puritan historian Neal, who, in his anti-episcopal bias, misconstrues the account in Strype, and so declares that Aylmer "always refused Wright a preacher's licence, because he was no minister, i.e., had only been ordained among the foreign Churches." This is a serious misrepresentation of Aylmer's actions which, at the most, only amounted to the similar caution displayed by Archbishop Sandys regarding Whittinghame's ordination, i.e., a laudable and proper desire to be convinced that Wright had really been ordained presbyterianly when abroad.

Certainly any real denial of the spiritual validity of foreign non-episcopal Orders by Aylmer would have been a gross breach of fellowship, absolutely inconsistent with his known views and sympathies and with his former friendship with the foreign Reformers when in exile during Mary's reign. A man who had declared of Luther that "through the mighty hand of God . . . he was able to set up the Cross of Christ, pull down the chair of anti-Christ, restore God's Word, banish the Devil's sophistry . . . and find out the cross of Christ hidden in the dunghill of devilish doctrine " (³⁶) was not likely to assert the theory of ' No bishop, no Church,' and thus deny the ministry of either the Lutherans or the foreign Reformed Churches.

(B) THE EUCHARIST

Let us turn now to that storm centre of Reformation controversy and consider the teaching of the ' Elizabethan Settlement ' of Anglicanism on the doctrine of the Eucharist. As we have already seen, while all the Reformers had rejected the medieval and Roman teaching of transubstantiation and the propitiatory Sacrifice of the Mass, they had not all agreed in their views on the nature and purpose of the Lord's Supper. Bucer had approximated to Luther's teaching of Consubstantiation. Cranmer had at first believed both in transubstantiation and the Real Presence, but in Edward VI's reign he had taught a ' Virtual ' or receptionist view, similar to that held by Calvin and not far removed from the views of Zwingli. There is no evidence to show that Elizabethan Churchmen differed materially in their teaching on the Eucharist from the declared opinions of Cranmer and Ridley on the subject, so Article XXVIII was re-written to assert that " the Body of Christ is given, taken and eaten in the Supper only after a heavenly and spiritual manner, and the mean whereby the Body of Christ is received and eaten in the Supper is Faith." It also definitely condemned transubstantiation as ' overthrowing ' the nature of a Sacrament and as having " given occasion to many superstitions." "The ' Sacrifices of Masses ' in the which it was commonly said that the priest did offer Christ for the quick and dead to have remission of pain or guilt," were declared to be, " blasphemous fables and dangerous deceits " (Article XXXI). The language of Article XXIX ruled out even a Lutheran view of the Eucharist, since it definitely asserted that those who were ' void of a lively faith,' even though ' they pressed with their teeth ' the ' sign or sacrament ' of the ' Body and Blood of Christ,' " yet in no wise were they partakers of Christ." There was no indication anywhere in the Elizabethan formularies of the teaching of a "real objective Presence of Christ in the elements by virtue of consecration and apart from the faith of the recipient." Article XXVIII makes it quite clear that 'the Body of Christ' cannot be 'touched' or 'handled' even by the faithful communicant, since it is 'given, taken and eaten' in the Supper, "*only* after a heavenly and spiritual manner." It should be remembered that even the explanatory section on the Sacraments in the Catechism was not added until the revision of the Prayer Book in 1604. Hooker seems to have correctly interpreted the positive authorised teaching of the Anglican Church on the subject in his familiar enunciation of the receptionist view that "the real presence of Christ's most blessed body and blood is not therefore to be sought for in the Sacrament but in the worthy receiver of the sacrament . . . I see not which way it should be gathered by the words of Christ when and where the bread is His Body or the cup His blood, but only in the very heart and soul of him which receiveth them " ([37]). This language merely amplifies the injunction to the Anglican communicant—" Feed on Him in thy *heart* by faith with thanksgiving."

We can safely say that the teaching of the prominent Elizabethan divines on the Eucharist, with the possible exception of Bishops Guest and Cheney, who were credited with Lutheran sympathies, goes no farther than that of a real Spiritual Presence of Christ in the Lord's Supper to the worthy receiver. Archbishop Sandys makes this quite clear when he says, " by faith He is seen, by faith He is touched, by faith He is digested. Spiritually, by faith we feed upon Christ when we steadfastly believe that His body was broken and His blood shed for us upon the Cross " ([38]). " When these words be said unto us "—" this is my Body "—" we say," declares Bishop Cooper, " it is most true. But mystically, sacramentally, figuratively, not really and according to the natural substance " ([39]). Bishop Jewel almost in the language of Article XXIX says definitely,

" Wicked men, and such as believe not, receive not the body of Christ, they have no portion in it " ([40]).

It was on this point that the Anglicans and the foreign ' Reformed ' parted company with the Lutherans owing to their theory of consubstantiation. The ' Formula of Concord ' (1576) declared quite clearly, " We believe, teach and confess that in the Lord's Supper the body and blood of Christ are truly and substantially present, and that they are truly distributed and taken together with the bread and wine." And it teaches that " not only believers in Christ . . . but also the unworthy and unbelieving receive the true body and blood of Christ " ([41]). Calvin, however, like the Elizabethan Churchmen, refutes this teaching—" It is no more possible to receive Christ without faith than it is for seed to germinate in the fire " ([42]). But Calvin, in common with Cranmer, Ridley, Latimer, and the Elizabethan divines, denied that the elements were merely naked signs or figures. While deliberately confessing that the ' mode ' was beyond his comprehension, he declares " yet are they not naked and empty figures, but have their truth and substance united to them." " In His sacred feast He bids me under symbols of bread and wine, to take His body and blood, to eat and drink. I doubt not but that He really offers and that I receive " ([42]).

The First Scotch Confession of Faith of 1560 uses similar language, " Whosoever slanders us, as that we affirm or believe scaraments to be naked and bare signs, do injury unto us, and speaks against the manifest truth " . . . " we confess and undoubtedly believe that in the right use of the Lord's Table, the faithful do so eat the body and drink the blood of the Lord Jesus that He remains in them and they in Him ; yea they are made flesh of His flesh and bone of His bones " ([43]).

The difference between the Lutherans and the ' Reformed ' was really one only of the mode of Christ's presence in the Eucharist. This was clearly brought out in the Preface of the ' Harmony of Protestant Confessions ' (1581), the chief author of which was supposed to have been Theodore Beza, the French Reformed divine, who succeeded Calvin as leader of the Church of Geneva from 1564-1605. Speaking of the Lutherans this ' Preface ' declares its agreement with them in " all particular points of faith," and it adds " For concerning that doubt about the Lord's Supper, in the thing and of the thing itself there is no strife. For we all acknowledge that the holy signs have not a bare signification ; but that by the ordinance of God they assure our consciences that the things themselves are as truly and certainly given of God to all that come as the signs themselves are given by God's minister. But this question remaineth, whether as the sign, so also the present thing itself be given to the body ; or rather the present sign be given to the body, but the present thing be given only to the mind of faith ; again whether, as both be given to all, so both be received of all, of some unto life and of other some unto death. . . In like sort we all believe the true communication of the true body and the true blood of our Lord Jesus Christ ; the controversy standeth in the manner of communicating " (p. xxxiii).

RESERVATION

There was, moreover, complete agreement amongst all the Reformers, both Anglican and foreign, on the question of the Reservation of the Sacramental elements. The practice was condemned either openly or silently by all ; although the foreign Reformed Confessions are occupied mainly with the condemnation of its use for purposes of Adoration and are silent on its use for the reservation for the Sick. As far as the Lutherans are concerned the practice of Reservation for any purpose naturally died out because of their definite teaching that outside their divinely appointed use, the elements have no signification at all. Melanchthon clearly states " the Sacrament has no significance beyond its divinely appointed use, and that Christ was not present for the sake of the bread, but of the recipient " (44). " From henceforth," declared the Synod of Homburg, 1526, " let it nowhere be reserved in tabernacles or pyxes, or carried about for any reason " (45), while the Confession of Saxony, 1551, says " It is a manifest profanation to carry about part of the Supper of the Lord to *adore it* " (Art. X). The Scotch Confession of Faith, 1560, similarly denounces " Adoration, veneration, bearing through streets and towns and keeping of bread in pyxes as a profanation of the use of Christ's sacraments, which should be duly used and not kept to be worshipped and honoured as God, as the Papists have done heretofore " ([46]). The Confession of Bohemia, 1573, also declares that " the body and blood of our Lord Jesus Christ must be distributed only and be received in common of the faithful, but it must not be sacrificed or set forth or lifted up, that it may be worshipped or exhibited or stored away, or carried about." " It ought to be received and administered without adoration and without that worship which is due to God alone, yet with a due kind of religion and reverence " ([47]).

The practice of Adoration of the reserved elements was very prevalent and popular at this time, of which the demand made by the Western rebels in 1549, affords a striking illustration—" We will have the Sacrament hang over the high altar and there to be *worshipped* as it was wont to be, and they which will not consent thereto we will have them die like heretics against the holy Catholic Faith " ([48]). In the First Anglican Prayer Book of 1549 permission had been given on a day when there had been an open Communion service in Church, for the priest to reserve as much of the elements as might suffice to administer the Communion to a sick person, which he was enjoined to do " as soon as he conveniently may " after the service in Church was ended. But as even this primitive custom of ' extended Communion ' encouraged the medieval abuse of veneration and adoration of the reserved sacrament, it was discarded in the 1552 and following revisions of the Prayer Book. Moreover the XXVIIIth Article of 1562 contained the definite declaration that the " sacrament of the Lord's Supper was not by Christ's ordinance reserved, carried about, lifted up or worshipped." Furthermore the Elizabethan Prayer Book of 1559 had made it clear that even this practice of ' extended communion ' authorised in 1549, was no longer allowed, since a post-communion rubric stated that " if any of the bread and wine remain, the Curate shall have it to his own use." Also in the Service for the ' Communion of the Sick,' the rubric clearly states " At the time of the distribution of the holy Sacrament, the priest shall first receive the Communion *himself*." Such an order presupposes the proper celebration of the Holy Communion and not the mere administration of the reserved elements to the sick person, as allowed by the 1549 book. It is true that in 1560 a semi-official Latin Prayer Book was published on royal authority only, but it was very little used. In this Book in the Service for Communion of the Sick, the 1549 rubric allowing ' reservation ' from the ' open Communion ' in church was inserted. But such permission directly contravened the actual provisions of the Statutory 1559 Prayer Book as well as the definite prohibition of the Act of Uniformity of 1559, which forbade under penalties any one to " use any other rite, ceremony, or order, form or manner of celebrating the Lord's Supper openly or privily . . . than is mentioned and set forth in the said (1559) Book " (Clause 4). But the Service for ' Communion of the Sick ' in the 1559 Book gave no directions as to " how much of the Communion Service was to be used " in administering to the sick person, and the omission led Bishop Anthony Sparrow, in his ' Rationale of the Book of Common Prayer,' published in 1655, to suggest that such directions should be sought for in the rubric of the 1549 Prayer Book for ' The Communion of the Sick.' Now this lengthy opening rubric, as we have seen, makes provision for reservation of the elements from the ' Open Communion' in Church. But Sparrow was not thinking of illegally reviving this discarded practice, but solely of the specified " parts of the Communion Service to be used " for the Communion of the Sick. This is quite clear when his whole statement is carefully read ; since he deliberately alters and adds to the directions of the 1549 rubric as to " what parts of the Service are to be used." This rubric read " Before the Curate distribute the Holy Communion, the appointed General Confession must be

made in the name of the Communicants, the Curate
adding the Absolution with the Comfortable Sentences of
Scripture, following in the Open Communion, and after
the Communion ended the Collect." But it is significant
to notice that Sparrow stops at the words—" following
in the open Communion " and adds " and so proceeding
in the Communion Service to the end of the *Consecration*
and distribution."* He thus shows clearly that Com
munion from the reserved elements was not permissible
under the 1559 Prayer Book, but that there must be a
fresh ' consecration ' for each occasion of ' Communion
of the Sick,' and so *that* ' part of the Service ' must be
used ([49]). It should not be forgotten that Sparrow was
one of the Revisers of the 1662 Prayer Book and that
this Book clearly set forth what ' parts of the Service '
were to be used in the ' Communion for the Sick,' while
a post-Communion rubric for the first time differentiated
between the consecrated and unconsecrated bread and
wine which might remain, and definitely forbade any
of the consecrated elements " to be carried out of the
Church," but ordered that they be " reverently con-
sumed " at the close of the service.

Moreover prominent Elizabethan Churchmen had condemned in no uncertain terms every form of reservation
for any purpose whatever. Bishop Jewel, in his
' Apology,' says " We justly blame the bishops of Rome
because without the Word of God . . . they do not only
set before the people the sacramental bread to be worshipped as God, but do also carry the same about " ([50]).
Bishop Bilson asks, " If you could not worship the ' rock '
without committing adultery, though the rock ' were
Christ,' how can you give divine honour to the bread
and wine, since they be Christ after the same sort that
the rock was ? " ([51]).

It is most unlikely that any Elizabethan bishop would
have endorsed the statement made recently by some
Anglican bishops at a Conference with the Eastern

*Chancellor Wordsworth in his Article on ' Reservation ' in
the ' Prayer Book Dictionary ' (page 662) overlooks this point,
and consequently misinterprets Sparrow's meaning on page 350
of his ' Rationale.'

Orthodox Church that "*after* Communion the consecrated elements remaining were regarded as the Body and Blood of Christ " ([52]). They would rather have agreed with Bishop Cosin, who ruled out all customs of reservation or adoration when he said, " though the bread and wine remain, yet the consecration, the sacrament of the Body and Blood of Christ do not remain longer than the holy action itself remains, for which the bread and wine were hallowed and which being ended, *return to their former use again* " ([53]). " Christ," he says, " in the consecrated bread, cannot be kept preserved to be carried about, because He is present only to the Communicants " ([54]). It is clear therefore that on the question of Reservation there was practical unanimity of teaching amongst the Reformed Churches, both Anglican and foreign. The authorised formularies of the Anglican Church since 1552, as the declared ' Opinion ' of the two English Archbishops in May, 1900, stated, leave no place for any kind of reservation since " the language of the XXVIIIth Article cannot be taken otherwise than as condemning the practice altogether. To say that ' the Sacrament of the Lord's Supper was not by Christ's Ordinance reserved, carried about, lifted up or worshipped,' is to say with clearly implied condemnation that those who do these things, use for one purpose what Our Lord ordained for another " ([55]).

On one outstanding subject connected with the Eucharist there was complete unanimity. Elizabethan Churchmen concurred fully with both Lutherans, and all ' Reformed ' in condemning the doctrine of the Sacrifice of the Mass and transubstantiation. The Lutheran ' Formula of Concord ' (1576) is most definite, when it says, " We reject and condemn by unanimous consent . . . the papistical transubstantiation . . . the papistical sacrifice of the Mass, which is offered for the sins of the living and the dead " ([56]). The Second Helvetic Confession of 1566 is equally explicit—" The Mass which is now used throughout the Romish Church . . . for many and just causes is quite abolished out of our Churches. Truly we could not like it . . . because that in it the Priest is said to make the very body of the Lord, and to offer the same really, even for the remission of the sins of the quick and dead " ([57]).   The purpose and effect are the same, although these condemnations are expressed in milder language than that used in the Anglican Article XXXI which describes ' Sacrifices of Masses ' as " blasphemous fables and dangerous deceits."   It has been contended that by this strong language Cranmer was only condemning " the erroneous developments of later times," and " deliberately leaving room for a basis of older and sounder doctrine " on the Eucharistic Sacrifice, since " he cannot have been ignorant of the distinction between ' offering for the quick and dead,' and ' offering for quick and dead, *to have remission of pain and guilt* ' " ([58]).   In fact, it is urged that by this definite statement " it is not ' the Sacrifice of the Mass,' but ' the sacrifices of masses ' that is condemned " ([59]).

It is unfortunate, however, for this rather subtle distinction between the singular and the plural, that the Ordination injunction to the Roman priest empowers him " to offer sacrifice and celebrate *masses* as well for the living as the dead."   It is also certain that neither Cranmer nor the Elizabethan bishops were ignorant of any of the subtle distinctions or of the popular errors in the medieval teaching on the Eucharist.   Cranmer expressly condemned the Eucharistic " offering for the quick and dead," as well as " for the remission of pain or guilt."   " The very body of the tree," which " is the corruption of the flock of Christ," was, he asserted, " the sacrifice and oblation of Christ made by the priest for the salvation of quick and dead."   There is not a shred of historical or documentary evidence to support the novel contention of (Cardinal) Newman that the Reformers in Article XXXI were merely condemning an extravagant and totally discredited view of the Sacrifice of the Mass, taught by Archbishop Catharinus (1489-1553), that " the Sacrifice on the Cross only availed for all actual post baptismal sins."   The Anglican Reformers were well aware that official Roman teaching had condemned this crude popular perversion of the Sacrifice of the Mass, and it is impossible to show that in Article XXXI they were condemning this theory and yet leaving room for a 'Eucharistic Sacrifice for the quick and dead.' It is worthy of notice that the very expression 'sacrifices of Masses' was used at the Council of Florence in 1438, when in a decree of Union, signed by both Eastern and Western bishops, it is stated of souls departed this life in venial sin, " that their souls are cleansed after death by purgatorial pains," and in order that they may be relieved of these pains the suffrages of the faithful living profit them, namely ' the sacrifices of Masses,' prayers, alms, and other works of piety" (⁶⁰). The Council of Trent also in 1562 (Sess. xxii, cap. 2) had clearly stated that in the Mass Sacrifice Christ is unbloodily offered " non solum profidelium vivorum peccatis, poenis satisfactionibus et aliis necessitatibus, sed pro defunctis in Christo nondum ad plenum purgatis, rite, juxta apostolorum traditionem, offertur." Such language is practically equivalent to that condemned in Article XXXI concerning the priest " who offered Christ for the quick and dead to have remission of pain or guilt."

Moreover, one of the articles charged against Ridley and Latimer at their trial was that they " had obstinately maintained that in the Mass is no propitiatory sacrifice for the quick and dead." Although in the 1549 Prayer Book the word ' Mass ' was retained as a ' popular ' name for the Eucharist—The Supper of the Lord, or Holy Communion, *commonly called* the Mass—yet the Reformers clearly intended to abolish the Mass Sacrifice. Bishop Gardiner, in 1550, had to subscribe an article which stated that " the Mass that was *wont to be said* of the priests was full of abuses, and had very few things of Christ's institution besides the Epistle, the Gospel and the Lord's Prayer and words of the Lord's Supper ; the rest for the most part was invented and devised by the bishops of Rome and other men of the same sort, and therefore justly *taken away* by the Statutes and Laws of this realm, and the Communion which is placed in *the stead thereof* is very godly and agreeable to Holy Scripture " (⁵³).

It is an easy task to prove that the Elizabethan Churchmen were equally strong in their condemnation of the Sacrifice of the Mass as the earlier Reformers.

In the Second Book of Homilies put forth in 1562 there is a warning concerning the Eucharist " to take heed lest of a memory it be made a sacrifice," because Christ on the Cross " had made a full and sufficient sacrifice for thee," and therefore " thou needest . . . no sacrificing priest, no mass."   And in commenting on the corruptions in the Church of Rome, the Homily for Whitsunday declares " Christ commended to His Church a sacrament of His body and blood, they have changed it into a sacrifice for the quick and dead " ([61]).

Moreover in the ' Eleven Articles ' of 1559, which Archbishop Parker imposed on the clergy the ' propitiatory sacrifice of the Mass ' is condemned as " most ungodly and most injurious to Christ's one sufficient Sacrifice." . . . Archbishop Parker and the leading divines also tell Elizabeth in a Petition for the removal of altars that their retention " would only serve to nourish the superstitious opinion of the propitiatory Mass in the minds of the simple " ([62]).

It seems strange that a modern historian should venture to assert that it was the ' declared policy ' of Elizabethan Churchmen " not to condemn the Mass as idolatrous " ([63]), when we find that the Elizabethan bishops were careful in their Visitation Articles to inquire " whether any openly or privily say Mass or hear Mass " ; and when popish recusants had to declare in their recantations " I also detest the Mass as abominable sacrilege being a sacrifice, as the Papists term it, for the quick and dead " ([64]).

Bishop Jewel declared the sacrifice of the Mass to be imaginary and injurious, and he tells Martyr " He who drinks of it is mad, depart from it all ye who value a sound mind " ([65]).   Bishop Guest, one of the ' highest ' churchmen of the day, declared that the " priest sacrifice was neither propitiatory, nor available, but sinful and insufferable " ([66]).   Archbishop Whitgift declares that those who resort to the Mass " offend God in being present at an idolatrous service."   Similar strong language is used by other prominent divines like Archbishop Sandys, Richard Hooker and Archbishop Bancroft.   This definite aim and intention of abolishing the Sacrifice of the Mass in the Anglican Church was confirmed by the statement made in the seventh Canon of 1640, which stated, " At the time of Reforming this Church from that gross superstition of Popery it was carefully provided that all means should be used to root out of the minds of the people . . . the idolatry committed in the Mass, for which cause all Popish altars were demolished " ([67]).

From this short survey we can see that there was a practical harmony in fundamental teaching on the Eucharist between all the Reformers, Anglican and Foreign. For while they all held " that the Body and Blood of Christ were sacramentally and spiritually received by the faithful in the Lord's Supper," they all, even the Lutherans, repudiated the theory of a localised objective Presence of Christ in the elements by virtue of priestly consecration. In the Eucharist they received a gift from God rather than offered Him any material Sacrifice. The ' Eucharistic Sacrifice ' was a definite offering of praise and thanksgiving for all the benefits of Christ's Passion which were so vividly represented in the whole Eucharistic rite. They rejected as unscriptural the view that in the transmuted elements Christ is offered to the Father as a sacrifice for the quick and dead, and that in this act the Church on earth is doing what Our Lord is supposed to be doing in heaven, i.e., presenting to God His once completed, but eternally present sacrifice. Or, in the language of a modern writer, " We as His members join with Him in presenting His Sacrifice before the Father. . . In the Eucharist we on earth join with Him in pleading His sacrifice, even as He pleads it above " ([68]).

In view of this harmony of belief it is well to observe what a clear division this question of Eucharistic teaching created between Reformed and unreformed Christendom. We see this serious difference well illustrated as we study the Eucharistic worship and doctrine of the Eastern Church. The Eastern Liturgies are largely patchworks based on the Early Liturgies of St. Chrysostom and St. Basil, but they are obviously full of medieval additions and alterations. They contain numerous prayers and commemorations for the departed and an excessive amount of ritual and ceremonial so that the whole service, with its multifarious ceremonies and symbolical acts, lasts at least two hours and must be exceedingly difficult for the priests to remember. Dr. Covel in describing this Liturgy in his ' Greek Church,' published in 1722, remarks rather sarcastically that with this intricate Liturgy to memorise, it is not strange that the Greek priests have no other learning ! Not until the middle of the XVIIth century was there any clearly defined teaching on the Eucharist in the Greek Church. The doctrine of the Real Presence was taught, as it was loosely and ambiguously held by the Greek Fathers. The Reformation had, however, an influence on the Greek Church and especially on one of its Patriarchs— Cyril Lucar (1572-1638). He was Patriarch of Constantinople from 1621-38. He was a great traveller and studied at Venice and Padua and resided for a time at Geneva. He was disgusted with the Romish religion and was much drawn to the Reformed, and he corresponded with Archbishop Abbot, of Canterbury and sent a priest to be educated at Balliol College, Oxford. He offered great resistance to the efforts of the Romanists in 1595 to win over the Russian and Polish Greek Churches, and he incurred the bitter hatred of the Jesuits, through whose machinations he was at length falsely accused of treason, and by the Turkish Emperor's orders he was strangled. In 1629 he drew up a Confession of Faith which was in conformity with the Reformed doctrine, and he succeeded in getting a Council of Greeks to accept it. It was, however, later on condemned by the Synod of Constantinople in 1638. It was owing to this attempt of Cyril Lucar to reform the Greek Church that an ' Orthodox Confession of Faith,' drawn up for the Russian Church by Peter Mogilla, was issued in 1643, by the four Patriarchs of Constantinople, Alexandria, Antioch and Jerusalem ; and this was finally sanctioned by the Synod of Jerusalem in 1672*

---

* See Appendix to this Chapter for a fuller account of ' The Career and Teaching of Cyril Lucar.'

Dr. J. Covel, afterwards Master of Christ's College, Cambridge, was appointed British Chaplain at Constantinople in 1670, while residing there he made careful enquiries into the worship and doctrine of the Greek Church and he published a very full account of their Eucharistic service at that time. From this we learn that before the administration, the priest prays " For Thou O Christ and God, art He who offerest and art offered, who receivest and art distributed or received." The elements are censed and a prayer of offering is made through " our most Holy Immaculate above all Blessed, Glorious Lady." The Epiclesis in the Prayer of Consecration asks—" We intreat and pray and beseech, send down Thy Holy Spirit upon us and upon these Thy Gifts proposed and make this bread the precious Body of Thy Christ, and what is in this Cup the precious blood of Thy Christ." A long list of prayers for the Dead or Tables of the Dead follows.

In administering the bread to the deacon, the priest says, " To . . . is imparted the precious and holy and immaculate Body of our Lord and God and Saviour Jesus Christ for the remission of his sins and for eternal life." After administering the wine in similar language, the priest adds, " This hath touched thy lips and will take away thy transgressions and thoroughly purge thy sins." Sacred loaves are brought to the priest by the people " who offers them to God for themselves and their friends, living and dead."

It is obvious in this liturgy that the consecration of the elements is regarded as being effected by the Epiclesis and not, as in the Roman rite, by the recital of the words of Institution ; since after these latter have been used, the prayer is made to the Holy Spirit for the gifts and the priest adds " changing them by thy Holy Spirit " ($\mu\epsilon\tau\alpha\beta\alpha\lambda\omega\nu$ $\tau\omega\nu$ $\pi\nu\epsilon\upsilon\mu\alpha\tau\iota$ $\sigma\upsilon$ $\tau\omega$ $\dot{\alpha}\gamma\iota\omega$).

Dr. Covel endeavours to show that this Epiclesis prayer was only that " a new and supernatural divine effect should be given to the elements," and not that they were by that prayer regarded as transubstantiated. It was not, he argues, a prayer to change the elements in substance but in effect, that they "might be made to all that receive them to soberness of mind to the remission of sins." . . . But although this is true as regards the object of the prayer for the receivers, he overlooks the fact that before this petition for the 'receivers,' is the definite general petition of the priest to "Make this bread the precious Body of Thy Christ, &c. . . . changing them by Thy Holy Spirit." Such clear language implies a change in the *elements themselves* apart from their effect on the receivers. And it is difficult to find much practical difference between the effect of 'changing' (metaballown) and transubstantiation. The one word is virtually equivalent to the other. It seems in the nature of special pleading therefore to assert, as Dr. Covel does, that this prayer must be interpreted only in a spiritual sense so that "make this bread the body and this wine the blood of Christ is not absolutely or literally meant, but so as to have the effect in the receivers" ([69]). This explanation is really untenable when we find that the real doctrine of the Greek Church is made clear from the definite statement on the consecration of the Eucharist given in the 'Orthodox Confession of 1643,' which says—

It is fitting that the priest should have this intention for the occasion when he consecrates the gifts, that the very substance of the bread and the substance of the wine are changed into the substance of the true body and blood of Christ through the operation of the Holy Ghost where He pronounces the Invocation at that time. After these words the change of substance takes place immediately, and the bread changes into the true body of Christ and the wine into the true blood of Christ, there remain only the accidents or appearances where they are seen and that in accordance with the divine economy.

In striking contrast to this language the 'Confession' of the Patriarch—Cyril Lucar—had defined the belief in the Eucharistic Presence in language which would have been endorsed by all the 'Reformed '—

"In the use and administration of this mystery we confess and believe," he says, "the true and certain Presence of Our Lord Jesus Christ, only that Presence which faith presents and brings to us, not that which a rashly invented change of substance teaches. For we believe that the faithful when they partake in the Supper eat the body of our Lord Jesus Christ—not

111

sensibly chewing with the teeth and finishing the participation, but having communion by the preception of the soul. For the body of the Lord is not that which is seen and received by the eyes in the mystery, but that which spiritually faith receives, presents and bestows upon us " ([70]).

That the Eucharistic teaching of the Eastern Church has not changed since the XVIIth century is clear from the statements of doctrine set forth by the Greek Archimandrite, Michael Constandinides, in his book, ' The Orthodox Church,' in which he describes " the change of the bread and wine into the Body and the Blood of our Lord," as a ' miracle.' Such a statement is definitely at variance with the ' Black Rubric ' of the Anglican Communion office which states dogmatically that " the sacramental bread and wine remain still in their very natural substances." Moreover, he declares that the Holy Eucharist is not only a sacrament, but also a sacrifice offered to God for ourselves. It is not only a sacrifice of praise and thanksgiving, but also a propitiatory sacrifice. As such it is offered for all present or absent, the quick and dead ([71]). This doctrine as we have seen, not only the Anglican Article XXXI but also the teaching of the Elizabethan and Caroline Churchmen definitely condemned.

We should, however, bear in mind that the definitions of the Greek Church do not assert, like those of the Roman Church in the Council of Trent, that " in the Sacrament of the most holy Eucharist are contained truly, really and substantially the body and blood, along with the soul and divinity of Our Lord Jesus Christ and therefore whole Christ," and also " whatever belongs to the true conception of a body, as bones and nerves " ([72]). But apparently the Greek Church teaches a mechanical view of the virtue of the Eucharist, for we are told that " all the faithful *including infants* must receive the Holy Eucharist, since " Except ye eat the flesh of the Son of Man, &c.," and so infants must not be deprived of life "—teaching directly at variance with the Anglican Articles XXV and XXVIII, which limit the benefits of Sacraments to such only as " worthily, rightly and with faith receive the same."

112

(C) THE AUTHORITY OF HOLY SCRIPTURE.

There is little doubt that the doctrinal Reformation in England was largely accomplished through the translations of the Scriptures into the vernacular by Tyndale and others in Henry VIII's reign. Many attempts have been made to prove that the Scriptures were fairly freely circulated in England in English in pre-Reformation times. Cardinal Gasquet quotes Sir Thomas More and others to show that the Scriptures were allowed to be read even before Wycliffe's day, and that there were English versions before that time. It is certainly true that there were extracts from the Bible in popular devotional books and there is evidence that there were a few sundry translations of the Psalms and other portions of Scriptures, which may have come within the reach of a very small minority of educated lay churchmen who were able to read, but it is most unlikely that even these were in wide or general circulation. It was not till late in the XIVth century that a distinct class of literate *laymen* existed. Before this date education was almost exclusively confined to ' clerks ' in minor or priests' Orders. Miss Deanesley tells us that " there is no single Will which mentions an English Bible before Wycliffe's death at all, nor is there any reference to one in any other historical source." And she adds also that " it is almost impossible to quote any instance of lay people who were acquainted with the Bible before Wycliffe's days " ([73]), other than what they may have heard from portions used in the services of the Church. Priests were not required to instruct the people in the Scriptures and sermons were very rare occurrences, while the average priest had great difficulty in translating the Latin of his service books or of the Vulgate. Wycliffe's claim that the laity should read the Bible was certainly regarded as a radical and dangerous innovation. " Every Christian," he declared, " has the right and the duty to study the Bible ; for not to know the Bible means not to know Christ." Therefore he urged that all had a right to have the Bible taught truly and clearly, " in our Mother tongue." But

until the issue of ' Wyclif's ' Bible,* which was translated mainly by Nicholas of Hereford and Dr. John
Purvey, this was not possible, as even the old versions
of the Gospels in Early English by Bede and others
were in his day unintelligible.

The evidence for the existence of other English Bibles
before Wycliffe's day has been shown recently by
Dr. Workman to be unreliable. It is evident that Sir
Thomas More mistook partial translations and even
Purvey's, for separate original versions. The Consti-
tutions of Oxford in 1407 forbade the translation of
the Bible into English without the express approval of
the Bishop, and licences to possess a copy of the English
Bible were, after this, only given to rich and powerful
laymen who were thought to be orthodox. Even Sir T.
More admits that only the "good and Catholic" were
allowed by special licence of the Bishop to read the
Scriptures, and an Archdeacon, in Mary's reign, admits
" that only such as had them in handling were allowed
by the Ordinary and approved as proper to read them."
As we have already seen, More sought to excuse this
prohibition by asserting that " the Scripture has of
necessity been kept out of lay people's hands " ([74]),
because of what he terms the false translations of

---

* This translation was popularly credited to Wyclif and it
is certain that he originated the idea and set the work in motion,
but it is doubtful if he himself was responsible for much of the
actual translation. . . . In the ' Chronicon of Henrici Knighton '
we read : " In those days (1382) the most eminent doctor of
theology . . . Master John Wycliffe translated from the Latin
into the English tongue . . . the Gospel which Christ gave to
clerks and doctors of the Church . . . through him it is become
more common and open to laymen and women who are able to
read than it is wont to be even to lettered clerks of good intelligence " ([74]). But Archbishop Arundel was probably more
accurate when in writing to Pope John XXIII in 1412 he referred
to Wycliffe as the " very herald and child of Anti-Christ," who
" to fill up the measure of his malice, *devised the expedient* of a
new translation of the Scriptures into the Mother tongue." It
was Wycliffe who ' devised the expedient,' but as Miss Deanesley
says, " the historical evidence shows that the lollards made
the translation of the Bible and consistently practiced its use,
while no orthodox person or manual ever suggested its use by
lay people " ([75]).

114

Wycliffe, Tyndale, and Friar Barnes. But the fact remains that for the ordinary layman to possess a copy of the English Bible in pre-Reformation days was usually a dangerous evidence of 'heresy.' Dr. Coulton sums up the actual position regarding Bible reading in the later Middle Ages in a clear statement, part of which we have before referred to—

"The rough truth may be put very simply, the best medieval writers knew their Vulgate very well, a great many more knew parts of it well enough, especially those portions which happened to come in their Service Books. The average priest knew nothing outside those service books and not even all that was inside; the lower priesthood, as Roger Bacon and other equally credible witnesses testify, understood little or nothing even of their Church offices, the laity could seldom read Latin with any ease outside a sort of hotel waiter's vocabulary with which a bailiff wrote his accounts . . . therefore the most educated and ambitious seldom got far beyond the Psalms and Sunday Gospels and Epistles. A few of the richest possessed Bibles in French or Psalters in French or English; but as soon as a general desire for the vernacular arose, this was opposed by the ecclesiastical authorities and for the rest of the Middle Ages vernacular Bibles were either explicitly condemned, or lay under a strong suspicion of heresy" ([77]).

As regards the authority and place of the Scriptures in the life and teaching of the Church, Wycliffe was in full accord with the position taken up by all the later Reformers, both Anglican and foreign. He certainly did not believe that it was necessary that the knowledge of the Scriptures should be confined to those whom the bishops considered to be 'approved and proper persons.' On the other hand, he agreed with Erasmus and Tyndale and Luther that the 'humble man'—'the husbandman following the plough'—might and should search and read the pages of the Bible to discover the way of life and salvation. "Every Christian," urged Wycliffe, "has the right and the duty to study the Bible" ([78]). The current view in his day was that "the Bible was a mysterious book, the literal sense of which was useless and which therefore could not be read by the simple." But Wycliffe believed that "the Holy Spirit teaches us the meaning of Scripture as Christ opened its sense to His disciples," so that it was "open to the understanding of the simple in all points necessary to salvation " ([79]).

Wycliffe also taught the supremacy and final authority of Scripture and thus enunciated the position of the doctrinal Reformers of the XVIth century—that " Scripture alone was the sufficient Rule of Faith for the Church." " Neither the testimony of Augustine or Jerome, nor any other saint should," he asserted " be accepted except in so far as it was based upon Scripture" ([80]). Cranmer makes a similar dogmatic statement on the position of the Anglican Reformers, when he says " the authority of the orthodox Fathers is by no means to be despised, but that the Holy Scriptures should be interpreted by their decisions we do not allow, for Holy Scripture ought to be to us both the rules and judges of all Christian doctrine "—" the true Word of God is the very touchstone which must try all doctrine and learning whatsoever it be."

Luther had been equally definite on the supreme authority of Scripture. Quite early in the ' Indulgence' controversy in 1518, he had told his great antagonist, Dr. Eck, that " if Christ and His Word are with me, I will not fear what the whole world may do to me." " No believing Christian," he declared, " can be forced to recognise any authority beyond the sacred Scripture, which is exclusively invested with the divine right, unless indeed there comes a new and attested revelation" ([81]). " If any one cannot found one's Creed on the Bible now," why, he asks, " did Augustine have the right to do it 1,100 years ago ? "

Melanchthon was just as clear in rejecting all other authorities—" he is deceived who seeks the form of Christianity anywhere else than from the Canonical Scriptures " ([82]). All the Reformed Confessions take up an identical position. The French Confession of Faith, 1559, declares that " no authority should be opposed to Holy Scripture . . . but that all things should be examined and regulated by them " ([83]). The Scotch Confession of 1560, inspired by John Knox, asserts that " the Scriptures of God are sufficient to instruct and make the man of God perfect " and their " authority is of God."

We should remember that it was this common appeal of all the Reformers to the supreme authority of the Bible which was the foundation of the Reformation movement. Moreover, it was this positive appeal to Holy Scripture, as the sole sufficient Rule of Faith, which originated the very name ' Protestant.' The ' Protest ' put forth in the ' Instrumentum Appelationis ' by the German Reformers at the Diet of Spires in 1529, declared that " the Word of God was the only truth, the sure rule of all doctrine and life and can never fail or deceive us." The same positive appeal to the Scriptures was made by a number of prominent martyrs in Edward VI's reign who, in a manifesto from prison, declared, " We confess and believe all the canonical books of the Old and New Testaments to be the very Word of God and the judge of all controversies and matters of religion " (84).

Similarly, Bishop Ridley wrote in 1555, " Call me ' protestant ' who listeth, I care not for it. My protestation shall be thus, that my mind is and ever shall be, to set forth sincerely the true sense and meaning of God's most holy Word and not to decline from the same " (85). All the Reformers, both Anglican and foreign, believed that in making this final appeal to Holy Scripture they were restoring the universal rule and practice of the early Catholic Church. St. Augustine had declared that " the holy Scripture fixes the rule of our doctrine," and St. Chrysostom warns his readers " to look for no other teacher " than Scripture. Bishop Jeremy Taylor, after making a full examination of the attitude of the early Fathers on this question, sums up by saying, " the Scriptures are a perfect rule, for that the Scriptures are the Word of God . . . is delivered by a full consent of the Fathers and no one Father denies it." " That Scripture is the rule of our Faith, is," he asserts " a main protestant doctrine and therefore certainly must not be quitted." And he adds that in this position Protestants are simply ' witnessing for ' Catholic teaching, since " that the Canonical Scriptures should be our only and entire rule, we are sufficiently convinced by the title which the Catholic Church always hath given

117

to the Holy Scriptures, for it is κανών the 'rule' of Christians for their whole religion" ([86]).

That the teaching of this eminent Caroline divine was held by all the prominent Churchmen of Elizabeth's reign is not open to question. Bishop Jewel in his 'Apology' voiced their convictions when he declared Scripture to be the "very sure and infallible rule whereunto all ecclesiastical doctrine ought to be called to account" ([87]).

The Elizabethan Reformers were most careful to emphasise the fact that they were conserving Catholic Teaching and introducing no novel views.

"We never departed," Bishop Horne emphatically declared at the 'Westminster Disputation,' 1559, "from the faith of the true and Catholic Church of Christ. We are of the true Catholic Church and maintain the verity thereof." (Foxe, "Acts and Mon.," VIII, 681, 690.)

Queen Elizabeth herself confirmed this definite aim of the English Reformation when she told the Emperor Ferdinand in 1563—

"We and our subjects, God be praised, are not following any new and foreign religions, but that very religion which Christ commands, which the Primitive and Catholic Church sanctions, which the mind and voice of the most ancient Fathers with one consent approve." (Bayne, "Anglo-Roman Relations," p. 307, 1913.)

But although the Reformers made their supreme Rule of Faith the appeal to Scripture, they did not neglect or deny a subordinate appeal to the teaching of Catholic antiquity. As Dean Field expressed it, "We do not therefore so make Scripture the rule of our Faith as to neglect the other (rules), nor so admit the other as to detract anything from the plenitude of Scripture in which all things are contained that must be believed" ([88]). The foreign Reformers also showed a similar regard and respect for the teaching of antiquity and the decisions of the early Catholic Church. The 'Former Confession of Helvetia,' 1536, speaking distinctly of the Holy Fathers and their interpretation of Scripture, says "We not only receive them as interpreters of Scripture, but we reverence them as chosen instruments of God."

The Confession of Wurtemburg (1552) declares that " Councils ought to have their judgments in the Church concerning the holy doctrine of religion, but that the authority of God's Word must needs be greatest, although the authority of lawful Councils is great." Similarly the Belgic Confession of 1566 says, " We willingly receive those three Creeds and whatever has been established by the Old Fathers according to the meaning of those Creeds." Again the eminent French Reformed divine, Peter Du Moulin, tells Bishop Andrewes—

" Think of me as of a man with whom the authority of antiquity shall ever be in great esteem." " Nor am I such a boldface as to pass sentence upon those lights of the Ancient Church, Ignatius, Polycarp, Cyprian, Augustine, Chrysostom, Basil, the two Gregories . . . all of them bishops, as usurpers of an unlawful office. The reverend antiquity of those first ages shall ever be in greater esteem with me than the novel device of any whomsoever " (89).

The Elizabethan Church also showed a very definite respect for the teaching of the Fathers and the early Councils. The Canons of 1571 were passed by the Upper Houses of Convocation, and one of them distinctly warns preachers not to preach anything as of the faith " except that which is in accord with the old and New Testaments and which the Catholic Fathers and the old bishops have collected from the doctrine of the old and new testaments " (90). A further reference was also made in a State document, which can scarcely claim full ecclesiastical or Synodical authority, to the teaching of the ' First Four General Councils,' as one of the tests by which the newly-formed ' High Commission Court ' could adjudge heresy. But it should be observed that this clause in the Act of Supremacy, 1559, definitely limited the reference to these Councils to matters " which only concern the Confession of the true Christian Faith and the doctrine of the Sacraments." Such subordinate references in no way weakened the fundamental appeal of the Reformed Anglican Church to the supreme Rule of Scripture. The Thirty-Nine Articles of 1562 not only subordinate the decisions of General Councils, but even the acceptance of the Three Catholic Creeds, to the final test of Holy Scripture—because " they may be proved by most certain warrants of Holy Scripture."

Elizabethan divines, in common with the earlier Reformers, were fond of appealing to the teachings of the Fathers on current controverted points of doctrine, as evidence that their own views were not *novel* but had been held in the early days of the Catholic Church. They were glad to be able to do this, but they did not regard this confirmatory evidence of their own interpretations of Scripture as in any way *essential*, or as an appeal co-ordinate with Holy Scripture. They, like their Continental brethren, were always anxious to show that the medieval teaching of their Romish opponents was a *departure* from the Faith of the early Catholic centuries. This was the main reason therefore for their frequent appeal to the opinions of the Fathers. They wished to make it quite evident that the Fathers also had continued faithful to the teaching of Holy Scripture, and thus were at one with them in their appeal to Scripture as the sole Rule of Faith.

It is true that immediately after the legal separation of the Church of England from the Roman see in Henry VIII's reign, the ' Ten Articles ' of 1536 defined the Rule of Faith as the Bible and the Three Creeds, interpreted according to the opinions of the ' holy approved doctors of the Church.' But neither in the doctrinal Reformation of Edward VI, nor in the ' Elizabethan Settlement,' was this Rule ever again ' set forth ' ; and it was entirely superseded by the clear declarations, concerning the absolute supremacy of Scripture, contained in the authorised ' Thirty-Nine Articles of Religion.' In 1604, the Fifty-First Canon confirmed this standard of appeal by enacting that preachers shall not publish any doctrine " disagreeing with the *Word of God* or the Articles of Religion and the Book of Common Prayer " ([91]).

We can therefore rightly say that the question of the place, authority and the right of interpreting Scripture, was a crucial and pivotal one at the time of the Reformation. Cardinal Bellarmine confessed that it marked the great fundamental dividing line between the Church of Rome and the Reformed Churches. The latter held that all necessary doctrine was contained in the Written Word, whereas the Church of Rome maintained the necessity of the Unwritten Word or Tradition. The Council of Trent made this point quite clear when it declared " the truth to be contained in the written books and in the unwritten traditions which having been received by the Apostles were handed down even to us." It goes on to assert that it " receives and venerates with an equal feeling of piety and reverence all the books of the Old and New Testaments *as well as* the traditions relating both to faith and morals dictated either orally by Christ or by the Holy Spirit and preserved in continuous succession in the Catholic Church " ([92]). When we turn to the official teaching of the Eastern Orthodox Church there is no question that on this subject it takes its stand definitely with the Unreformed Church of Rome. In the ' Full Catechism ' of Philaret, 1840, the questions dealing with the Holy Tradition and Holy Scripture make it clear that Tradition is more important than Scripture, because it is available to all, whereas books are only available to ' a small part of mankind,'—a striking allusion to the large proportion of illiteracy in Russia at that time. Again, this Catechism asserts that " Tradition is necessary even now as a guide to the right understanding of Scripture," and that Scripture is to be read " in the sense in which it is interpretated by the Church and the Fathers." It should not be forgotten in this connection that the Synod of Jerusalem 1672 (of the Greek Church) even condemned the reading of the Scripture by the laity. Identical teaching is given by the Archimandrite M. Constandinides, in his ' Orthodox Church,' where he says, " Holy Tradition is essential to the completion of Holy Scripture ; it is essential also for a true interpretation of those truths to which there is only a brief allusion in Holy Writ " ([93]).

In the ' Declaration of the Eastern Church ' made at the ' World Conference on Faith and Order,' at Lausanne, in 1927, we find similar assertions. For instance, in direct contradiction to the Anglican Article VIII, that the Creeds are accepted because they may be proved " by most certain warrants of Holy Scripture," the Orthodox Declaration accepts the Creeds because " the Church has affirmed their validity in her Œcumenical Councils." Moreover it definitely denies the right of private judgment on matters of Faith (a claim so strongly asserted by the Reformers) by declaring that " the limits of individual liberty of belief are determined by the definitions made by the whole Church." It also refuses to conceive of a United Church in which some would hold that Holy Scripture is the sole source of divine Revelation, while others affirmed that " Apostolic tradition is the necessary completion of Holy Scripture " ([94]).

For practical purposes, therefore, the position of the Roman and Orthodox Eastern Churches on the authority and interpretation of Scripture and its relation to Tradition is the same. They both place Tradition on a level in authority with, and therefore practically, as *superior* to, Holy Scripture. And they both assert that Scripture can only be correctly interpreted by the Church or by Tradition, and not by the individual-spiritually enlightened Christian. On the other hand, the Reformers, as we have seen, both Anglican and foreign, assert the supremacy and sufficiency of Scripture and the right of its private interpretation. For instance, the Anglican Homily on the ' Knowledge of Holy Scripture,' definitely encourages " the humble man to search *any* truth boldly in the Scripture without any danger of error." And if he be ignorant, it tells him, not to go to ' Tradition ' or consult the ' Church,' but simply that he " ought the more to read and search Holy Scripture to bring him out of ignorance " ([95]). Similarly the Anglican Ordination Service for priests asks the candidate whether he will promise " to teach nothing as required of necessity to eternal salvation but that which *he* (not the Church) shall be persuaded may be concluded and proved by Scripture." Nowhere in any of the authoritative formularies of the Anglican Church is the individual priest or layman told to rely on the teaching of the Church or on Catholic tradition for additional knowledge, or for the correct interpretation of Scripture. It would seem therefore that the definite statements which were made by the Anglican ' envoys ' during the ' Malines Conversations ' of 1924-6 were seriously misleading. For they declared that

Anglicans and Roman Catholics agree that Holy Scripture needs to be interpreted, and that it belongs to the Church alone to give an authoritative interpretation of it in matters affecting faith and morals. For guidance in this task the Church has recourse to the works of the Fathers of the Church " [96].

The acceptance of a similar statement by the Anglican representatives in the Conference with the Eastern Church in 1931 that " Holy Scripture needs completing by tradition " is equally misleading. For both these affirmations are definitely at variance with the express teaching of official Anglican formularies and are therefore merly the expression of the individual views of the delegates, which can in no way affect the authorised teaching of the Church.

Moreover, the view that the Scripture needs ' completing by tradition ' and ' authoritatively interpreting by the Church,' is in effect destructive of the whole Reformation position. For ' tradition ' practically applied, stands for Church teaching. It therefore implies that the Scripture needs to be explained and interpreted by Church Teaching. Now undoubtedly one of the main purposes and the great achievement of the Reformation, was the subordination of Church teachng to Holy Scripture. The Bible must take precedence over the Church. But this theory of the function of ' tradition ' or of ' Church teaching ' would reverse this position, and once again subordinate the Scriptures to the Church. In practice such a solution would go far to restore the medieval status of Church dictation, against which the Reformation was a deliberate revolt. For there is no question that the supremacy of the Bible over the Church is the core of the protestant witness for Catholic Truth.

THE CAREER AND TEACHING OF CYRIL LUCAR.

THE career of Cyril Lucar is in some respects like that of St. Athanasius, especially in the sudden fluctuations of his fortunes, although the 'end' of Athanasius was far happier. Cyril was born in 1572, at Crete, and he studied as a youth at Venice and Padua. He then visited the chief European cities, specially with a view to study at first hand the true teaching and character of the Reformed Churches. He went to Geneva, Holland, and possibly also to England, and returned to Alexandria, having formed a strong aversion from the Romish Faith, but with a definite sympathy with the Reformed Churches and with Calvinistic teaching. He was ordained priest and soon appointed Archimandrite. Later, he was sent on a mission to Poland where the King was anxious for his subjects to embrace Romanism and break with the Eastern Church. Cyril was unsuccessful in preventing this Union, while a conference between the Greek Christians and the Lutherans came to nothing. The King of Poland then strove for a reunion of the Eastern Church with the Western. Cyril strongly opposed this project, especially as by this time he had realised the need for a reformation in the Greek Church and was therefore eager for a Concordat with the Reformed Church of Geneva. In 1602 Cyril was appointed Patriarch of Alexandria. Ten years later he went to Constantinople where he found the Jesuits busy trying to ' convert ' the Greeks. Cyril opposed their secret efforts and thus earned their deadly enmity, which followed him throughout his life.

In May, 1612, Cyril commenced a correspondence with a Dutch Reformed minister at the Hague. He addressed him as ' Brother in Christ.' He reminds him that as both are pastors appointed by the Chief Shepherd, it is not well that one does not recognise the calling of the other. He claims, however, that the Eastern Church always remains the same and always preserves and keeps untainted orthodoxy. He received a most cordial reply from the Dutch pastor, and then in a further very full and most brotherly epistle, Cyril refers to the two Sacraments of Baptism and the Eucharist, which he describes as seals conferring the grace of the Gospel, but which should not be totally separated from the Gospel. He also explains some of the special Greek ceremonies connected with the Eucharist, but admits that they must be subject to the judgment of Scripture, because being only of men, they are indifferent and fallible. Later on in 1616 he also corresponded with Archbishop Abbot, and he responded to Abbot's suggestion and sent a Greek priest to study at Oxford. Unfortunately, however, this young student after an expensive five years' course at the University, borne by the Archbishop, turned out a very worthless and unreliable character.

Abbot wrote in most brotherly terms to Cyril, and rejoiced in the " unity of the faith which binds each to each." He also told Cyril that as regards ' discipline ' " we differ from other churches which have been purged from the dregs of popery, we retain the ancient form of ecclesiastical rule and the distinct orders of Ministers. God, the giver of all good things, preserve them to us for ever." He tells Cyril that he has placed his protégé in " a pleasant garden," i.e., at Oxford, where " there is a most excellent library and seventeen Colleges, and where a numerous race of men are supported at the public expense." He asks for Cyril's prayers that the British Church may be preserved from Romish emissaries, whom he describes as " foxes and rapacious wolves."

In September, 1618, Cyril wrote a long letter to Mark Anthony de Dominis, Archbishop of Spalato, who had at that time left the Roman Church and was on a visit to

England, coquetting with the Anglican Church. In this epistle, Cyril refers to his own spiritual enlightenment through reading the writings of the ' Evangelical Doctors,' so that " for three years he had compared the doctrine of the Greek and Latin Church with that of the Reformed." Previously, he said, that with the exception of the dogma of the supremacy of the Pope, he, in common with the Greek Church, had accepted " the dogmas of the Roman Communion " as true, and had " abominated the doctrine of the Reformed Churches." This admission affords very clear evidence that at this time there was a recognised sharp and serious dividing line on matters of *doctrine* between the Reformed and Unreformed Churches, including the Eastern. Cyril then tells the Archbishop that as the result of his studies, " I left the Fathers and took for my guide Scripture . . . and at length, through the grace of God, because I discovered that the cause of the Reformers was more just and more in accordance with the doctrine of Christ, I embraced it." And as a convincing proof of this avowal he emphasises the cardinal tenet of all the Reformers, when he declares, " I can no longer endure to hear men say that the comments of human tradition are of equal weight with Holy Scripture." He then outlines his view of the Lord's Supper which appears to be similar to that held by Bucer, Calvin and the English Reformers ; since although he asserts that " Christ is present . . . truly and properly, essentially and really ; " yet with respect to the manner of the Presence he says, " Our Greek Church is at variance both with those who adopt the chimera of transubstantiation and with the erroneous opinion of the Ubiquitaries." And he asserts, in language very similar to that of the Anglican Article XXIX that " the faithful alone receive the Lord's Body and Blood in the Holy Eucharist." On another occasion Cyril explains what he calls the ' Orthodox ' view that " he who approaches in faith to the Table of the Lord, receives not only the visible Sacrament of the Body and Blood, but participates internally and spiritually in the very Body and Blood of our Lord Jesus Christ."

It is very doubtful, however, as we have seen, if the

phraseology of the Greek Liturgies will bear this spiritual and Evangelical interpretation. Cyril also declares that it is wiser and safer to abstain altogether from Image Worship, since the vulgar, at least, are by it " carried away from the true and spiritual worship and latria which is due to God alone." He also rejected the Invocation of Saints, since he perceived " how they eclipsed the glory of our Lord Jesus Christ," and he confesses to the Archbishop of Spalato, " the great pain it gives him to hear the Saints invoked in reciting the Greek Public offices " to " the dereliction of Jesus Christ and the great detriment of souls."

Cyril now definitely worked, but apparently with rather a forlorn hope, for the reformation of the Greek Church ; since in 1619 he writes to a Dutch layman, declaring that " if I could reform my Church, I would do it willingly ; but God knows that it is talking of impossibilities." In November, 1621, Cyril was unanimously elected Patriarch of Constantinople, and from this time his life was one of constant unrest and insecurity. The Jesuits had been peculiarly active in proselytising efforts at Constantinople and Cyril's first action was to conjure the faithful to cease communion with all Romanists. The Jesuits retaliated by appointing an anti-Patriarch, and then Cyril, with his archbishops and clergy, solemnly excommunicated this intruder, who was banished and then executed by the government. The Jesuits then made false accusations against Cyril, with the result that he was banished to the island of Rhodes, when the Jesuits tried to elect another patriarch and actually succeeded in raising Archbishop Anthemius to the dignity. But through the influence of the English ambassador, Sir T. Roe, Cyril was recalled in 1622, and Anthemius abdicated in alarm, after seeking Cyril's Absolution. Cyril was re-instated to his office on the payment of a large sum to the Government. Still further subtle Jesuit plots were hatched against him, which usually could only be defeated by bribery. On one occasion, Cyril was compelled to retire for a time from Constantinople, until the Turkish Government were convinced of his innocence.

After the arrival of a printing press from England in 1626, a ' Confession of Faith ' on behalf of the Greek Church, which Cyril had drawn up, was published, and the articles in this are very similar in their doctrinal intent to those in the ' Confessions ' of the Reformed Churches.   For in it the authority of Holy Scripture is asserted to be far greater than that of the Church, since, " it is a different thing to be taught by the Holy Spirit from being taught by man."   " The Catholic Church," another Article asserts, " contains all the faithful in Christ, both those who, having fallen asleep have removed into their Country, and those who are yet strangers in the way."   Of this Church " Christ is Head alone."   But besides this mystical Society there are " particular Visible Churches," in which "the chaff is mingled with the wheat."   In the administration of the Eucharist, " we confess a true Real Presence of Christ, but such a Presence as Faith gives, not such a one as the rashly devised doctrine of transubstanitation affirms." " But we believe the faithful eat the Body of Christ in the Lord's Supper, but by receiving it with the sense of the soul."   Moreover, this Confession expressly condemns the doctrine of purgatory.   The publication of this ' Confession ' by a Greek Patriarch caused a definite sensation in Europe.

In 1632 Cyril wrote to a friend that " we wish the world to know that we will have no communion with the Roman Church, which is the mother of errors, the corrupter of the Word of God and the nest of superstitions."

In 1634, owing to a disgraceful bargain for the Patriarchate, Cyril was deposed and exiled, but a month later he was able to return on payment of 70,000 dollars. In 1635, he was again banished and a rival seized the patriarchate, but in a little over a year he was again restored.   It was about this time that Cyril, in writing to the Senators at Geneva told them that " he embraced their doctrine which was orthodox and Catholic," and that " he abhorred the false and corrupt Roman doctrine."   And a little later he wrote, that " by the favour of God the state of the Church will be restored, the orthodox faith propagated, the truth shine forth, and everything be reformed according to the rule of the Word of God." This undoubtedly was the vision which he cherished and the hope he had set before him, but it was never destined to be realised in the Greek Church. His relentless enemies, the Jesuits, being unable by plots and false accusations to silence him, finally determined on his death. So in 1637 a most infamous accusation was hatched against him, and the Sultan was persuaded to sign his death warrant, and he was strangled on board a ship. The following year a Council of Constantinople, whose decisions were signed by three Greek Patriarchs, with many anathemas, definitely condemned the Articles of Cyril's 'Confession' as heretical. Calvinistic teaching was not, however, thus easily stamped out of the Greek Church, especially as the lives of its opponents were peculiarly worldly and corrupt and in striking contrast to the outstanding piety and holiness of Cyril's character. But at an Eastern Œcumenical Council or Synod, at Bethlehem, in 1672, the statements of Greek Orthodox doctrine set forth were far removed from Cyril's 'Confession.' In the Eucharist, it was asserted, " the Bread is really and truly and properly changed into the very body of our Saviour Christ and the wine into His life-giving Blood, and the Holy Eucharist is offered up as a sacrifice for all Christians both quick and dead." In treating of Church government it is baldly stated " that without Episcopal government there can be neither Church nor Christian." The infallibility of the Church is asserted and the Invocation of Saints and Image worship are both justified. It was also definitely stated that Cyril's 'Confession of Faith' was not the Confession of the Eastern Church, and an attempt was made to declare that this 'Confession' misrepresented Cyril's real views and was in fact a forgery.

The life and teaching of Cyril Lucar furnish a most interesting and remarkable chapter in the history of the Eastern Church, and they afford an example of a sincere and courageous, but at the same time, futile effort to range that Church on the side of Reformed Christendom.

That Cyril's courageous effort at reformation was practically 'still-born' reflects no discredit on his sincerity or his zeal. Its failure was mainly due to the fact that the 'soil' in the East had not been prepared, as it had been in the West, by a great intellectual Movement of honest scientific inquiry and the study of origins. It was this 'Renaissance' movement, which led to the widespread study of the Scriptures and an eager search after spiritual truth, which immediately produced the great awakening of the Reformation.

There had been in Eastern Christendom no 'Lollard' or 'Hussite' or German 'Mystic' movements as in Western Europe, and moreover the political condition of the Eastern Church at Constantinople under the complete domination of a strong Infidel Power was not conducive to fearless religious leadership, individual initiative or independence of thought.

CHAPTER VI

WORSHIP AND USAGE

" **A**ND in these our doings we condemn no other nations nor prescribe anything but to our own people only." This was the guiding principle regarding ' Ceremonies ' adopted by the Anglican Reformers and enunciated by Cranmer. Their successors in Elizabeth's reign submitted this thesis to their Romish opponents for debate at the ' Westminster Disputation,' in 1559—" That every particular church hath authority to institute change or abrogate ceremonies and rites in the Church, so that it be to edify."

This statement was added almost verbatim, in Article XXXIV in 1562. Consequently we find that there was from the first a diversity of usage and services and ceremonies amongst the different Reformed Churches, an illustration of which we have already seen in considering the unedifying squabbles of the Marian Exiles, at Frankfort. A careful examination of the different Reformed Liturgies will, however, prove that, while there were varieties of expression and differences of emphasis on this or that aspect of worship, and closer adherence to exact Scriptural phraseology in some, the divergencies only affected minor questions—mainly those of ritual or ceremony—and did not exhibit any serious difference of doctrine.

This statement is of course definitely challenged today by the disciples of the Tractarian Movement, who contend that the inclusion of the ' Ornaments Rubric ' in the Anglican Prayer Book, requires the ritual use of what are popularly called ' Mass Vestments ' for the Holy Communion service. Thus in their view the Anglican

131

Church symbolically teaches that " the administration of the Lord's Supper is neither more nor less than the Mass in English " (Lord Halifax in 1906). For the use of these vestments are " an outward sign that in fundamental (Mass) doctrine the Church of England today is at one with the rest of the Catholic Church in the past and in the present " [1].

But as we have already seen, the Elizabethan Churchmen and their successors in the Caroline age, were just as clear and definite as their Continental Reformed brethren in repudiating as unscriptural the Roman and Greek doctrine of the Sacrifice of the Mass. And this condemnation was expressed in the statements made in the Articles and canons of the Church. It requires therefore a large amount of credulity to accept the theory that the Anglican Reformers deliberately and intentionally authorised the liturgical use of vestments to teach through symbol, a doctrine which they were never weary of denouncing.

While not wishing to enter on an exhaustive inquiry this very controversial question, on which much ink and paper has been used on both sides, there are one or two outstanding facts to be borne in mind in connection with the correct interpretation of this rubric—

(1) An ' illegal ' rubric ordering in effect the ritual use of albs, copes or chasubles for the Communion Service was inserted in the Elizabethan Prayer Book of 1559, contrary to the Act of Uniformity.

(2) Royal Visitors acting as ' Commissioners for ecclesiastical causes ' as required by the ' Proviso ' of the Act of Uniformity, carried out, in July, 1559, a drastic Visitation, during which they destroyed or burned these very vestments as ' monuments of superstition.'

(3) That clergy, like the Provost of King's College, Cambridge, were actually deprived for ' papistry ' for resisting this order to destroy these vestments, which are now asserted by some to be the authorised vesture for Holy Communion at the time.

(4) That the Elizabethan and even Caroline bishops, like Archbishop Laud, made searching inquiries in their Visitation Articles, whether these " Mass Vestments," " Not allowed by law," remained undestroyed, or " whether any have heard Mass since it was abrogated by law."

(5) In 1566 Archbishop Parker issued the " Royal Advertisements ' by the Queen's command, to stop the " sundry varieties and novelties " then being practised by the Puritan clergy, who were refusing to wear the surplice ; so " the whole realm should be brought *to one manner of uniformity* " ([2]).

This uniformity ordered the surplice only, for all ministrations, except that a cope was added for the Communion services in Cathedrals and Collegiate Churches. This was no ' minimum ' use, as an ingenious, but fantastic, modern theory would suggest ; but it was the ' one manner of uniformity ' ordered by the Queen, who, we are told, was " unable to bear the least alteration in matters of religion " ([3]).

(6) The wording of this rubric was deliberately altered by the Bishops at the revision of the Prayer Book in 1661, at a time when these ' Vestments ' had not been in ' ritual use ' for 100 years, and therefore its language that " such ornaments of the Ministers should be *retained* and be in use as were in this Church of England by authority of Parliament " in 1549, could not possibly refer to the alb or chasuble, but only to that one ' ornament of the Minister ' —the surplice—which had been continuously worn in the services of the Church. ' Mass Vestments ' which like the chasuble had been consistently destroyed, would have had to be *re-introduced*, if this rubric was intended to order their use in the Holy Communion Service.

(7) There is no record of any of the bishops or clergy ever using or wishing to use these Vestments till about the middle of the XIXth

century, and the Supreme Ecclesiastical Court has ruled that they are illegal in the Church of England. (Ridsdale and Clifton Judgments.)

In face of such facts it cannot be seriously maintained that the anomalous appearance of this singular rubric in the Anglican Prayer Book separated Elizabethan churchmen, as far as teaching through worship and ceremony was concerned, from the general doctrinal position of the foreign Reformed Churches.

As we have already seen (Chapter 3) the Anglican Liturgy of 1549, while taking the ' Sarum Use ' as its groundwork, was largely indebted to Lutheran Service books, especially in the Baptismal and Communion offices ; while the 1552 Prayer Book had in the main, been acceptable to the leading foreign Reformers, although it had incurred certain strictures from Calvin, who had been given an unfair account of it.

SCOTCH REFORMED WORSHIP

Although John Knox, the leading spirit directing the course of the Scottish Reformation, was noted for his strong puritan views and his personal dislike of the 1552 Prayer Book, it is interesting to notice that, at least at first, the Scotch Reformers desired the same form of worship as the English. In 1557 the Protestant ' Lords of the Congregation ' resolved that " it is expedient in all parishes of this realm, the Common Prayers be read weekly on Sundays and other festival days publicly . . ." and " conform to the order of the Book of Common Prayers." This resolution was duly put into force, since in 1559, Kircaldy of Grange writes that the parish churches are being cleansed of " images and all other monuments of idolatry that no Mass be said in them, in place whereof the Book set forth by godly King Edward is read in the same churches " [4]. This obviously referred to the 1552 Book, as a correspondent in 1560, says that in Glasgow the Common Prayers " are the very same or differ very little from those in England."

The General Assembly ordered in 1562 that the Sacraments, Marriages and Burials, should be celebrated according to the Book of the Church of Geneva (drawn up by Calvin), but there is evidence that the English Liturgy was in use for several years after this in many places. This ' Book of Common Order ' contained set liturgical prayers and forms of services for special occasions, although their use was generally optional. It remained in use in the Church of Scotland for nearly 80 years until the ill-fated attempt of Archbishop Laud to impose an English Liturgy on Scotland, in 1637, produced a strong reaction against all Prayer Books. It is interesting to notice that the ' Order of Public Worship,' in the ' Book of Common Order,' starts, like the Anglican Liturgy, with an Exhortation, followed by a ' Confession ' of sin, and after the sermon there is the Prayer for the ' whole estate of Christ's Church,' followed by the Lord's Prayer and the Apostles' Creed.

It is often asserted that there was a real distinction between the Anglican and foreign Reformers, in that the former wished to proceed by the way of careful and conservative ' reform ' while the latter desired clear-cut radical ' revolution.' The one, we are told, paid great deference to antiquity and especially to the life and teaching and customs of the Catholic Church of the first six centuries, while the other completely disregarded such a standard and wished to break with everything which could not claim the sanction of the actual Apostolic age. Such a theory is, however, not supported by the attitude of the Scotch Reformers, who in a petition to the Regent in 1558, desired that the " wicked, scandalous and detestable life " of Prelates and of the *State ecclesiastical* " should be reformed according to the rules and precepts of the New Testament, the *writings of the ancient Fathers* and the goodly approved laws of Justinian the Emperor." But in settling doctrinal controversies, like their Anglican brethren, they claimed that the appeal to Scriptural teaching " should decide all controversy " ([5]).

There is no evidence that in the Primitive Church there was any limitation of the administration of the Sacraments to any special officer of the congregation. It was apparently a restriction which grew up with the development of Church Order and organisation and there was no exclusive rule on the subject even in Tertullian's day. The Scotch Reformers had no desire to discard traditional and historic usage in this respect, and just as the Anglican Article XXIII declared the unlawfulness of any one " ministering the sacraments in the congregation," before he is " lawfully called and sent," so the Scotch ' Book of Discipline ' 1560 requires that " strict laws be made against stubborn contemners of Christ Jesus and *against* such as dare presume to minister His Sacraments not orderly called to the office." They even add that such conduct is a " crime deserving death " ([6]).

With regard to the method employed in calling men to the Ministry, although it would appear that for a short time the Scotch Church was inclined to neglect the Scriptural and primitive imposition of hands of the presbytery in Ordination, the names and titles of bishops and archbishops were retained ; and in the Second Book of Discipline, 1578, Ordination was to be performed with ' imposition of hands of Eldership,' accompanied by prayer and fasting. Even before this date the Scotch Assembly approved of the ' Second Helvetic Confession of Faith ' 1566, which enjoined that candidates are to be ordained by the presbyters with public prayer and laying on of hands. This rite had evidently been in general use in the Scotch Church, because John Morrison who was Minister of Bara in 1574, and then later migrated to England, was described, in his licence given him by Archbishop Grindal in 1582, as having been " admitted and ordained to sacred orders and the holy Ministry by the *imposition of hands*, according to the laudable form and rite of the reformed Church of Scotland."

We get also an incidental testimony to the close accord and harmony in doctrine and fellowship then acknowledged between the Churches of England and Scotland, since this licence further asserts that " the congregation of that county of Lothian is conformable to the orthodox faith and sincere religion now received in this realm of England and established by public authority " ([7]). This testimony is very significant, since episcopacy was at this time abrogated in the Scotch Church, yet Grindal told Bullinger in 1567 that in Scotland " the true religion of Christ is established and the impious superstition of the papists abolished." This was not an individual opinion only, as Parkhurst confirms it five years later, in testifying to Bullinger that " the true religion is flourishing in Scotland," and similarly Bishop Jewel declares in 1571 that " the affairs in Scotland are under the direction of those who profess the Gospel " ([8]).

If we turn to the prescribed services in the Scotch ' Book of Common Order ' we find further evidence of a conservative respect for antiquity. Thus the Consecration Prayer in the Communion Service contains the Catholic usage of a definite commemoration of the original institution of the sacrament, which is even fuller than that in the Anglican Prayer Book of 1552, since it includes, like the 1549 office, the Passion, Death, Resurrection and Ascension of our Lord. Moreover the ' Manual Acts ' were apparently performed, and in the sentences of delivery of the elements, the words were, " Take ye, eat ye, this is the Body of the Lord which is broken for you, do it in remembrance of Him." It is rather surprising to observe that the ancient ceremony of the ' lavabo ' was retained till well into the XIXth Century, in many of the Scotch churches, in the form of a basin of water and towel placed on the Communion Table, so that the minister could wash his hands before admininstering the Sacramental elements. An ancient form of dismissal after the administration is also in use in the Scotch Church.

Apparently also the medieval custom of the fast before the Communion was continued for long after the Reformation, while in many churches unleavened bread was used and the mixed chalice, but the latter probably *before* the service. A custom which was possibly derived from Eastern sources, also survived, of the deacons bringing in the elements at a certain stage in the service and placing them on the Table.

In the baptismal service not only were sponsors retained, but the medieval custom of the sponsor, and not the minister, holding the child at the font. Although the observance of the great Festivals and Saints' Days was condemned in the FIRST Book of Discipline,* the Book of Church Order retains them and they were considerably observed in spite of their condemnation. Fasting during Lent was rigorously enforced, but more on prudential grounds than ecclesiastical—" because all kinds of flesh grow out of season then." But the ' Book of Common Order ' contained the ' Order of the General Fast ' which was prefaced by a treatise on fasting. During the fast week only bread and drink were permitted, and all games and marriages were prohibited. Catholic custom is also fully observed in a strict ' Order of Excommunication ' and Order for ' Public Repentance ' and a ' Form of Absolution.' The indicative character of this latter Form, certainly assumes the full exercise of the ' Power of the Keys,' and it is interesting to learn that it was drawn up by John Knox in 1567, although derived from John à Lasco. On profession of repentance the Minister says, " I in His Name pronounce and affirm that thy sins are forgiven not only in earth, but also in Heaven, according to the promises annexed with the preaching of His Word and to the power put in the Ministry of His Church."

We cannot, therefore, say that a review of the rites and ceremonies preserved in the Scotch Reformed Church show much evidence of the adoption of a line of radical cleavage from the Anglican Reformers in their respect for the historic and traditional customs of Christian antiquity.

SWEDISH REFORMED CHURCH

Turning to one of the most interesting of the Reformed Lutheran Churches we are faced with the historical fact that the Reformation in the Swedish Church was carried

* In 1566 a number of leading Scotch Ministers and divinity professors wrote a long letter to Theodore Beza at Geneva voicing their warm appreciation of the ' Latter Confession of Helvetia, 1566,' but they mention that at the present time the festivals of Christmas, Circumcision, Passion, Easter, Ascension and Pentecost are not observed in Scotland.

out on the most careful and conservative lines, in the first instance by Laurentius Petri, who was consecrated Archbishop of Upsala in 1531. The actual breach with the Church of Rome occurred in 1527, when most of the ecclesiastical property was confiscated, and the Church was brought practically under the control of the Crown. The historic episcopal government and succession was, however, preserved, and it was not until 1593 that the Swedish Church accepted the Augsburg Confession of Faith. This was accomplished at the Upsala 'Mote' of 1593, which at the same time laid down the rule of Holy Scripture as the basis of doctrine. Luther's Catechism was authorised for religious instruction and the 'Church Order' of Laurentius Petri became the standard of worship. The second general resolution of this historic Synod asserted the catholicity of the Swedish Church—"We further declare the unity and agreement of the Swedish Church with the Christian Church of the primitive ages, through the adoption of the Apostolic, Nicene and Athanasian Creeds." Strong insistence was from the first placed on the necessity of preaching and reading the Scriptures in the public Services of the Church. For some time, however, the Latin Mass continued side by side with the new Swedish Mass Book of 1531.

Although some of the medieval ritual and ceremonial, including the priestly mass vestments, were retained in this 'Swedish Mass,' the whole aim and trend of the changes were Evangelical, and the modern Swedish rite for Communion bears great resemblance to the Anglican. It thus contains many familiar features of the Ancient Liturgies. The 'Sursum Corda' is retained and the rehearsal of the 'Words of Institution,' The 'Agnus. Dei' is sung during the administration of the elements. The Words of delivery are simply "The Body of Christ given for thee," "The Blood of Christ shed for thee," and each row of communicants is dismissed with "The Lord Jesus Christ whose body and blood ye have received preserve you unto everlasting life. Go in the peace of the Lord." Although the name 'Mass' is retained, the idea of the 'Sacrifice' in it is that of praise and thanksgiving for the benefits of the one great sacrifice for sin offered by Christ alone.   Archbishop Laurentius Petri, in 1542, in his 'Dialogue,' declares " the Sacrament used of old to be called the Thanksgiving or Eucharist, and I doubt not at all that the old Doctors called the Mass a Sacrifice for no other reason."   " If," he says, " you will call the mass a sacrifice because it signifies or represents the sacrifice which Christ made on the Cross, and not as you do now, appropriate the office of Christ to yourself or the priests who are said to offer it, it might be well suffered that you call it a sacrifice." Laurentius Petri was the author of the Swedish ' Church Order ' of 1571, which clearly sets forth the work of the Swedish Reformation.   In this the use of the term Mass, as well as of Mass Vestments, altars and frontals, crossings and signings are all defended as innocent and Evangelical in intent, since the whole aim of the Swedish Reformation was to restore Communion in the Mass.   In this way it would be used " rightly according to Christ's command, by eating and drinking."   Consequently the same rule was laid down, as in the Anglican Communion Service, that Mass was not to be celebrated unless there be some to communicate with the priest for " the right use of the Sacrament does not consist in this, that he sees and gazes with his bodily eyes, but in eating and drinking."   Voluntary private confession before Communion was retained and was especially encouraged at the season of Easter.   But Masses, as sacrifices for sins, and masses for the dead were condemned.   Again in the ' Nova Ordinatio Ecclesiastica ' of 1575, although the mystery of the real, spiritual Presence, even locally attached to the elements, is maintained, yet the practices of Adoration or of Processions with the Host or its offering for the living and the dead are most strongly condemned as " appalling misuse and idolatry."   The Swedish Reformers were anxious to emphasise both the ' Memorial ' and ' Communion ' aspects of the Eucharist, but at the same time they were most careful, as the Anglican Homily expresses it, " lest of the memory it be made a sacrifice, lest of a communion a private eating." Thus the Swedish Reformed Church, which went

through a period of sharp controversy concerning its
liturgical worship and ceremonies, gives striking evidence
of its determination and even anxiety, to preserve, consistently with Evangelical Truth, as much as possible
of ancient traditional ritual and usages.

DENMARK AND NORWAY.

By the Union of Kalmar, 1397, a law was enacted
that the three kindred kingdoms of Norway, Sweden
and Denmark should always be under one ruler. But
although this close unity was not destined to be permanent, the fortunes of these three Scandinavian countries
were closely bound up together. It is not therefore
surprising that the Reformation of the Church in these
three countries was derived and initiated from the same
Lutheran source and synchronised in its incidence.

It was through intercourse with Germany and
Lutheranism that the Evangelical truths penetrated
into Denmark and Norway as well as into Sweden, and
the translation of the New Testament into Danish was a
great factor in the spread of the movement. The
greatest preacher and advocate of reform was John
Tausan, a monk, who was most popular. The King,
Frederick I, espoused Lutheranism, and thus favoured
the Movement, and he also protected its preachers
against the antagonism of the Romish bishops. In 1530
a Conference of the two parties met at Copenhagen,
when the Protestants put forth their Confession of
Faith, which was accepted as that of the Danish
Lutheran Church. Like their brethren in Sweden, and
like the Reformers generally, Holy Scripture was set
forth by the Danish Church as the Rule of Faith, and
Christ was accepted as the only Head of the Church.
The propitiatory Sacrifice of the Mass for the living and
the dead was condemned, and " the true Mass of Christ "
was declared to be " the commemoration of His sufferings and death, in which His body is eaten and His blood
is drunk in certain pledge that through His Name we
obtain forgiveness of sins."

In 1536, King Christian III, by the ' Recess of

Copenhagen,' abolished the ancient episcopal government, and formally proscribed the Romish worship and publicly established the Reformed Lutheran Faith. There was, however, very little iconoclasm and most of the churches still retained their medieval ' ornaments ' and the clergy still wore the medieval vestments. But a new Lutheran liturgy was compiled and, as in Sweden, the Augsburg Confession was adopted. In 1537 the King appointed seven ' Superintendents ' or bishops, to exercise episcopal oversight over the dioceses. These were described as " other Christianlike bishops or superintendents who can teach and preach the Holy Gospel." But these ministers only received presbyterian ordination from Bugenhagen, a Lutheran divine. So that as regards its polity, the Church of Denmark, and also of Norway, differed in this respect from that of Sweden. On the accession of Christian III to the throne of Norway, a similar inauguration of Lutheranism was effected, and all the bishops except two were expelled. But in Norway this reformation was unfortunately accompanied by a considerable spoliation and destruction of churches and religious Houses. Inasmuch as the Reformation in the three Scandinavian countries was carried out on Lutheran lines, with the acceptance of the ' Augsburg Confession ' in each case, it cannot be charged against any of these Churches that antiquity or ancient rites and ceremonies in worship and usage were completely discarded or deliberately disregarded. The XXIInd Article of the ' Augsburg Confession ' is most insistent that Lutheran doctrine was not inconsistent " with the Church Catholic," or even with the Roman Church so far as that Church is known from the writings of the Fathers. The rites of the Churches, it urges, were never " at any time the same," " although among us in large part the ancient rites are diligently observed. For it is a calumnious falsehood, that all the ceremonies, all the things instituted of old are abolished in our churches." All they have done, the Confession declares, is to " omit a few of certain abuses which are novel . . . and have been received by the fault of the times " (Part 2). " The

Mass," they explain " is retained still among us and celebrated with great reverence and almost all the ceremonies that are in use " (Art. III, Pt. 2).

Moreover, the Augsburg Confession makes frequent appeal to the customs and teaching of the early Fathers of the Church. Certainly Luther's ' Order of Divine Service ' included many ancient features, such as the observance of Holy Days with Epistle and Gospel. The use of the Te Deum, the Benedictus and Magnificat, Feast and Fast Days and Holy Week were to be observed. The Sunday Eucharistic rite is not unlike the order of the Anglican, with a psalm or hymn, the Kyrie, Collect, Epistle, Gospel, Creed, Sermon, Lord's Prayer, Exhortation to the Communicants, and Prayer of Consecration which includes the recital of the Words of Institution. The ' Sanctus ' was sung and also the Agnus Dei and even the elevation of the host was not forbidden, while men and women were required to sit, and also receive, apart.

It should be carefully borne in mind that Luther asserted that the Reformed German Evangelical Church " was a member of the old true Church, inasmuch as it possessed the Sacraments of Baptism and the Lord's Supper, the power of the Keys, the Word and preaching, without any addition of man, the ancient faith as contained in the Apostles' Creed " ([9]). It is not unimportant to notice that Lutheran teaching directly influenced our English Reformers on the subject of Confession and Absolution. For the ' Augsburg Confession ' declared that " Confession was retained " for " the great *benefit* of Absolution." And Melanchthon's ' Apology ' distinctly declares that " enumeration of sins in Confession is not necessary " because " the ministry of absolution is a *benefit* or grace, not a *judgment* or law." And it defines Absolution as " the voice of the Gospel remitting sins and consoling consciences " and affirms that this " does not require knowledge of sins " (Von Hase Lib. Symb. p. 181, Lips. 1846).

In the Thirteen Articles of 1538 this view was also accepted by the Anglicans who declare for the retention of Confession " principally for the sake of the *benefit* of Absolution " . . . " which is the voice of the Gospel by which the Minister through the Word, not in his own but in Christ's name and authority, announces and offers remission of sins to the person confessing."

This Lutheran teaching was again specially emphasised in the Exhortation in the Communion Service of 1552, where the invitation to the troubled soul, not to ' confess ' his sins, but . . . to consult a " discreet and learned Minister of God's Word," to receive " ghostly counsel and advice," adds " that by the Ministry of God's Word he may receive comfort and the *benefit of Absolution*," using the exact phraseology of the Lutheran Confessions.

THE ' REFORMED ' CHURCHES

CHURCH OF ZÜRICH

Turning to the Evangelical ' Reformed ' Churches, let us notice first the Church of Zürich, where Zwingli is supposed to have carried out a Reformation on radical lines, and to have made a clean sweep of all medieval superstitious teaching and ceremonial. It is interesting to notice that even here there was no deisre to discard the traditional and ancient forms of worship and usage which were innocent, helpful and Scriptural, simply *because* they were old and had been used in papal times. In the Order of celebrating the Eucharist given in the ' Fidei Christianae Expositio, 1531,' we find several familiar and ancient features. The Service starts with the invocation of the Trinity and with a prayer. The Minister then reads the Epistle standing to the left of the Table. The ' Gloria in Excelsis ' follows and the Te Deum, and the Response. The deacon then reads the Gospel from St. John vi. 47-63, and at the conclusion the Minister kisses the book and the Apostles' Creed is recited. The Minister then reads the Invitation to the Communicants and a prayer follows on the lines of the Anglican ' Prayer of Humble Access.' The Minister then proceeds to the Consecration by a recital of the Words of Institution in which the Manual acts

144

are performed. After the administration the Service is closed with sentences and a prayer of thanksgiving ([10]).

There was unfortunately in the early days of the Reformation much unchristian hostility and intolerance displayed between the Lutherans and the ' Reformed.' It is interesting therefore to find that Calvin was able to act as a sort of ' bridge ' between them. He voluntarily signed the ' Augsburg Confession,' and Luther even approved of his explanation of Eucharistic doctrine, yet he was able to defend Zwingli against a Lutheran doctor's attack on his Eucharistic views. He declared that Œcolampadius and Zwinglians were induced by the best of reasons, nay compelled by urgent necessity, to refute a gross error which had long before become inveterate, and was connected with impious idolatry, but that while intent on this one object only, they lost sight of another, as often happens in debate, and he denies that he meant to imply from this that Zwingli " contended for empty symbols without thinking the reality was combined with them " ([11]).

Although Calvin rather adversely criticised the disparaging account given him by the Puritan party of the 1552 Prayer Book of Edward VI, it was certainly not on the ground of a definite dislike of ancient forms and prayers, since the Genevan Forms of Prayer preserved many familiar catholic features. For instance, the language used in the service of Holy Communion in the Puritan or ' Middleburgh ' Prayer Book of 1584, which was based on Calvin's Liturgy, seems to have been borrowed largely from the Anglican Liturgy. For in the ' Exhortation ' the Minister warns the communicants " diligently to try and examine themselves before they presume to eat of that bread and drink of that cup." The language then proceeds almost verbatim with the third Exhortation in the Anglican Communion Service with the addition of the significant sentence (after " not considering the Lord's Body "), " which is offered in the Sacrament to the worthy receiver."

Again in administering the elements the Minister is directed to break the bread and deliver it to the people

145

with the words, " Take and eat, this bread is the body of
Christ that was broken for us, Do this in remembrance
of Him . . Likewise he shall give the cup, saying Drink
ye all of this . . . This cup is the New Testament in the
blood of Christ which was shed for the sins of many."
But strong as this language appears, in reality it goes
no farther than the injunction in the Anglican Words
of Delivery to " feed on Him in *thy heart by faith* with
thanksgiving," since the Address definitely instructs the
worshippers that they " are not to seek Christ in the
elements " as " if He were enclosed in the bread and
wine or as if these elements were turned and changed
into the substance of His flesh and blood." They are
told that " the only way to dispose of our souls to receive
nourishment," is by a Sursum Corda—" to lift up our
minds by faith above all things worldly and sensible,
and thereby to enter into heaven that we may find and
receive Christ where He dwelleth undoubtedly " [12].
With regard to the ancient and apostolic rite of Confirmation Bishop Bancroft at the Hampton Court Conference,
1604, declared that Calvin " wished earnestly for its
restitution in those reformed Churches where it had been
abolished." Again, in discussing Confession and Absolution as used in the Church of England, Bancroft
asserted that not only the Lutheran Confessions abroad
retained and allowed it, but that " Calvin did also
approve such a general kind of Confession and absolution
as the Church of England useth, and withall did very
well like of those which are private, for so he terms them "
(Cardwell, ' Hist. of Conferences,' 173). Again, Henry
Bullinger, the celebrated leader of the Church at Zürich,
counsels Lawrence Humphrey to accept the ' habits ' and
surplice, since they are ordered by authority, and he
reminds him that " the same things were in use among
the ancients." He also finds no objection to the sign of
the Cross in baptism which he describes as a primitive
ceremony. Peter Martyr, although disliking the surplice, counselled the ' puritan ' brethren " to bear with
it " rather than forsake their ministry, and he also
fully approved of the use of unleavened bread for the
Communion, which, he said, was in use in all the Swiss

Churches. Rodolph Gualter, Bullinger's successor at Zürich, regarded Confirmation as Scriptural and sponsors for baptism lawful.

It is manifestly incorrect to charge the leading Swiss Reformers with a deliberate disregard for the standards and teaching of Christian antiquity when we recall their warm appreciation of Bishop Jewel's ' Apology.' This famous Anglican treatise was designedly an appeal to the customs and teaching of the Catholic Church of the first six centuries, and yet we find Peter Martyr in his congratulations to Jewel declaring that this ' Apology ' " appeared to Bullinger, Gualter and Wolfius, so wise, admirable and eloquent, that they think nothing in these days hath been set forth more perfectly " [13]. But like Jewel himself they regarded this appeal to antiquity as subordinate to the ultimate appeal to the final authority of Holy Scripture, and there is abundant evidence in other foreign Reformed ' Confessions ' that this attitude was general. For instance, the ' Confession of Wurtemburg,' 1552, in speaking of ' Ecclesiastical Writers ' (Chap. 34), says " We do reverence the grey hairs of our ancestors, who, ever since the Gospel began to be revealed and published, have in the world taken upon them the travail of furthering the Church by their preaching and public writings ; that their posterity might from the Apostles, even unto this time, have manifest and certain testimonies of the holy doctrine." This is exactly the same attitude towards the writings of the Fathers as that taken by the Anglican Reformers, who delight to appeal to their teaching as confirmatory of the true Catholic Faith which they had restored. And this ' Confession ' goes on to say, " And so we embrace their writings, as both holy Scripture alloweth us to use man's authority, and *as themselves* would have their writings acknowledged " : and it quotes St. Augustine in explanation, who says, " Neither ought we to esteem of the writings of any men, although they be Catholic, *as of the Canonical Scriptures*."

Similarly, the ' Confession of Bohemia ' (1573), while declaring that all " human writings whatsoever " " must give place to the holy Scripture," adds " We likewise teach that the writings of holy Doctors, especially of those that are ancient, are also to be esteemed for true and profitable . . . yet only in those things wherein they agree with the holy Scriptures " (chap. 1).

DUTCH REFORMED CHURCH

If we turn to the Dutch Reformed Church, we find that its Liturgy was a distinctly Protestant production. It probably owed its origin to the labours of two well-known Dutch Reformed Ministers of the XVIth Century —Petrus Dathenus and Caspar van der Heyden—and it was entitled ' De liturgie der Gereformeerde Kerke in Nederlant.' In the main it was a compilation from two distinct sources. The first was a liturgy composed by Martin Micronius, who was Minister of the Dutch Strangers' Church in Austin Friars, London, in Edward VI's reign. This was called ' The Christian ordinances of the Dutch Christian Community,' and it was an adaptation of John à Lasco's ' Forma ac ratio tota ecclesiastici ministerie in peregrinorum,' of 1550. The second source from which this Dutch Reformed Liturgy was drawn was the ' Paltz-ische ' liturgy written by Olevianus, which in its turn was a combination of Calvin's Geneva Liturgy and the Lutheran Wurtemburg Liturgy. But in spite of its definitely protestant origin this Dutch Liturgy retained elements and features familiar in the traditional worship and usage of the Catholic Church. In an edition published at Dordrecht, by Joris Waters, in 1609, it is bound up with the New Testament. It is a full and very comprehensive liturgy comprising besides the usual public service and Occasional Offices like Baptism and Holy Communion, Matrimony, Visitation of the Sick, The Catechism and Ordination, special services for Excommunication and Reconciliation of Penitents and also Family Prayers and personal prayers for sick people and daily duties.

It is well to examine some of these Services in a little more detail, not only as evidence of doctrinal unity with other Reformed Churches in their language, but also as an illustration of the many conservative elements which are so freely included, and which certainly indicate no revolutionary desire to break needlessly with ancient forms of worship. For instance, the Baptismal Service is fairly lengthy, containing Scriptural explanations of the origin and purpose of the rite and a reminder that Baptism has taken the place of Circumcision. Sponsors are used and there are definite questions to these godparents that they will promise to instruct the children in the Christian Faith. The Minister takes the child in his arms, as in the Anglican rite, and baptizes him in the name of the Trinity.

Candidates for Confirmation are carefully questioned as to their belief, on the lines of the Apostles' Creed, and it is customary for them to receive Memorial Cards of their Confirmation with such words as " He that will confess Me before men I will confess before My Father, who is in heaven."

The Marriage Service follows the lines of the Anglican Prayer Book with similar questions to the couple. The ancient ceremony of taking of hands is performed and the ring is given. There is a beautifully appropriate concluding ceremony in the presentation of a Bible to the pair with the words, " This is a letter from your Father to teach you how to guide your future life."

There is a lengthy Catechism in which the various Articles of the Creed, as well as the Sacraments and the Lord's Prayer are fairly fully expounded. In the Ordination Service there is a long address by the presiding Minister with a reference to Ephesians iv. 11-12, and the candidates are exhorted as ' shepherds of souls ' to tend their flocks with godly words and with the ministry of prayers and Sacraments and the preaching of God's Word. There is also a long Charge to the ordinands on similar lines to that given in the Anglican service for the Ordering of Priests, in which they are reminded of their authority for discipline in the Church—" seeing you have been entrusted with the keys of heaven." The questions to the candidates are very similar to those in the Anglican Service concerning the necessity of teaching the way of salvation from Scripture only, and maintaining discipline and observing the rules of the Church. The Laying on of Hands by the Ministers present then follows with the words—

God our heavenly Father who has called you to this holy service enlighten you through His Holy Spirit, strengthen you with His hand and guide you in all your work that you may profitably and fruitfully walk to the glory of His Name and the building up of the Kingdom of Christ Jesus His Son.

There is also an exhortation to the congregation to help and support their pastor and attend his Ministry, and a concluding prayer for the newly ordained, closing with the Lord's Prayer which, as in the Anglican Liturgy, is introduced into every service. There is a separate service for the Ordination of Deacons, Elders and Readers. In it they are reminded of the two types of ministry in the Apostolic Church—one for preaching and administering the Sacraments, the other for help and service to the Minister, the congregation and the poor. The candidates are specially warned against attempting to administer the sacraments which is the office confined to the Minister only. The questions to them refer to the acceptance of Scripture as the Word of God and for true doctrine, and faithful service, and a prayer is offered for them " for faithfulness and fruitfulness in this your service." An address to the congregation is concluded by the Lord's Prayer.

The Service for Excommunication is of a most definite character. It rehearses the great disgrace and sin of the erring member and the great sorrow of the congregation that he has been deaf to repeated warnings. Then the solemn sentence is delivered by the Minister—" I declare to you all that N . . . is shut away and shut out of this congregation of the Lord and is a stranger to the fellowship of Christ in the Holy Sacraments and all spiritual blessings that God has promised to His Church." The Congregation is also warned to treat the offender as a ' heathen and a publican ' as long as he is ' stiffnecked ' and impenitent—" by the command of Christ who has bound in heaven whatsoever His ministers bind on earth."

There is also a special Form of Reconciliation of Excommunicate persons of a most appropriate and helpful character. After inviting any objector to come forward, the Minister reminds the congregation of the authority given to the Ministry—" Whosoever sins ye remit they are forgiven "—and then the pentitent sinner is " solemnly received by the Minister " back into the congregation of the Lord and "restored to the fellowship of Christ and His holy Sacraments."

There is a special service of preparation for Holy Communion and the actual service itself is much longer than the Anglican form. It commences with the rehearsal of the Words of Institution—" Beloved in the Lord Jesus Christ—Hear the Words of the Institution of the Holy Supper." The Minister reminds the people that they must prove their title to partake and also they must understand the meaning of its institution. To this end the communicants are exhorted to self-examination—

(1) That they believe in God's promise of forgiveness to us through the sufferings and death of Jesus Christ.

(2) That out of gratitude to God they will live an upright and godly life. And in similar language to the Anglican ' Invitation ' they are exhorted " henceforth to live in love and unity with their neighbours."

(3) To think over their sins.

A long Exhortation follows, first of all warning all blasphemers and evil livers that they must not approach the Lord's Table—an injunction paralleled by the Anglican rubric against " open and notorious evil livers." This is followed by a further appeal for penitence and a warning that no one " must come to the Lord's Table who is under any sin." The Exhortation then proceeds on the lines of the Exhortations in the Anglican office (but at much fuller length) to rehearse the reasons of the institution of the Lord's Supper. The Words of Institution are again recited, and language similar to the Anglican Prayer of Consecration is employed, and the communicants are reminded that " we are to regard His full and perfect sacrifice once for all offered on the Cross " as the " one and only ground of salvation," and that " as oft as we eat this bread and drink the cup " we may have the " eternal certainty " —that . . . " I gave my body and shed my blood on the Cross that your hungry and thirsty soul might be fed with my crucified Body to eternal life."

Then there is a reminder of the ' fellowship and communion ' aspect of the Sacrament, similar to the language of the Anglican post-Communion prayers, that we " are through the Spirit, members of the same community bound together in brotherly love." " We all in the true faith in Christ are as one body and affection not only in words but in deeds and actions." This is followed by a prayer for grace on these lines and it is concluded with the Lord's Prayer and the recital of the Apostles' Creed.

A further injunction incorporates the idea of the ' Sursum Corda,' since the communicants are exhorted to depend on the ' heavenly Bread ' and not on the ' visible bread and wine,' but on " that. which is above in heaven, exalted where Christ Jesus, our Advocate, is at the right hand of the Heavenly Father . . . " " not doubting that we shall truly, through the working of the Holy Spirit, be fed and satisfied with His body and blood as we receive the holy bread and wine."

The Minister, in breaking the bread and administering the elements, says, " The bread which we break is the fellowship of the Body of Christ," and " the Cup of thanksgiving whereby we give thanks is the fellowship of the blood of Christ." After the reception the Minister exhorts to praise and thanksgiving, and most of the 103rd Psalm is sung. After a further short exhortation the service is concluded by a prayer of thanksgiving, in which the congregation join, and which is a sort of parallel or substitute to the ' Gloria in Excelsis,' and ends with the petition that " we may be daily led into a right belief and go forward in blessed fellowship with Christ."

In the Catechism there is also an explanation of the Sacraments in which the catechumen is instructed that " just as the Water in Baptism is not changed into the

Blood of Christ for the washing away of sins," neither are the "bread and wine the actual body and blood of Christ," but they are all "godly tokens and assurances."

In answer to the question, Why Christ called "the bread His Body and the cup His Blood," it is explained "that Christ's crucified Body and shed Blood are the true meat and drink of our souls to eternal life," and "much more" that "through these visible tokens and signs we truly partake of the true body and blood of Christ through the working of the Holy Ghost."

In explaining the difference "between the Supper of the Lord and the Popish Mass," we are told that the first assures us of the forgiveness of sins through Christ's one offering, but the Mass "teaches us that the living and dead are not forgiven by Christ's Suffering, but that Christ is literally under the bread and wine and these must be prayed to." It is doubtful today if the Anglican Service for The Visitation of the Sick is ever used in its entirety, but it is still more doubtful if the similar service in the Dutch Reformed Liturgy could often have been used as it was enjoined. For it contains twelve and a half pages of exhortation which are overburdened with a multiplicity of Scripture quotations which must have been far too wearisome for persons at all seriously ill.

THE FRENCH REFORMED CHURCH.

As regards the French Reformed Church we have an easy task to prove that it possessed the same regard for antiquity and for historical customs, worship and usages as the Anglican. For the learned Joseph Bingham devotes the best part of the eighth volume of his ' Origines Ecclesiasticae ' in an exhaustive comparison of the Anglican and French Reformed Churches. His immediate objective was to convince the English Nonconformists that—

" the methods and measures of reformation in the Church of England, are the same that the French Church did take or would have taken if she could : that our expedients for preventing and healing schisms in the Church are no other than what are laid down and prescribed in these (French) Synods : that our

Articles and Homilies contain no other doctrine, but what is publicly taught in the articles and homilies of the French Church : that the obligations against our Liturgy and Rubrics will hold as well against the Liturgy and public offices that are used among them " ([14]).

This statement in itself is a striking testimony of this late XVIIth Century Anglican divine and scholar, to the very close unity which was recognised between the Anglican Episcopal and French Presbyterian Reformed Churches. And this recognition was mutual. For the Frenchman Theodore Beza had told Archbishop Grindal, " we believe your churches do in all points of doctrine agree with ours," and " as to what concerns your faith or doctrine received by public consent, I suppose there is no man that thinks rightly of these matters, but will embrace it as true and certain." A little later the celebrated French Reformed divine, Peter du Moulin, in defending the French ' Confession ' against Jesuit attack, declared—

" Our adversaries under pretence that the Church of England hath another form of discipline than ours is, charge us that our religion is diverse ; but experience confuteth this accusation; for we assemble with the English in their churches, we participate together in the holy Supper of our Lord, the doctrine of their Confession is wholly agreeable unto ours " ([15]).

Again with reference to the regard for the teaching of the historic Catholic Church, du Moulin in his correspondence with Bishop Andrewes, declares—

" Think of me as of a man with whom the authority of antiquity shall ever be in great esteem. Nor am I such a boldface as to pass sentence upon those lights of the ancient Church—Ignatius, Polycarp, Cyprian, Augustine, etc., all of them bishops . . . the reverend antiquity of those past ages shall ever be in greater esteem with me than the novel device of any whatsoever" ([16]).

That these professions of reverence for ancient customs and teaching were genuine in the case of the French Reformed Church is amply proved by Bingham's comprehensive and thorough examination. He quotes from the Confession of the French Church, a similar statement to the Anglican—that " the Church hath power to decree rites and ceremonies " (Art. XX) ; and he instances the different ceremonies ordained in the French Church for order, decency and dignity. " Upon this account," he says, " she gives many rules about praying and preaching and adminstering the sacraments. That all men should pray kneeling, that baptism should not be administered but in Church assemblies—that Communion shall be received standing, that the minister shall deliver it singly into every man's hand, and use a certain form of words at the distribution of it to every individual; with many like prescriptions in her Liturgy and Canons, but especially her Book of Discipline, which contains above two hundred Canons." Bingham points out the strictness of the French Church in the use of its prescribed Liturgy. Calvin himself had ' highly approved ' of a fixed form of prayers, and a Canon of the French Church suspends from office any pastor who questions or varies the forms of " catechising or administering of the Sacraments, or of common prayers and celebration of marriage." And Bingham quotes the exact words of the consecration prayer in the Ordination of Ministers. He also reminds the English Dissenters that the French Church follows the English in accepting the Athanasian Creed and in reciting the Apostles' Creed in her public services, and that it recommends Sponsors in Baptism as " profitable and conforming to a very ancient and accustomed order " in the Church, and although unlike the Lutherans and Anglicans, it has discontinued the sign of the Cross in baptism, it does not condemn its use. Bingham also points out that the French Church observes with appropriate services the great Festivals of the Church, and that although circumstances forced it to employ presbyterian ordination, it admitted fully the Scripturalness and antiquity of episcopacy, and in no way condemned that form of Church government. He also quotes a most instructive statement made by a French Reformed Professor of Divinity at Saumur, which gives clear evidence that amongst the Continental Protestants, both Lutheran and Reformed, there was no desire whatever to break with ancient forms and standards of ritual or worship, in so far as they were not repugnant to Scripture, or superstitious. It is also interesting to notice that all the Reformed Churches continued the custom of liturgical services. "At the Reformation," says this French Professor, " the Liturgy, or service of the Church was purged from all popish superstition and idolatry, and all such ceremonies as were either too burthensome, or of no use towards edification." We get here an echo of Cranmer's statement concerning the ' multitude ' of " uprofitable and dark Ceremonies "—which " obscured the glory of God " rather than set forth " Christ's benefits unto us." But Capellus goes on to say, " And then set forms of Liturgy were composed and prescribed, by the several authors of the Reformation, in the countries where they lived, as in Germany, France, England, Scotland, Belgium, &c., *varying as little as might be from the ancient forms of the Primitive Church.* And these set forms have hitherto been happily used with profit and advantage, by the Reformed Churches of every nation." He then continues to censure a " sort of morose, and froward, nice and scrupulous " set of men in England, who for " very slight and slender reasons " have substituted " the Directory as they call it in its room," which left " every pastor to express himself in what words he pleased." And he concludes by referring to " other furious and mad men," who actually taught that it was unlawful for a " godly man " to use " any prescribed form of prayers, either in public or private " ([17]). In a French Reformed Psalm and Prayer Book (published in 1690, at Amsterdam, and not in France, probably on account of its prohibition after the Revocation of the Edict of Nantes in 1685* we find many features similar to our English Liturgy. The service starts with the Exhortation and Confession and the Creed is recited. In the Communion office a Long Exhortation to the Communicants recalls in its language the Prayer of Humble Access and the Sursum Corda of the Anglican service—

---

* Even before the fateful edict of Revocation on Oct. 18, an Ordinance of July 9, 1685, had excluded the French 'Reformed' from all printing trades, so as to suppress their books of devotion ; and shortly after this, all such Service Books and Bibles were confiscated and publicly burned.

Premièrement donc croyons à ces promesses que Jesus Christ, qui est la verité infallible a prononcees de sa bouche, assavoir, qu'il nous veut vraiement faire participans de son corps et de son sang ; afin que nous le possedions entiérement ; en telle sorte qu'il vive en nous et nous en lui. Et bien que nous ne voyons que du pain et du vin, toutefois ne doutont point qu'il n'accomplisse spirituellement en nos ames tout ce qu'il nous demontre exterieurement par ces signes visibles ; c'est a dire, qu'il est le pain celeste pour nous repaître et nourir a vie eternelle.

And the Exhortation goes on to speak of the ' dignity ' of " this precious gift," and exhorts the communicants " pour ce faire élevons nos esprits et nos coeurs en haut ou est Jesus Christ en la gloire de Dieu son Père."
It concludes by adding

Et ne nous amusons point à ces élemens terriens et corruptibles que nous voyons a l'oeil et touchons a la main, pour le chercher là comme s'il estoit enelos au pain ou au vin. Car alors nos ames seront disposées à estre nourries et vivifiées de la substance, quand elles seront ainsi élevées pardessus toutes choses terrestres, pour atteindre jusque au ciel et entrer au Royaume de Dieu ou il habite. Contentons nous donc d'avoir le pain et le vin pour signes et temoignages, cherchent spirituellement la verité ou la Parole de dieu promet que nous la trouverons.

The Catechism is much fuller in its teaching and covers more subjects than the Anglican, but its instruction is given on identical lines of question and answer. In the section dealing with the Sacraments, in answer to the question, " How many sacraments are there in the Christian Church ? " we have " Il n'y en a que deux communs que le Seigneur Jesus ait instituez pour toute la compagnie des fidels." The catechumen is then asked to distinguish between the two Sacraments and answers.

Le Baptisme nous est comme une entree en l'Église de Dieu. Car il nous testifie que Dieu au lieu que estions étrangers de lui, nous recóit pour les domestiques. La Cene nous est un témoign-age que Dieu nous veut nourrir et repaître, comme un bon pere de famille a le soin de nourrir et refecuionner ceux de sa maison.

In describing the meaning of Baptism we have—

Elle a deux parties car le Seigneur nous y represente la remis-sion de nos pechez et puis nôtre regeneration ou renouvellement spirituel.

A long and fuller explanation of this sacrament follows. The section on the Holy Communion is also full. In answer to the question as to its meaning, we have—

Notre Seigneur l'a instituée pour nous asseurer que par la communication de son corps et de son sang nos ames font nourries en l'ésperance de la vie eternelle.

After a much fuller explanation there are two closing questions—

" Selon tes responses, la Céne nous renvoye à la mort et passion de Jesus Christ, afin que nous communiquions à la vertu d'icelle ? " The Answer is—" Oui car alors le sacrifice unique et perpetuel a este fait pour notre redemption. C'est pourquoi il ne reste plus sinon que nous en aions la jouissance."

Question—" Le Cene donc n'est pas institue pour faire une oblation du corps de Jesus a Dieu son Pere ? "

Answer—" Non, car il n'y a que lui seul a qui appartient cet office, entant qu'il est sacrificateur eternel. Mais il nous commande seulement de recevoir son corps, non pas de l'offrir."

Reviewing the liturgies and usages of the different foreign Reformed Churches, we may therefore confidently affirm that as regards respect for Christian antiquity and the profitableness of ancient and primitive worship and usages, there is certainly no marked difference or dividing line between Anglican churchmen and their Reformed brethren on the Continent.

CHAPTER VII

LATER EVIDENCES OF FELLOWSHIP.

THAT the close friendship and fellowship between the Anglican Exiles and their Swiss brethren was not built on a foundation of sand, but on solid doctrinal unity and common interest, was very manifest during Elizabeth's reign. The gratitude felt by both clergy and laity for their preservation from persecution, and for their sustenance and hospitality during the troublous and perilous days of the Marian reaction was both deep and enduring. Moreover, in their close intercourse with the Swiss divines they had formed most intimate and affectionate relationships of which a continuous correspondence for nearly twenty years gives us abundant evidence. It is pathetic to read the real laments of the survivors as they record to each other in their letters the death of one and then another of these close friends of twenty years standing, until the correspondence ceases as they all pass away. Thus William Cole, the president of Corpus Christi College, Oxford, laments in his letter to R. Gualter in 1579, that scarcely five now remain of all those who were with him in exile at Zürich.

When Henry Bullinger, the acknowledged preceptor of both Anglicans and Swiss, died in 1575, Bishop Cox wrote that by his death " the whole Christian Church is disquieted with exceeding regret, that so bright a star is forbidden any longer to shine upon earth " [1].

The relationship between Bishop Jewel and Peter Martyr seems to have been like that of St. Paul and Timothy, or of David and Jonathan, since he regarded him almost as his father in Christ. He describes him as " his soul's better half," and " his father and most esteemed Master in Christ " ; and he longs for him once more to occupy his divinity Chair at Oxford. On Martyr's death, in his eulogistic lament to Bullinger concerning his piety and attainments, Jewel adds " the like of whom I can scarce believe to have existed " (¹).

We can form a good idea of the happy and satisfying fellowship that existed in the anxious years of exile, when in a letter to Martyr, Jewel exclaims, " O Zürich, Zürich, how much oftener do I think of thee than I ever thought of England when I was at Zürich " (¹). And after the death of Martyr Jewel exhorts Bullinger not to entertain " the thought that either the school of Zürich or your exceeding kindness can so quickly have passed away from my mind. Indeed, I have you all in my eyes and in my heart, and yourself especially my father, who are now the only light of my age " (²).

The solidarity of the Reformed cause and their common loyalty to primitive and Scriptural and Catholic teaching created the closest bond between them. Archbishop Grindal tells Bullinger in 1572 that in future he will write twice a year as he longs to hear how things are with them in Zürich and to give him information about the religious condition in England, for he adds, " we are members of the same body." Jewel had emphasised this point when he told Martyr that as the result of the Elizabethan Religious Settlement, " the full light of the Gospel shone forth " in England, and that " we do not differ from your doctrine by a nail's breadth " (²). This unity of doctrine was also emphasised by Bishop Parkhurst, who described the ' Latter Confession of Helvetia, 1556 ' as " that confession of true religion." We also get a very welcome human touch when Jewel, in a letter to Martyr, ends with " give a kiss to your little son, Isaac, whom I can fancy I hear bawling even here " (³). Moreover, circumstances tested this friendship and affection in a very practical way. Several Swiss youths were sent over to England by their parents to enlarge their outlook and complete their education. Amongst these students we find a nephew and grandson of Bullinger, and a son of Rodolph Gualter, who had himself been in England in Edward VI's reign.

The Anglican ' Exiles,' many of whom were now bishops, showed the greatest anxiety to befriend these young foreigners and help them with money and find places for them in the Colleges at Oxford and Cambridge.

Bishop Parkhurst, of Norwich, who had been for four years a guest with Gualter, at Zürich, was specially active and solicitous to help his son. He wrote in 1568 to the father, that whenever he thought well to send his son he would support him at the University at his own expense and care for him as if he were his own boy. And apparently he was as good as his word, for when young Gualter came to England a few years later, Parkhurst sent him first to Cambridge, and then, as the young man soon got tired of that seat of learning, he sent him to Oxford to Magdalene College and kept a close fatherly eye on his career there. He was most indignant with Gualter for wishing to repay him for his outlay on the boy. " Can I accept a return from you ? Do you not think you satisfied me at Zürich. Do you consider me as having cast off all generous feeling ? Let me never again hear any such thing from you ! He shall live in England at no expense to you. I will entertain him here and liberally too." At first he tells the father, " Your Rodolph is in great favour with everybody." But apparently this universal popularity somewhat disturbed the young student's balance, so that he became careless and extravagant, or at least wished to improve his opportunity by seeing as much of English life as possible. He spent several months loitering in London on his way to Oxford, so that Parkhurst had to reprimand him severely for this loss of time, and " the vain expense of money." But later on he pleads with the father to forgive " for his sake " this rather pardonable lapse—" he is a young man and the young do many juvenile things." The youth, however, succeeded in getting his M.A. before his father recalled him home. But Parkhurst's warm personal interest in him continued, for he writes both to Bullinger and Simler urging a marriage alliance for young Gualter with Bullinger's daughter. Evidently this ' match-making ' materialised, since two years later in 1576, John Rainolds, the President of Corpus, Oxford, writes congratulating young Gualter on his marriage.

It is interesting to notice that even after the generation of Anglican ' Exiles ' had passed away this friendship for the Swiss Church did not disappear. A grandson of Martin Bucer came to England in 1593 and the Queen defrayed the cost of his training at Cambridge, as an acknowledgment of the merits of his grandfather. The State of Zürich also recommended another student for the Queen's support and interest, and when this youth visited Oxford the Vice-Chancellor was most gratified to receive a " letter from the famous Church of Zürich," and the University granted the young man— Caspar Thoman—a yearly stipend of £20 and he became one of the first students of the new public Library at Oxford.

It is a striking testimony to the great respect and esteem in which the divines of the Zürich Church were held that both the Anglican bishops, and also the Puritan divines, appealed to them, almost as arbiters, in the unfortunate ' habits ' or vestiarian controversy, which the Puritan faction stirred up, and which raged furiously during the early part of Elizabeth's reign. It should be explained that neither the Anglican party nor the Puritans had any love for these ' habits,' and that both wished that the outdoor square cap and the surplice for divine service might be discontinued. But the Queen was obdurate on these points, and so the Anglicans quietly acquiesced in them as ' things indifferent.' The Puritans, on the other hand, strongly objected to them as " relics of the Amorites," or " rags of popery " or " Aaronic vestments " ; and they wrote in anxiety and alarm to the Swiss divines for their advice and decision on this burning question. Sampson and Humphrey, in 1566, sent a long list of queries to Bullinger, and they were by no means pleased with his reply. They could not they declared, regard the ' habits ' as " things indifferent," but as " against Christian liberty."

Bullinger simply told them that the wearing of the surplice was a matter of civil concern and did not savour of popery or Judaism. Gualter gave similar advice, urging the Purtian ministers not to desert their churches for matters of so little importance.

Sampson, who was Dean of Christ Church, Oxford, was at length deprived for his persistent nonconformity on this question. There is almost a humorous irony in this prominent and obdurate Purtian champion being, a few years earleir, sternly reprimanded by the Queen for his ' popish ' leanings ! He had to preach at St. Paul's before the Queen on the Feast of the Circumcision in 1561. He thought it would be a fitting opportunity to make a small New Year's gift to Elizabeth which would specially gratify her. Accordingly he caused some pictures and wood-cuts of the stories and sufferings of saints to be beautifully bound up with the Prayer Book, which he placed on the Queen's prayer desk. He had, however, underestimated the strength of her protestant prejudices, for Elizabeth refused to use the book and ordered the Verger to bring her an old copy. After the service she severely rated the unfortunate Dean for disobeying her " proclamation against the superstitious use of Images in Churches and for taking away of all such relics of popery." The astonished Puritan Dean pleaded his innocent intentions, but Elizabeth impressed on him her ' aversion to idolatry,' and to images and pictures of the kind representing Angels and Saints and the Blessed Trinity. The Dean excused himself that he had procured the pictures from a German, and so the Queen dismissed him with the warning—" Pray let no more of these mistakes be committed within the churches of our realm for the future " ([4]).

To return to the ' Vestiarian ' controversy, the Bishops also wrote for the advice of the Swiss leaders on this dispute over the ' habits,' and Bishop Sandys, in 1573, wrote to Bullinger and asked him to act as arbitrator between them and a new party of presbyterian puritans which had just developed. This section wished to overthrow episcopacy altogether and to leave the choice of ministers to the people, and they also condemned all liturgical or set forms of prayer. Sandys asked the opinion of Bullinger, Gualter, and Simler, " and the rest of the Brethren," respecting these things, and added, " which for my own part I shall willingly follow as being sound and agreeable to the Word of God. For if the whole matter in controversy were left to your arbitration, it would doubtless much contribute to the peace of our Church." " These good men are crying out that they have all the Reformed Churches on their side " ([5]). But although the Swiss themselves had no sympathy with the use of surplices or square caps, they soon discovered that they were being ceaselessly worried by a restless and irreconcilable set of extremists, whose scrupulous consciences did not, however, keep them from misrepresenting the aims and principles of their opponents in order to obtain their own way. Bullinger had told Beza in 1567 that Sampson had " a restless disposition," and was apparently always longing to find some grievance ; and he adds a remark which shows that certain types of mind are not peculiar to any special age, when he says, " England has many characters of this sort who cannot be at rest, who can never be satisfied and who have always something or other to complain about. I have certainly a natural dislike to men of this stamp " ([5]). Many will re-echo his antipathy ! But it reminds us of James I's estimate of Archbishop Laud as a man of " restless mind who does not know when things are well."

Gualter had at first been deceived by two Puritan emissaries, and therefore had written a mild reproof to Bishop Parkhurst on the harsh and unyielding policy displayed by the Bishops. But when he heard the true account from Bishop Cox, he retracted his strictures and apologised to the bishops, declaring that from henceforth " he would have nothing to do with those vain brawlers," who had filled Beza's ears " with calumnies and false accusations " ([5]).

We get an incidental testimony to the regard for ancient usage in Gualter's answer to Cox, concerning set forms of prayer.

" If," he says, " the Puritans condemn certain forms of public prayer in the Church, I should say that they are mad with their wits about them, and that blinded with an excessive desire of innovation, they look upon everything with envious eyes, for the purpose of finding out some occasion of calumniating. For that such prayers have been *in use in all ages* no one can deny, and it is more than necessary that they should be retained, forasmuch as most persons are either so unfitted or even perplexed in their minds that they can scarce conceive their prayers in their thoughts much less in words " (⁶).

As we review this close intercourse and prolonged correspondence between Anglican and Swiss divines, we discover that ecclesiastical problems and disputes have not greatly changed in principle, and that the protagonists then were evidently men of like passions and prejudices with ourselves. But we also get most convincing evidence of the absolute unity of spirit, interest and outlook in all the main essentials of the Faith and its preservation, which bound together the Evangelical Churches of England and Switzerland at this time. Further evidence of this solid unity between members of all the Reformed Churches was seen in the protection and patronage afforded the foreign Reformed congregations which were allowed to settle and use their own special form of worship in England during Elizabeth's reign. Some of the persecuted Dutch Protestants from Flanders were welcomed at the beginning of the reign and worshipped in special London churches and were ministered to by Adrian Hamsted. Another congregation, which had been granted the use of the Augustine Friars Church in London, under the superintendency of John à Lasco in Edward VI's reign, now petitioned for a renewal of this privilege. Elizabeth granted their request and John Utenhovius, their minister, received special letters of commendation from Bullinger. The Queen, to avoid an appearance of a dual ecclesiastical authority or order in the Nation, placed these churches under the jurisdiction of the Bishop of London as Superintendent. Grindal was soon called on to exercise this authority, and in 1560 he had to excommunicate Hamsted for denying the doctrine of the Incarnation. After the awful Massacre of St. Bartholomew in 1572, many of the persecuted Huguenots, of France, escaped to England and were given a church in London. Grindal tells Bullinger that " Many exiles from France have sought refuge in London, and among them many ministers of the Churches, who are there kindly received with hospitality and supported by the alms of the godly " (7). Apparently, however, this tender solicitude and sympathy for the persecuted foreign Protestants was abused and exploited by many undesirable immigrants, who came to England in the guise of religious refugees. Consequently, in 1574, a register of all aliens and of the causes of their immigration was ordered to be kept. " Her Majesty," it was stated, " by her gracious favour doth protect such as repair hither sincerely for their conscience' sake and for religion." But the Proclamation well declares that there is no reason to harbour others, and endanger the occupations and trades of Englishmen, " for such as make Religion the colour of their coming, and are in truth irreligious and frequent no church at all "(8).

While the sharp controversy with the Puritans had not in any way weakened the warm regard and close fellowship between the Anglican clergy and their Reformed brethren in Switzerland, it had the direct effect of changing somewhat the attitude of the next generation of Elizabethan and Caroline churchmen on episcopacy, so that they no longer advocated it, as Archbishop Whitgift did in controverting Cartwright, merely on grounds of antiquity and national expediency. An extreme party of Puritans had denounced episcopacy as unscriptural and asserted the divine right of presbyterian government. Challenged in this directly provocative manner, the Anglicans retorted by asserting the Scripturalness and divine authority of the episcopal polity, and they soon advanced the counter claim that episcopacy was normally necessary where a Church could obtain it without danger of error or idolatry. A defence on these lines was, singularly enough, first made by a Dutch Reformed divine, Adrian Saravia. He had been forced to fly from popish persecution in the Low Countries in 1560 and he settled at first as a schoolmaster in Guernsey.

He was a friend of Richard Hooker, and after going back
to Holland for a time as Divinity Professor at Leyden,
he returned to England and at various times held several
livings and was appointed successively prebendary of
Gloucester, Worcester, and Canterbury. In 1566 he wrote
a tract against the Puritans in defence of diverse ranks
of ministers in the Church. He affirms his belief that
normally and properly the Ordination of ministers
belongs to bishops, but he admits that in cases of
necessity ' orthodox presbyters ' may ordain a presbyter. He justifies the action of the foreign Reformers
in adopting presbyterian government, on the score that
" when all bishops fall away from the true worship of
God unto idolatry, without any violation of the government of the Church the whole authority of the episcopal
government of the Church is devolved upon the pious
and orthodox presbyters, so that a presbyter may ordain
presbyters." On this plea he maintained that Beza and
others had received for their ministry a " legitimate
calling in the Churches of Christ " ([9]).

It was on practically identical grounds that Archbishop Bancroft in his ' Survey of the Pretended Holy
Discipline ' (1593) of the presbyterians, defended
episcopacy as " a lawful calling appointed in the Apostles'
time for the right order of Christ's Church." But he
added that this Apostolic succession of bishops is only
valuable so long as the Church possessing it remains
true to the Apostolic doctrine.

But it is clear that these very definite claims for
episcopacy were not intended to create any breach in the
fellowship between Anglicans and foreign Reformed
Churches. For Canon 55 of 1604 expressly acknow-
legdes the presbyterianly governed Church of Scotland
as a branch of " Christ's Holy Catholic Church." And
Bancroft himself refused a suggestion of Bishop
Andrewes in 1610 that three presbyterian ministers, who
were to be consecrated bishops to restore episcopacy in
Scotland, should first be re-ordained presbyters, saying
that " where bishops could not be had, orders given by
presbyters must be reckoned lawful," significantly adding
that otherwise " the calling and character of the ministry

in most of the Reformed Churches might be questioned "
(¹⁰).

It is also clear that this 'higher' claim for episcopacy
gave no real offence to the foreign Reformed divines,
even though they may have held that a presbyterian
policy was best suited for their own Churches. Theodore
Beza seems at first to have taken exception to Saravia's
spirited defence of episcopacy, but later on he is careful
to explain to Grindal that in his writings he was only
opposing the hierarchy of Rome " and had no intention
of reflecting on the English ecclesiastical polity or to urge
conformity to the Genevan discipline " (¹¹). He
lamented with 'bitter sorrow of heart' that some in
England were separating from the Church, and declared
that he was not of "those ignorant men who think
nothing right done but what they do themselves " (¹²).
He freely admitted that " the Church of England after
the reformation, was supported and stood by the
authority of archbishops and bishops, of which order she
had many, not only famous martyrs, but excellent
doctors and pastors and may she for ever enjoy that
singular blessing of God upon her " (¹²).

An interesting and instructive correspondence took
place in 1618 and 1619 between Bishop Andrewes and
the learned French Reformed divine, Peter du Moulin,
which proves to us that these later Anglican divines
had no desire to break the spirit of fellowship with, or
to 'unchurch' the foreign Reformed non-episcopal
Churches on a point of ecclesiastical polity. A Jesuit
had made a virulent attack on the French Reformed
Church, and du Moulin in writing a defence, had laid
down three propositions—

(1) That the name of bishop is not distinct from
presbyter in the New Testament.

(2) That bishop and presbyter is the same order.

(3) That the superiority of bishops arose from
the judgment of the primitive Church and was
not of divine right.

Not only James I, but also Bishop Andrewes took
exception to these statements as calculated to encourage

the English 'presbyterian' party in their hostile attitude to the Anglican polity. Du Moulin explained that it was due to the necessity of his controversy with the Jesuit that he had referred to the origin of episcopacy, and that he had no thought or wish to reflect on the Anglican order, which he held in great honour. Andrewes, however, in a most friendly spirit, challenged his three propositions. In his arguments, Andrewes appeals confidently to all the unproved assumptions, assertions, inferences and strained interpretations of Scripture made by the Fathers, concering the origin of the different orders of the Christian Ministry, many of which modern scholarship and research would by no means confirm. For instance Andrewes baldly asserts that "bishops were formerly instituted by Christ in the Apostles, and presbyters in the Seventy-Two." Episcopacy, he maintains, is by divine right and " from the Holy Spirit," although he reluctantly admits that du Moulin's first proposition was correct—that the names of bishop and presbyter were originally identical in the New Testament. Du Moulin had stated that episcopacy was not a " point of faith or of divine right." Andrewes admitted the former statement, but denied the latter. Episcopacy, he said, was not of 'faith' but of order. Though bishops be " by divine right, we do not say these things belong to *faith*. They belong not to the *credenda* but only to the practice of the Church." Thus when du Moulin pressed him with the question whether they of the French Church " sin against the divine right " because they wanted bishops, Andrewes replied, " I did not say this, this only I said, that your churches wanted somewhat that is of divine right, wanted but *not by your fault*, but by the *iniquity* of *the times*, for that your France had not your kings so propitious at the reforming of your Church as our England had." " But the name bishop ought not to have been abolished by you, though to what purpose is it to abolish the name and to retain the thing ? (for even you retain *the thing* without the title) and they two (Calvin and Beza) whom you named, while they lived, What were they but bishops *indeed*, though not in name ? " This is a conclusion regarding Calvin and

Beza which would certainly not be accepted by a modern 'Anglo-Catholic' view of the exclusive necessity of Apostolic succession for a true Church. But it proves conclusively that Andrewes did not wish to mar the common protestant unity on this score, and he heartily endorsed du Moulin's earnest desire that "all the reformed Churches *who are united by one faith* may be united by one and the same bond of ecclesiastical government" ([13]).

Travelling a few years farther in the XVIIth Century we find that such prominent leaders as Bishop Joseph Hall and Archbishop Bramhall took a similar line and refused to break the bonds of fellowship with the foreign Reformed Churches of Sweden, Denmark, Bohemia, Poland and Hungary or the Lutheran Churches in Germany, just because some of them lacked episcopacy but had retained "an ordinary succession of pastors, some by the name of Bishops, others under the name of seniors or Superintendents" ([14]).

Bishop Hall, although strenuously advocating "Episcopacy by divine right asserted," is careful to explain that 'Divine right' does not mean "an express law of God requiring it upon the absolute necessity of the being of a Church," but rather that which "imports the well or better being of it" ([15]). Therefore Hall adds a testimony to the real unity existing with other Reformed Churches when he says, "Blessed be God there is no difference in any essential matter between the Church of England and her sisters of the Reformation." Similarly Dean Field refused to condemn non-episcopal ministries —"There have been and may be true Churches," he declares, "without succession of bishops, therefore such succession of bishop and pastors cannot absolutely and without limitation truly be said to be a note of the Church" ([16]).

JOHN DURY AND REUNION.

It is appropriate here to refer to a little known, but most remarkable XVIIth Century divine who devoted practically all his life, as an enthusiastic pioneer, to the cause of Christian Reunion. His one consistent aim and effort was to promote full intercommunion and fellowship between all the Evangelical Churches of Christendom which embraced the principles of the Reformation ; and it has been asserted that John Dury " did and suffered more for the cause of peace than probably any other man." He was born in Edinburgh towards the close of the XVIth Century. His father was an ex-monk, who became a celebrated presbyterian divine, but his sermons were so polemical and political that he incurred the anger of the Government. Prudence therefore dictated flight to Holland, and he became a pastor at Leyden. His son, John was educated there and embraced ' Separatist ' or ' Independent ' views, probably on account of intercourse with the English ' Separatist ' exile congregations then in Holland, some of whom in 1620 became the ' Pilgrim Fathers ' of the *Mayflower*. This ' guess ' becomes almost a certainty when we recall the fact that Leyden was the chief centre of ' Separatist ' or ' Brownist' activities at the time, and that the ' Separatist ' or Independent Church there was under the pastorate of the celebrated John Robinson. In 1628 John Dury accepted the post of pastor to the English factory at Elbing in Prussia, which at the time formed part of the dominions of Gustavus Adolphus, King of Sweden. Here Dury became very intimate with one of the Swedish Privy Councillors—Dr. Godeman—who suggested to him the urgent need of achieving fellowship and intercommunion between all Protestants. Dury was enthused with the project and gave the rest of his long life with most self-denying zeal to this laudable endeavour. Sir Thomas Rowe, who had seconded the similar efforts of Cyril Lucar, when he was ambassador at Constantinople, heard of Dury's design and recommended it warmly to the Swedish Chancellor.

Oxenstein and Rowe both agreed that the project should receive the support of Gustavus and Charles I. Sir T. Rowe then interested many influential people in England on the subject, so that Dury gladly accepted an invitation to visit England and advocate the cause there. He was most cordially received by both Archbishop

Abbot and Bishop Laud, who counselled him to see both Gustavus Adolphus and the Protestant Princes of Germany and to take such action as they advised to carry out the design. Fortified by a Commendatory letter signed by 38 English divines, Dury saw Gustavus in 1631, at a time when, owing to the Battle of Leipsic, he was the Protestant dictator of Europe. Gustavus strongly supported the scheme, but all that was then accomplished was a recommendation to divines to prepare for such unity by suitable sermons.

Dury next turned his attention to the Calvinists and visited the Palatinate and the Wetterau and brought about a colloquy between the Lutherans and Calvinists at Leipsic in March, 1631. But the fall of Gustavus at Lutzen in 1632, was a great setback to the Movement, and Dury again appealed for help to Abbot and Laud ; and he represented England at a general meeting of the Protestant States at Heilebron. By this time consider-. able interest was aroused throughout Europe, and there were many friends to the Movement in Switzerland, France, and Germany. Dury then tried to gain over the Dutch pastors in Holland. In the autumn of 1633 he returned to England to find Laud had become Archbishop of Canterbury. He was received most kindly and Laud inquired from whom he had received Holy Orders. Dury, whose one consuming passion was the achievement of Protestant intercommunion, did not concern himself overmuch with questions of Church polity. But he admitted to Laud that he had always had scruples as to the validity of ' Independent ' ordination. These ' scruples ' were certainly shared by Laud and the Anglicans generally, since the English ' Separatists ' or Independents had from the first denied the validity of Anglican Orders and sacraments and had created their own Ministry in a decidedly ' irregular ' manner. A prominent Anglican divine therefore advised Dury to obtain Anglican Orders and thus secure a wider field of service. Dury was quite agreeable to this proposal, since as he said he " looked upon the Church of England as a Church of Christ, true in respect of the doctrine professed therein, and eminent for all spiritual gifts bestowed upon it, that I judged the government thereof by bishops with indifference, and that I took *them as men commissioned by the King to be his delegates*," an Erastian view of Orders which although it might be quite acceptable to the Caroline supporters of the ' divine right ' of Kings, would be so to few others ! It furnishes us, however, with additional evidence of Dury's early association with the Leyden Separatist Church, and it tells us that he still retained the views of episcopacy which these Independents propounded. For in 1617 the Leyden Brownists sent ' Seven Articles ' of their faith to the Council of the English Virginia Company, and it is interesting to notice that their language concerning the King's ecclesiastical authority is practically identical with that used by Dury. " The authority of the present bishops in the land we acknowledge, so far forth as *the same is indeed derived from His Majesty unto them and as they proceed in his name* " ([17]).

Dury was accordingly ordained priest by Bishop Joseph Hall, at Exeter, in February 1634. There is no record of his ordination to the diaconate, and possibly this step was dispensed with in view of his previous ' call ' to the Independent Ministry ! But it should be noticed that this is not a case of a re-ordination of a regular foreign Reformed (presbyterian) divine, in which, it is certain, Bishop Hall—any more than Bishop Morton —would " have had no hand."

Laud presented him to a living in Devonshire, giving him a special licence of non-residence so that " thus you may be able to pursue your negotiations with more effect." Dury now sought for further testimonials and further definite encouragement from prominent Anglican bishops for his great undertaking. Laud wrote a kind of circular letter to both the divided and contending parties. In his letter to Dury of February 10, 1634, for the Calvinists, Laud praises Dury's great zeal in his self-imposed task, and adds, " Assuredly as soon as I heard there was a hope conceived of the peace of the Reformed Churches I was filled with joy and my daily prayers are not lacking beseeching the God of peace to bring to fruition any hope whatever of a harvest so glorious and fruitful." " As far as I am concerned I will strive with all my might not to seem lacking in a work so worthy of the name of Christ. Moreover, I know honestly that this undertaking will be most acceptable to the Anglican Church." His letter to Dury for the Lutherans is couched in a similar strain.

" I approve up to the hilt," he says, " of this desire for Christian peace . . . greet in my name these brethren beloved in Christ and let them know that I am and always will be most eager for Christian reconciliation . . . I commend to you and to them this undertaking with my utmost earnestness " (18).

Dury also appealed to his episcopal supporters to publish their ' Opinions ' as to the best methods of securing this Protestant unity and intercommunion. One result of this appeal was a tractate by Bishop J. Davenant called ' An Exhortation to brotherly Communion betwixt the Protestant Churches.' In his ' Introduction ' Davenant discusses what are the essential ' fundamentals ' of the Catholic Faith, and he is most eager to give some advice " which may serve to advance so holy a work " as Dury's. He wisely declares that a full and *perfect* agreement between the opinions of divines is not to be expected, but that this should not prevent a " brotherly holy communion " between them, and he instances the concordat recently achieved in the Polonian Churches. He longs that they should " bid farewell to all dissensions and establish so near a Communion betwixt themselves that they refuse not to admit each other into their congregations either to the hearing of the Word preached or receiving of the sacraments." He further asserts that the three obstacles to unity are :

(1) The tyrannical jurisdiction of one Church lording it over the Faith of others.

(2) The approving of idolatrous worship on one side and detesting it on the other, although he adds that there was no fear of the least ' spot or stain of idolatry ' on either side in the Reformed Churches.

(3) The assertion of a Fundamental Article necessary to salvation. He declares that the common faith

is sufficiently set forth in the Apostles' Creed. "Other differences of opinion and interpretations of the Scripture are not sufficient to cause a break in Communion between one Church and another." He concludes that none of these obstacles really block the way to union between the Lutheran and 'Reformed' or Calvinistic Churches. Such 'brotherly Communion' he declares to be incumbent on all Christians, and he adds that "I doubt not at all that the Saxon and Helvetian Churches . . . acknowledge to have and to desire to retain brotherly Communion with the English, Scottish, Irish, and other foreign Reformed Churches. Surely as concerning us, although we consent not with them in all points and titles of controversial divinity, yet we acknowledge them Brethren in Christ and protest ourselves to have a brotherly and holy communion with them." "If," Davenant concludes, "they are like minded towards us, why do they (the Lutherans and Calvinists) deprive each other of that brotherly communion?"

He then advises a peaceable conference between the divines, and the disuse of bitter terms such as 'heretic,' and adds a plea which all sincere disciples of reunion will re-echo to day, that "it were to be wished that those sirnames of Lutherans, Zwinglians, and Calvinists, were packed away and utterly abolished, which are rather ensigns of faction than badges of brotherly union."

Dury also secured Opinions from Bishop Morton and Bishop Bedell of Kilmore, and the latter allowed him a pension for the rest of his life to prosecute his mission.

Bishop Hall, in a Tract, entitled "Good Counsells for the Peace of the Reformed Churches," declared that "the Articles of religion wherein the Divines of both sides do *fully agree* are abundantly sufficient both for a Christian man's salvation and likewise for the establishing of a firm and lasting peace in the Churches of God." In the same tractate we find a Sermon preached before King James I, by Archbishop Usher, wherein the same sensible advice is given. If, said Usher, we leave the points wherein Christians differ from one another and " gather into one body the rest of the articles wherein they do generally *agree*, we should find, that in those propositions which without all controversy are universally received in the whole Christian World, so much truth is contained, as being joined with holy obedience, may be sufficient to bring a man into everlasting salvation." It is interesting to discover that learned and pious divines three hundred years ago had such a breadth and charity of outlook and such a true Christian vision, and that they were then advocating the same healing principles for achieving Christian unity, which are today, in our Reunion efforts, being propounded as " fresh and enlightened " views, by modern pioneers in the Cause.

We must follow these persistent and sincere efforts of Dury a little farther, although they are largely a record of the difficult and disheartening nature of attempts to secure religious Concordats, and the healing of the Broken Fellowship of Christendom, of which we have had many examples in past years. In 1634 he returned to the Continent and he held repeated Conferences with Protestant States and divines. He also pleaded his cause in Scotland and in the Netherlands before Dutch Synods, and in most places he received many fair words and resolutions of sympathy, which, however, resulted in no practical action.

Special mention must be made of his effort with the Church in Sweden, where he want in July, 1636. The Chancellor Oxenstein accompanied him on a tour throughout the kingdom, and he attended a large Synod of divines at Stockholm. The Swedish Church was not only Lutheran but it had also retained the ancient epsicopal government. We have, however, sufficient evidence to prove that it held no rigid theory of the essential necessity of episcopal polity. Indeed its official actions, at times, certainly go to prove that it regarded this ancient, catholic and scriptural Order with singular laxity. On various occasions or emergencies the Swedish Church practically assumed the identity of the offices of bishop and priest even to the extent of ordination. Thus in 1758, 1764, and 1775, the Dean of Upsala, during the vacancy of the See, ordained numbers of candidates to the ministry of the priesthood.

There was not therefore any barrier on the score of 'Order' which hindered the Swedish Church from furthering Dury's scheme of general Protestant Intercommunion, and in fact the main obstacle centred round the Lutheran doctrine of the Eucharist. The Swedish churchmen demanded that the 'Reformed' should accept fully the teaching of the Confession of Augsburg, and although Dury tried to prove that the difference was mainly one of words, he was quite unsuccessful. In February 1638, he was told that his proposals were quite unacceptable, and a Royal Edict expelled him from the country, declaring that "he had resided sometime not without the great scandal of our ecclesiastics and he should depart without delay." The effect of this disappointment was so great that Dury became seriously ill in Stockholm, but vowed that if spared, he would devote the rest of his life to this sacred cause. He recovered, and continued his difficult and often disappointing task. He visited many German States and Princes and also the German Lutheran Universities of Wittenberg, Jena, Leipsic and Bremen. He then advocated his Mission in Denmark and Holland. But although much approval was given to the Scheme no real progress was effected. He returned to England in 1640 and was selected as Tutor to the Princess Royal, at the Hague, where he remained till 1643, when he was invited to the Westminster Assembly of Divines. The Prince of Orange refused to allow him to accept this invitation, and so Dury resigned his post and became Chaplain to a Merchant Adventurers Company at Rotterdam. He returned to England in 1645 and pleaded the cause of Christian Unity before the House of Commons. He remained in England for the next nine years, during which time he married a lady with comfortable means—a fact which must have greatly facilitated his work.

He exerted his utmost efforts to save Charles 1, but he was able to accept both the "Covenant" and the "Engagement." In 1654 he secured recommendations from Cromwell and the English divines, and he then pleaded his Cause before the Swiss Protestant Cantons. He visited Germany again in 1655, but his association with Cromwell rendered him unacceptable to the Elector Palatine. He visited many cities and also attended Synods in Holland, and in spite often of a luke-warm reception, he doggedly persisted in his efforts to bring about Conferences between the Lutherans and the ' reformed.' He even again tried in vain to interest the Prince of Sweden in his Mission. Returning to England in 1657, at the Restoration he endeavoured to secure the sympathy of Charles II, who was already secretly a Romanist. It was not therefore surprising that he received no reply. He appealed to Archbishop Juxon who, although most sympathetic, declined to move unless the foreign Princes would ask for the mediation of the Anglican Church. Baffled in this attempt, but still persevering Dury, now an old man, re-visited Holland, Sweden, Belgium, and Switzerland, always ceaselessly and strenuously advocating his Cause. In 1664 he settled in Cassel and from thence visited many States ; but in the end he found that he could make very little progress with the Lutherans. In 1672 he published an Eirenicon, in which he reduced the necessary terms of belief to the ' Apostles' Creed,' and he was apparently on this basis willing to embrace even the Roman Catholics in his scheme of reconciliation. In 1678 he was visited by the Quaker—William Penn ; but beyond this date there is no authentic record of his career. He is supposed to have lived till 1690.

It would be easy to refer to other prominent Caroline divines who showed their concern lest their strong insistence on the necessity of retaining the ancient episcopal polity for the Anglican Church, should be construed as a condemnation of the regimen of the foreign Reformed Churches, or should interfere with the close harmony and fellowship which had existed between them since the common breach with Rome. This anxiety was specially manifest during the Commonwealth period when many Anglican churchmen sought shelter from Puritan persecution by a sojourn in France. Bishop Cosin was especially concerned that these temporary exiles should associate with the French Reformed Churches and thus maintain their close historic and doctrinal connection, and " make no schism between their Church and ours " (¹⁹)[19]. He advises English churchmen abroad to communicate with the French Reformed Churches, and he pertinently asks, " If the Church and kingdom of England have ackonowedged them (the French Protestant Ministers) as they did in admitting of them when they fled hither for refuge, and placing them by public authority in divers of the most eminent cities amongst us*, without prohibition to any of our own people to go and communicate with them, why should we, that are but private persons utterly disclaim their communion in their own country ? " And he goes on to point out that " as there is no prohibition of our Church against communicating with them (as there is against communicating with the Papists and that well grounded upon Scripture and the Will of God)," that they, in order to declare their unity " in professing the same religion " may " communicate reverently with them of the French Church " [20]. In another recently discovered letter, Cosin brings forward the same plea for presbyterian Orders as other Caroline divines. " If," he says, " Bishops become enemies to God and Religion, in case of such necessity, as the care and government is devolved to the presbyters remaining Catholics, so the duty of ordaining such as are to succeed them in the work of the Ministry pertains to them likewise." " Who then," he demands, " dare condemn all those worthy ministers of God that were ordained by presbyters in sundry Churches of the world at such times as Bishops, in those parts where they lived, opposed themselves against the Truth of God and persecuted such as professed it ? " And he goes on to apply this plea of necessity to the

---

* One of these foreign Reformed divines was Peter du Moulin's son—Peter du Moulin the Younger—who was instituted Rector of Adisham, in Kent in 1662 in place of an ejected Minister and held the benefice for 22 years.

Scottish and especially to the French Reformed Churches* [22].

But although Caroline Churchmen were thus anxious to retain a bond of close unity with their foreign Reformed brethren who lacked an episcopal polity, they were not slow to condemn English and even Scotch presbyterians or ' sectaries,' who had neglected or refused episcopacy where it could be had in a pure Scriptural form. Thus the Scotch Church had reinstalled episcopal government by receiving bishops, consecrated in England in 1610. Then a few years later they had repudiated them. This action the Caroline divines regarded very seriously, and as Archbishop Bramhall and Bishop Ferne, of Chester, told them, there was a wide difference between wanting and not having bishops, and casting them out when they have them." So Bishop Hall told the Scotch—" We can at once tenderly respect them (the foreign Reformers) and justly condemn you " [23].

This attitude explains what might otherwise seem an inconsistency in the re-establishing of the episcopate in Scotland in 1661, when the presbyters consecrated as bishops were first re-ordained deacons and priests—a procedure definitely rejected by Archbishop Bancroft in 1610. But in 1660 the Church of Scotland was regarded, as Bishop Burnet tells us, as having been " lately in a state of schism." It is significant, however, that when these new Scotch bishops consecrated other presbyterian ministers as bishops, they did not first re-ordain them as deacons or priests. Bishop Burnet states definitely of this period, " No bishop in Scotland, during my stay in that kingdom ever did so much as desire any of the Presbyterians to be re-ordained " [24].

Clearly the Caroline churchmen of this period had no intention of denying the essential or intrinsic validity of presbyterian ordination, and it is interesting to notice

* Cosin evidently translated his convictions into practice, since even after the passing of the Act of Uniformity 1661, he only silenced one preacher in his diocese of Durham, and that was because of his " having neither Episcopal *nor presbiterall ordination.*" The inference is obvious regarding his willingness to have accepted presbyterian Orders [21].

that the practice followed in this revived Scotch Episcopal Church has evidently suggested a precedent for the proposed ' South India United Church.' Under that Scheme of Union of Anglican and non-episcopal Churches, existing non-episcopal ministers are to be recognised, without re-ordination by Bishops, as fully accredited Ministers of the United (Episcopal) Church, and other members are at liberty to communicate in these churches served by non-episcopal ministers. This was exactly the practice followed in Scotland after 1662. No attempt was made to re-ordain existing presbyterian ministers who, if so minded, were allowed to continue their ministrations, and administer the sacraments to all in their parishes, whether presbyterians or episcopalians. A clause in the South India Church Scheme, however, forbids a non-episcopally ordained minister to celebrate the Holy Communion in any previous ' Anglican ' church, if the congregation raises any objection.

We find that even after 1661, when the Act of Uniformity rigidly enforced episcopal ministries for the Anglican Church, the proposals set forth by the Bishops and clergy in 1689, in the ' Comprehension Scheme ' at the Jerusalem Chamber Conference, still recognised the fellowship and unity with the foreign Reformed Churches. For foreign divines were to be allowed to minister in England without re-ordination, although a conditional ordination was to be imposed on the English Dissenters because " many still doubt the validity of presbyterian ordination where episcopal ordination *may be had and is by law required* " ([25]). Moreover, the later Caroline divines still retained the same brotherly regard for the foreign Reformed Churches, and clearly differentiated between their position and that of the English Dissenters who had separated from the National English Church. Dr. H. Maurice, Lady Margaret Professor of Divinity at Cambridge, writing towards the end of the XVIIth Century, clearly emphasises this distinction when he says—

the ordination of our dissenters is peculiar and they do the foreign Churches great wrong, when they concern them in their quarrel. For first your Independents have no root of orders, but their pastors are of lay extraction. The Presbyterians have ordination from presbyters not only without, but *in opposition* to, bishops, against the established rules of this Church, against the laws of the country, as well as the practice of ancient Churches. And if upon this account we pronounce them void, we do no more than what all Protestant Churches abroad would do in like case. If some deacons or laymen would take upon them to ordain pastors in the French Churches for separate congregations, in opposition to the received discipline professed in their synods, I would appeal to any minister of those Churches whether he held such ordination valid. . . . Nay though a presbyter deposed by their synod should take upon him to ordain, I still appeal to the ministers of those Churches, whether they would account such an ordination valid. If we therefore do judge such ordinations here to be nullified because administered by subordinate officers against the laws of the Church, in opposition to their superiors, and against the practice and discipline of the primitive Christians, we cannot be thought singular in this judgment since all the ancient Churches would have done the same thing, and *all the Protestant Churches in Europe* in like case would follow our example. Those persons therefore who plead for ordination by presbyters without bishops here in England, are desired to show that their case is the same with that of the foreign Churches ([26]).

Prominent Churchmen were prepared to give practical expression to this spirit of fellowship with the foreign Churches. Thus Archbishop Sharp declared that he would willingly communicate with them if he were abroad, and Archbishop Wake described as " mad writers " those who would " cut off " their members " from our Communion " ([27]).

There certainly was no real desire to sever the historic bond between the Anglican and foreign adherents of the Reformation movement. We get a good illustration of this in Wall's treatise on ' Infant Baptism,' written in Queen Anne's reign. Speaking of the schism involved in separating from the National Churches for mere non-essential matters of ceremony or order, he illustrates his argument by a reference to the ' foreign Protestant Churches.' Though he admits " their ways of worship are not the same as ours," yet he confidently asserts that " we should communicate with them if in their nation," and that " they, when they come hither, do the same with us." Then in striking contrast to this definite recognition of their ministries, he asserts that the

Scripture makes it necessary to separate from the Roman Church since it has incurred the charge of idolatry " [28].

Another practical illustration of the continuance of this brotherly relationship, with the foreign non-episcopal Churches is furnished in the Report of the Society for the Propagation of the Gospel for the year 1705. We find that the Genevan clergy were in such full sympathy with the aims of the Society that they had " already proceeded to render the divine service in their Church as comformable as might be to the English liturgy and will imploy their lives to bring it nearer if possible. The Society also sent financial aid to a Dutch Minister for carrying on his evangelistic work amongst the Red Indians and wished to engage a Dutch Reformed minister as a colleague for one of their own missionaries" [29].

Caroline Churchmen, in common with their Eliza-. bethan predecessors, were most definite in their repudiation of and condemnation of what they freely described as the unscriptural and idolatrous teaching and worship of the Roman Church. But we get a striking and conspicuous illustration of their readiness to have full fellowship with ' proselytes ' from that Communion. We have already referred to a certain Antonio de Dominis, who was Archbishop of Spalato, in Dalmatia, for 14 years. This ingenious ecclesiastic came to England in 1616. He professed to have discovered innumerable errors in doctrine and practice in the Church of Rome, which, he declared, were burdening men's consciences and were contrary to Scripture. In his book he described the Roman Church as " mystical Babylon and Sodom " and the Pope as a " tyrant, schismatic, heretic, yea even Anti-Christ himself." Not unnaturally, with such pronounced anti-Roman sentiments, he was favourably received and most generously treated by Anglican Churchmen. His subsequent career however, soon disclosed him as a clever, mean, grasping, and unscrupulous hypocrite, who grossly deceived the Anglican authorities and grievously imposed on their credulity and hospitality. Afterwards, it transpired that the cause of his ' conversion ' was merely resentment at a pension which he was ordered to pay one of his suffragan bishops. In a fit of avaricious indignation he left his see, and went to the Low Countries to try his fortunes with the Dutch Reformed Church. Not however finding sufficient inducements or favour in that presbyterianly governed Communion to satisfy either his ambition or his cupidity, he came to England, where he soon struck a far more profitable ' quarry.' His ' conversion ' was fully credited, and both the King, nobility and clergy combined and rejoiced to honour and bestow on this most welcome ' jewel ' both presents and preferments. He was entertained by the Archbishop and soon made Dean of Windsor, Master of the Savoy Hospital and Rector of West Ilsley. His controversial writings were esteemed as most valuable for the Protestant cause, but his avaricious designs soon alienated his tenants and aroused suspicion. And this dislike and suspicion were confirmed when Gondomar, the Spanish ambassador, denounced him to James I as a daring deceiver, who was still at heart a Romanist. As evidence for this accusation, Gondomar procured from the Pope a pardon for De Dominis and also a promise of a wealthy bishopric and a Cardinal's hat, if he would abjure his writings. This ' bribe ' was eagerly welcomed by the shamelessly grasping Archbishop, especially as he had just failed to secure the richer ' plum ' of the archbishopric of York ! He asked leave of the King to depart so as to accept the Pope's offer, alleging that the English climate was injuring his health ! And he pretended that his stay in England had " advanced and furthered the union of all Christian Churches." But he also perfidiously asserted that he had lately discovered " many errors in our English Church," although he confessed unblushingly that he was " allured with the reward of a salary eight times as great " as his present revenues. In the end he was brought before a special Commission of bishops and others at which his perfidy and his secret treacherous correspondence with the Pope were fully exposed, and he was ordered to quit the country within twenty days and never to return. Arriving at Brussels, he recanted his

' conversion ' and railed on the Anglican Church, calling his adventures in England a " pestiferous and devilish voyage."

But as he had so grossly deceived others, so he received his just deserts. For the Pope failed to redeem his promises, and when De Dominis reached Rome, as Fuller quaintly puts it, " returning to Sodom he became unsavoury salt, cared for of no side." For a time he received a pension from the Pope, and when this ceased he again in anger ventilated his ' heresies,' and was consequently imprisoned and apparently met a violent death there ([30]).

His career in England is, however, of interest to our investigation for his attempt to disturb, if not alienate, the affection of Anglicans for the foreign Reformed Churches. For in 1620 he suggested to Bishop Morton that he should re-ordain a foreign minister in presbyterian Orders. But the Bishop at once indignantly refused the proposition declaring that " it could not be done but to the scandal of the Reformed Churches in which he would have no hand." The right of ordination was, Morton maintained, " the jus antiquum of the Presbyters " ([31]).

Although it is well beyond the Reformation period it is not unimportant to glance at the XVIIIth Century and see what evidences there are, allowing for the changed conditions, of the continuance of this same spirit of unity and fellowship, especially between the Anglican and foreign Protestant Churches.

In 1706 an attempt was made to effect some sort of working union between the Lutheran and Reformed Churches. Frederick I, of Prussia, wished that such an alliance should be effected on the basis of a Lutheran episcopate, and therefore negotiations were started with the Archbishop of Canterbury and the project was received most sympathetically in England. But the Lutherans objected to the Thirty-Nine Articles as savouring " of a little too much Geneva stamp," and so the Conferences came to nothing, although in 1714 a translation of Baron Pufendorf's book on the ' Principles of the Lutheran Church,' was published in England to show

how far they agreed with those of the Church of England. A practical illustration of close fellowship between the Anglican and Lutheran Churches was, however, afforded in the ' Jerusalem Bishopric Scheme,' which was inaugurated in 1841. Under this arrangement between England and Prussia, the appointment to the newly-formed bishopric was to be made alternately by the Lutheran and Anglican Churches. In the Royal licence for the consecration of the first Bishop in Jerusalem, a clause, which is still in force to-day, provided for the exercise of his jurisdiction over " other Protestant congregations desirous of placing themselves under his authority." The application of this reference was explained in the letter of the Archbishop of Canterbury to the King of Prussia (June 18, 1842), which stated that the Bishop would " consider it his duty to take under his pastoral care all the congregations of the German Protestant Faith who may desire it." The condition of membership for such congregations was the signing of the Confession of Augsburg.

Archbishop Wake was specially active and concerned for the cause of Christian reunion and professed the most friendly sentiments towards the foreign Reformed Churches, and declared in 1719 that " he would welcome a closer union amongst all the Reformed bodies at almost any price." He told Fr. Courayer, a most tolerant French Romanist, that although he was convinced that episcopal government " had been established in the Christian Church from the very time of the Apostles," yet he would not like to affirm that " where the ministry is not episcopal there is no Church nor any true administration of the sacraments "([32]). Most friendly relations also existed during this century between the Anglican Church and the Moravian Brethren. In 1715 Archbishop Wake procured a Royal *Brief* ordering collections in churches for " the relief and for the preserving of the episcopal Churches in Great Poland and Polish Prussia." On the representations of the Moravian bishop, Jablonksy, to the Archbishop, the needs of the Moravian Church were warmly advocated by the Anglican bishops. Later on in 1737 on the consecration of Count

Zinzendorf, Archbishop Potter wrote a warm letter of greeting and congratulation, declaring that he was always ready " especially to love and embrace your Church, united with us in the closest bonds of love, and which has hitherto, as we have been informed, invariably maintained both the purest primitive faith and the discipline of the Primitive Church " ([33]). On another occasion, Potter asserted that he believed the " Church of the Brethren is a truly apostolic and episcopal Church, whose doctrines contain nothing whatever militating against the Thirty Nine Articles of the Church of England " ([34]). In 1749 a Bill was passed in Parliament to encourage the Moravians to settle in the Colonies and the ' United Brethren ' were described as " an ancient Protestant Episcopal Church," whose doctrine differed " in no essential article of faith from the Church of England " ([35]).

An interesting but fruitless attempt was made in 1717 towards establishing a fellowship with the unreformed Church of France. The Pope in the Bull *Unigenitus* had attacked the Jansenists and also the greatly cherished liberties of the Gallican Church. Several leading French Romanists urged a right of appeal from the Pope to a General Council, while the celebrated Church historian, Du Pin voiced a desire for union with the Anglican Church. He declared that " the differences between them, on most points, were not so great as to render a reconciliation impracticable, and that it was his earnest wish that all Christians should be united in one sheepfold." As a result a correspondence ensued with Archbishop Wake, who insisted on the orthodoxy and purity in doctrine and discipline of the Anglican Church and declared that it possessed plenary and independent authority, and had no need to consult any other Church " what to retain or what to do." Wake demanded as an essential preliminary the repudiation of Papal Supremacy, and urged that on points of doctrine they should endeavour " to agree as far as possible in all articles of any moment and for other matters to allow a difference till God shall bring us to a union in these also." But he made it quite clear that although he was "a friend to peace " he was "more so to truth " ([36]).

The bitter hostility of the Jesuits prevented any fruitful issue to the effort, and Wake, as might have been expected in an age which was still extravagantly and even violently anti-Roman, incurred suspicion as an enemy to the Protestant position of the Anglican Church. Very shortly after, however, Fr. Courayer, a French Professor of Theology and chief Librarian at the Augustan Abbey at St. Geneviève, at Paris, published an able treatise in which, after a careful historical examination, he declared that, even from the Roman view of catholicity, Anglican Orders were unassailable ; since the proofs for Barlow's consecration and for Parker's, and the comparison of the Roman Pontifical with Edward VI's ritual, form in a matter of this kind demonstrations in favour of the English Ordinations with which no reasonable doubts can subsist." This honest and charitable conclusion was the cause of his exile to England, especially as he asserted that the validity of Anglican Orders should make us long "with greater ardour for reunion " with the English Church. "Though separated from us they are," he dared to affirm, " still our brethren, nor is anything foreign to us of that which is marked with the seal of Jesus Christ " ([37]). This dissertation was published in Paris in 1723 and naturally aroused considerable opposition, especially from the Jesuits. At length in 1727 his book was condemned by an ecclesiastical Assembly of bishops, and to avoid more serious consequence Courayer was compelled to escape to England, where he was warmly received and hospitably entertained by Archbishop Wake and other Anglican bishops and members of the nobility. A State pension of £100 a year, which was soon afterwards doubled, was settled on him. Although a Roman priest refused to hear his confession, Courayer regularly attended the services of the Roman Church, except when he retired occasionally to the village of Ealing, where he " constantly attended the parish church, and always expressed great satisfaction in the prayers of the Church of England." We are told that while he defended the doctrine of a Commemorative Sacrifice in the Mass " he doubted of the correctness of a large proportion of the doctrine and discipline maintained by the Church of Rome "(37). He died in London in 1776 at the advanced age of 95.

About the same date as this negotiation with the unreformed French Church, a similar effort was made, not indeed by the Anglican Church, but by its offshoot, the Non-Jurors Schism, for a Concordat with the unreformed Orthodox Eastern Church. It should be remembered that these Non-Jurors were distinctly ' high ' Church in their principles, and that a section of them had abandoned the English Prayer Book for something akin to the 1549 Liturgy. They were therefore prepared to make most liberal concessions in order to reach an agreed union with the Easterns. They were most anxious " that all endeavours should be made to heal the breaches of Christendom." In view of the efforts now being made towards a rapprochement with the Eastern Church, it is specially interesting to recall the history of these sincere negotiations set on foot by the Non-Jurors. The Scheme was first started by some Anglican and Scottish Non-Jurors in 1716 and was carried on by Bishops Collier, Brett and Griffin and the Scotch Bishops Campbell and Gadderer. The Non-Jurors were warned at the outset that " the Greeks were more corrupt and bigoted than the Romanists," but they entered with great zeal into the project which was also warmly approved by the Czar of Russia. It was styled a " Proposal for a Concordat betwixt the orthodox and Catholic remnant of the British Churches and the Catholic and Aspostolic Oriental Church." The Church of Jerusalem was to be acknowledged as the " true Mother Church and the principal of ecclesiastical Unity," "whence all other Churches have been derived and to which they owe a peculiar regard." The Non-Jurors also declared their profession of the Catholic Faith explained in the Councils of Nicea and Constantinople, and thus claimed that they should be "reciprocally acknowledged with the Easterns." They also urged as " near a uniformity as possible " in worship, allowing for the different national customs and rites. They emphasised their repudiation of the ' Twelve Articles ' which the Latin Church have added to the Creed. They agreed that the Holy Communion must be administered in both kinds and that " the Latin Church hath transgressed the Institution of Christ by restraining from the laity one kind." They further agreed " that there is no proper purgatorial fire in the future state for the purgation of souls." But on the following points they could not agree with the Eastern Church :—

(1) Although " they have a great reverence for the canons of ancient General Councils yet they allow them not the same authority as is due to the sacred text."

(2) They " are afraid of giving the glory of God to a creature . . . by blessing and magnifying the Virgin Mary."

(3) They " cannot use a direct invocation to any of the Saints."

(4) Though they believe " the faithful do verily and indeed receive the body and blood of Christ, they believe it yet to be after a manner which flesh and blood cannot conceive, seeing no sufficient ground from Scripture or Tradition to determine the manner of it, so that everyone receive the same in faith and worship Christ in spirit without being obliged to worship the sacred symbols of His Presence."

(5) They are fearful of encouraging idolatry by the worship of Images and " of giving scandal to many well meaning Christians."

If the Greeks will meet them in these objections the Non-Jurors proposed that a Union Church be erected in London where occasional united services of Greeks and Non-Jurors could be held.

But in a lengthy letter of August 16, 1721, the four Greek Patriarchs refuse all these concessions. They require the Non-Jurors to use the Greek Liturgy and not the 1549 Prayer Book. They adhere to the worship of the Blessed Virgin Mary and the Invocation of Saints, and they declare that the statement of the Non-Jurors concerning Eucharistic worship is 'blasphemous,' and in contra-distinction they assert their belief in transubstantiation. They say that these conclusions "were drawn up by a Synodical Judgment and determination of the Eastern Church after the most mature deliberation in a Council assembed in April 1718."

The Non-Jurors in another reply again decline " to give the worship even of 'dulia' to angels or departed Saints." Neither can they agree with the 'corporal presence' in the " bread and wine in the Holy Eucharist after consecration, which you call transubstantiation, as it has no foundation in Scripture." Nor can " they be convinced of any liberty for invocating the Saints and paying religious worship to them." " We conceive," they say, " the argument lies strongly against giving relative worship or religious respect to their images, since the prototype cannot be thus addressed 'tis still more difficult to imagine the bare representation of such a being can claim any such honour." In conclusion they ask for a ' compromise,' and wish " the Patriarchs to give them liberty not to be obliged to the invocation of Saints and angels, the worship of images, nor the adoration of the host." If they can obtain such assurances they have hopes of a favourable conclusion to the negotiations. The Patriarchs however displayed a most rigid and unyielding attitude. For in January 1723, they merely state that " they have nothing to add to their previous letter," except that the Greek doctrines must be accepted and submitted to " with sincerity and obedience and without any scruple or dispute " [38].

The negotiations therefore came to nothing because the Non-Jurors refused to acknowledge the decrees of Councils as on a level with Holy Scripture, or to accept the other doctrines and practices, which they regarded as a corruption of the Catholic Faith. Their decision is specially interesting and significant since it demonstrated their adherence to the cardinal principles of Reformed teaching in their insistence not only on the superiority of Faith to Order, but on the final supremacy of Scripture as the Rule of Faith and practice.

CHAPTER VIII.

CONCLUSION.

THE foregoing investigation should be sufficient to enable us to arrive at certain clear conclusions on the precise relationships which existed between the different sections of Christians, who in different countries repudiated the authority and governance of the Roman Church at the period known as the Reformation. We have, it is contended, discovered sufficient evidence to assert that :—

(1) The closest doctrinal unity existed between all the orthodox Reformed Churches, both Anglican and Continental, with the single exception of the divergence on Eucharistic doctrine between the Lutherans and the rest of the ' Reformed.'

This unity amounted to, and was commonly recognised as a ' Protestant Solidarity,' as against the teaching and claims of the Roman Church, and it was testified to not only by the foreign Reformers, but by Anglican Churchmen of varying types. For instance, the Puritan divine, Richard Baxter declared " The Reformed Churches called Protestants are a party indeed, but deserve not the name of a sect ; for their religion is nothing but simple Christianity, protesting against the papal corruptions " [1].

It is probable that Baxter uses the term ' protesting' here, in its original positive derivation of ' witnessing for.' There is abundant evidence to prove that the Protestant Reformation did not consist of a mere protest against Papal ' abuses.' Bishop Hall emphasises the same note of doctrinal solidarity when he speaks of the foreign

Reformed Churches as agreeing with the Anglican Church "in every point of Christian doctrine without the least variation."

Bishop Cosin also refers to the French Reformed Church "as professing the same religion " as the Church of England, while Archbishop Sancroft asks for prayer for ' the universal blessed union' of all Reformed Churches both at home and *abroad against our common enemies "*(²).

(2) The fullest fraternal fellowship and friendship was maintained between the Anglican and foreign ' Reformed' Churchmen during Elizabeth's reign, and also later into the Caroline period.

(3) The question of Church polity, whether episcopal or presbyterian, was certainly at first regard mainly as one of circumstances, expediency and national polity, and thus a ' thing largely indifferent,' and as creating no barrier to full and free intercourse, intercommunion and fellowship between the different Reformed Churches.

(4) The view that the foreign Reformed Churches in their worship and usages deliberately discarded all the customs and practices of historic Catholic antiquity and tradition, is not borne out by the known facts.

(5) Certain divergencies arose on questions of discipline and ceremonies, but these minor non-essential matters created no barrier to fellowship between the different regional or national Reformed Churches, although ' dissent ' from a National Reformed Church was regarded in the serious light of an unlawful 'schism,' and on the ' cujus regio ejus religio ' principle it was also often treated in the light of ' sedition.'

(6) All the Reformed Churches emphasised the New Testament doctrine of the priesthood of all believers, and therefore rejected the claim of the hierarchy alone to dominate the Church and to dictate to the faithful laity. This was, for instance, one of the main truths which Luther reiterated in his first three Reformation treatises published in 1520. " We are all," he declared, " consecrated priests by baptism." " All we who believe on Christ are kings and priests in Christ." " It belongs to each and every Christian to know and judge of doctrine " (³).

It was the exclusive claim of the Romanists that it belonged to the hierarchy and not to the laity to judge concerning the faith and discipline of the Church, and it was this claim which was practically repudiated when the Act of Uniformity was passed in 1559 by Anglican *laity* in Parliament in face of the unanimous opposition of the bishops. It is also denied by implication in the Anglican Article VI.

(7) A crucial line of cleavage on what were regarded as fundamental matters of doctrine, such as transubstantiation and the sacrifice of the Mass, was clearly recognised between the Reformed and unreformed Churches, whether Roman or Eastern Orthodox, and this was also accepted by the Anglicans, at least till the rise of the Tractarian Movement.

As we have seen, the Reformers had definitely opposed the medieval dogmatic definitions of the mechanical conveyance of grace through the sacraments, and especially the crude materialistic implications of the theory of transubstantiation. The Tractarians, with their assertion of the real Objective Presence of Christ in the Elements in the Eucharist, in effect revived this mechancial view of the conveyance of grace. Bishop Samuel Wilberforce, in opposing such teaching in Keble's ' Eucharistic Adoration,' touched the core of the whole controversy when he said that the predicating of a local Presence of the Eternal Priest in the elements was surely " the peculiar distinction between the Reformed and the Unreformed Faith " (Art. in " Quarterly Review," July 1866). The Reformers did not quarrel with the spiritual purpose and value of the Sacraments, but with this precise, mechanical, and materialistic definition of their operation. It was unfortunately an age which overstressed dogmatism, and much unchristian bitterness and condemnation could have been avoided if contending theological dogmatists would have been content with a general acceptance of the simple yet sublime belief that " in the Holy Communion Our Lord Jesus Christ Himself gives us the spiritual food of His body and blood " ([4]).

(8) This deep cleavage was conspicuously illustrated on the vital question of the position of Holy Scripture.

Was Holy Scripture to be accepted as the sufficient supreme and final Rule of Faith ?—the position of the Reformers, or had Scripture to be supplemented and interpreted by Tradition or by the decisions of the Pope, Fathers or Councils—the position of the Unreformed Churches ?

As we have seen (p. 121) Cardinal Bellarmine tersely and correctly expressed this irreconcilable antithesis when he said, " The controversy between us and the heretics is this that we assert that all necessary doctrine concerning faith and morals is not necessarily contained in Scripture and consequently beside the Written Word is needed an unwritten one, whereas they teach that in the Scriptures all such necessary doctrine is contained and consequently there is no need of an unwritten word " (⁵).

That this latter assertion was the uniform teaching and position of all the Protestant Churches we have clear and abundant evidence. We also get a very full and definite statement on this point in the ' Formula of Concord,' drawn up in 1576, to unite the Lutheran Churches. " Holy Scripture," it declares, " alone is acknowledged as the only judge, norm and rule according to which as by the only touchstone, all doctrines are to be examined and judged, as to whether they be godly or ungodly, true or false." " Other writings, whether of the Fathers, or of moderns, with whatever name they come are in nowise to be equalled to the Holy Scriptures but are all to be esteemed inferior to them, so that they be not otherwise received than in the rank of witnesses to show what doctrine was taught after the Apostles' times also, and in what parts of the world that more sound doctrine of the Prophets and Apostles has been preserved " (⁶).

The Anglican Reformers were always eager, in their controversial writings, to refer and appeal to the decisions of early Christian Councils and to the teaching of the orthodox Fathers. But it is quite clear from their statements (cf. Ch. V) that this appeal is by way of confirmation, and for the purpose of adding generally accepted ' witnesses ' to early catholic doctrine, which their fundamental appeal to the final authority of Scripture had compelled them to restore. For instance, Bishop Jeremy Taylor was most emphatic that—

the Scripture is a full and sufficient rule to Christians in faith and manners, a full and perfect declaration of the Will of God, and is therefore certain because we have no other . . . we have no reason to rely upon tradition for any part of our faith . . . The fulness and sufficiency of Scripture in all matters of faith and manners is the principle that I and all Protestants rely upon."(7)

In conformity with this reformed position we find that the Anglican Canons of 1604 forbid preachers in their sermons " to publish any doctrine disagreeing from the Word of God or from any of the Articles of Religion, or from the Book of Common Prayer " (Canon 51).

This addition of the standards of the Articles and Prayer Book does not imply any departure from the Protestant appeal to the final supreme standard of Holy Scripture, since the Canons of 1571 had definitely asserted that the Thirty-Nine Articles " are without doubt collected from the sacred books of the Old and New Testaments and agree with the heavenly doctrine which is contained in them in all points." And they add that the Prayer Book " contains nothing different from that very doctrine " (8). We may without hesitation assert that this 'Protestant' view of the position of Holy Scripture was the 'watershed' which clearly divided Reformed and Unreformed Christendom. Consequently the recent ' Agreement' drawn up between the representatives of the Anglican and Eastern Orthodox Churches in October 1931, was not only misleading but, if it should ever become the official teaching of the Anglican Church, it would for the first time since the Reformation place that Church definitely on the ' Unreformed ' side of this ' watershed.' To say, as this ' Agreed statement ' does, that " we receive the Divine Revelation in Our Lord Jesus Christ through Scripture *and Tradition*," and that we regard Holy Scripture as " completed, explained, interpreted and understood in the Holy Tradition, by the guidance of the Holy Spirit residing in the Church," seems to be practically equiva-

lent to the decree of the Roman Tridentine Council that
" the truth is contained in the written books and in the
unwritten traditions which having been received by the
Apostles were handed down to us " ([9]).

This modern statement, it is not unimportant to
notice, is directly at variance with the clear incidental
acknowledgment of " the Holy Scriptures as our supreme
rule of Faith and Practice," made by Archbishop
Davidson in his Kikuyu ' Judgment ' in 1913 ([10]), and
also of Resolution II of the Lambeth Conference of 1888,
which regards the Holy Scriptures as " being the rule and
ultimate standard of faith."

This ' Statement ' also in effect contradicts the cardinal
doctrine of the Reformation concerning the supremacy
and sufficiency of Holy Scripture. It is one of serious
doctrinal import. For the Reformed position asserts a
Catholic obligation for the acceptance of Holy Scripture
as the sole rule of faith, although it fails to discover any
Catholic authority for the essential necessity of one
special form of Church polity. It would seem also, on
careful examination, that this historic Reformed position
on Scripture has been jeopardised, if not forsaken, by
the pronouncements of the Lambeth Conference of 1930,
concerning the authorised ' Profession of Faith ' of
the ' Old Catholic Church.' This small body of Christians is composed of members of the Roman Church who
seceded in 1870 as a protest against the dogma of Papal
Infallibility. It received its episcopate in 1871 through
the friendly action of a remnant of the Jansenists, of
Holland—the little Church of Utrecht—which had for
200 years preserved an ' Old Catholic ' tradition
together with the historic episcopate. In 1889 an
assembly of Old Catholic Bishops drew up a " Profession
of Faith," entitled the " Declaration of the Church of
Utrecht," as the official doctrinal pronouncement of the
Old Catholic Church. The Lambeth Conference of 1930
considered the negotiations in progress for fellowship
with the Old Catholics, and its Committee reported that
" there was nothing in the terms of the Declaration of
Utrecht which would be an impediment to union between
the two Churches " ([11]). Also a Resolution of the

Conference agreed that " there is nothing in the Declaration of Utrecht inconsistent with the teaching of the Church of England " (11). It is very surprising that such definite statements could have been made by responsible Churchmen in view of the first assertion made in this " Old Catholic Declaration." For this accepts the Faith of the primitive Church " as formulated in the œcumenice symbols and specified precisely by the unanimously accepted decisions of the Œcumenical Councils held in the Undivided Church of the first thousand years."

This is a serious addition to the Reformed ' Rule of Faith ' in Scripture alone. The Anglican Church, as far as an Act of the State can effect this, has recognised the decisions of the first four General Councils on matters of faith or as a test of heresy, but it distinctly states that General Councils " may err and sometimes have erred, even in things pertaining unto God " (Article XXI).

Moreover the Second Nicene Council ordered that " the worship of salutation and honour " should be paid to ' holy images,' and such a decree is definitely condemned by the clear language of Article XXII, that such worship is "a fond thing vainly invented and grounded upon no warranty of Scripture, but rather repugnant to the Word of God." It was the learned Caroline divine Dean Jackson, who declared that the Faith of a Church which accepted the decree of this Second Nicene Council, " can be no Catholic Faith " (12). Moreover a Catechsim of the ' Old Catholic ' Church specifically condemns the primitive Catholic doctrine of the sole supremacy of Scripture. It describes those holding it as ' Protestant sects,' " que toutes rejettant l'authorité de la tradition, *n'admettent que celle de la Bible*, soumise au libre examen de chacun, olles rejettent aussi le sacerdoce, n'admettent que deux sacraments, rejettent enfin l'invocation des saintes et les prières pour les defunts " (13). As appears from this condemnation, the ' old Catholic ' Church practises Invocations of Saints, and in the Collect for St. Thomas of Canterbury's Day, prays that " all who implore his assistance, may find comfort in the grant of their petitions." Further the Old Catholic Church believes in the propitiatory Sacrifice of the Mass, the rejection of which sent the compilers of the Anglican Liturgy and Articles (Cranmer and Ridley) to the stake. In its ' Missal ' it prays, " Have mercy, O Lord ; we beseech thee on the soul of thy servant N., for which *we offer this victim of praise*, humbly beseeching thy majesty, that by this propitiatory sacrifice he may arrive at eternal rest." In the ' Communion of the Sick,' the host is administered with the words, " Brother receive the viaticum of the Body of our Lord Jesus Christ, which can conduct thee to everlasting life " ([14]) ; and perpetual Reservation and Adoration are also practised.

In Ordination the Bishop blesses the newly-ordained priest with the petition that he " may offer propitiatory sacrifices for the sins and offences of the people to Almighty God."

By adopting such practices and teaching, the Old Catholics may be maintaining, as their ' Declaration ' asserts, the " faith of the Undivided Church " till 1054, but in view of the significant omission of the Invocation of Saints and of Prayers for the Dead from the Reformed Anglican Prayer Book, and the definite condemnation of Invocation of Saints and " sacrifices of masses for the quick and the dead," in Articles XXII and XXXI, as well as in the Homilies, it is clearly incorrect to assert that the ' Declaration of Utrecht ' is not " inconsistent with the teaching of the Church of England."

The foregoing evidence justifies us in arriving at a further conclusion. For we may legitimately infer that before a Concordat has been reached with other orthodox non-episcopal Churches—

(9) Anything in the nature of a Union of the Anglican Church with either the ' Old Catholics,' or the Eastern Orthodox Churches, in which any of the common historic protestant principles are sacrificed, would be a complete reversal of the traditional position of the Reformed Anglican Church and would place it in an entirely new orientation.

Evidently, however, the serious divergence in doctrine and practice between the Anglican and Old Catholic Churches was recognised by the Anglican Commission,

till this date, Anglicans had maintained the historic distinction between the foreign Reformed Churches and the English Dissenters in favour of fellowship with and recognition of the Ministry of the former. Even one of the more moderate of the early Tractarians refused to excommunicate the foreign Reformed Churches for their lack of episcopal government. " It seems impossible," wrote W. Palmer in his ' Treatise on the Church ' (p. 301), " to deny that the Churches of the Foreign Reformation constituted on the whole a portion of the Catholic Church." That this close doctrinal unity with the foreign Reformed Churches was still recognised, was illustrated by the ' Charge ' which Bishop Coplestone, of Llandaff, delived in 1842. Coplestone was a ' High Churchman,' yet in speaking of the surprising " tenderness for Rome—the very centre and core of corruption "—which the Tractarians were displaying, he contrasts it with the ' harshness ' exhibited ' toward the Continental Churches—Lutheran and Genevan, and he declares that the defects of these Churches, i.e., specially their lack of episcopacy —are faults of a trivial character as compared with " the gross superstitions and idolatries of Rome, its creature worship, its withholding of the Scriptures, its exaltation of the power of the priest, and its load of ceremonies, all contrived to rivet that power and hold its votaries in blind subjection " [15].

The teaching of the Reformed Churches had emphasised the truth that every baptized Christian was necessarily a member of the Catholic Church, apart from the question of Church organisation, since " by one Spirit we are all baptized into one body." Newman and the Tractarians practically restricted the work of the Holy Spirit to one outward visible and specially organised Christian Society. The properly ordained officers of this Society alone could dispense the Sacraments of Christ's Church. Only those ordained by bishops, who claimed to trace their descent from the Apostles of Christ, could be Ministers of this Catholic Society. " We must necessarily consider," asserted Newman, " none to be really ordained, who have not been *thus* ordained."

Such a theory of the Ministry immediately condemned

the foreign Reformed non-episcopal Churches as possessing no valid Orders or Sacraments and as being outside the Catholic Church. But Tractarian teaching also contradicted the basic principle of the whole Reformation appeal, since it claimed that the Rule of Faith was not Scripture alone, but Scripture and *Tradition*. The Faith must be interpreted and explained by Tradition, and thus, in this way, tradition would complete Scripture; and of course the true exponents of Tradition would be the clergy, the accredited teachers of the Church. This theory would in effect restore the Medieval position of the clergy to teach the Faith, and the laity to listen and receive it, and it would thus virtually destroy the Scriptural teaching of the priesthood of the laity. This subtle attack on the great fundamental principle of Protestantism was soon perceived at the time, for Dr. T. Arnold, of Rugby, in a letter to Dr. Pusey, in February, 1834, in reference to the Tracts then being issued wrote :

You are lending your co-operation to a party second to none in the tendency of their principles to overthrow the truth of the Gospel . . . I stand amazed at some apparent efforts in this Protestant Church to set up the idol of Tradition, that is, to render Gibbon's conclusion against Christianity valid, by taking like him, the Fathers and the second and subsequent periods of Church History as a fair specimen of the Apostles and of the true doctrines of Christ [16].

The Report of the Royal Commission on Ecclesiastical Discipline in 1906 enumerated some practices, then being observed in Church worship, which it declared " lay on the Romeward side of a *line of deep cleavage* between the Church of England and that of Rome." That such a line of " deep cleavage " had been the clear teaching of the Anglican Church and of its leading theologians since the Reformation there is more than abundant evidence. In fact the unrestrained language of the Homilies sounds even coarse and uncharitable to our modern ears, when they describe the Church of Rome as " the foulest and filthiest harlot that was ever seen " [17].

The Homily for Whitsunday (Part II) uses no less definite language when it calls the Popes of Rome " false prophets and false Christs which deceived the world a long time," and prays that " they may be utterly confounded and put to flight in all parts of the world," since " they and their adherents are not the true Church of Christ much less to be taken as the chief heads and rulers of the same."

The Thirty-Nine Articles are content with the milder course of expressing condemnation of the Church of Rome as having " erred not only in its living but also in matters of faith " (Art. XIX.)

Again Canon 66, of 1604, speaks of the Church of England " being purged from all Popish error and superstition," an official condemnation which, it should be observed, is never used in connection with the foreign Reformed Churches, while Canon 7, of 1640, refers to " the time of reforming this Church from that gross superstition of Popery."

Now the teaching of the Tractarians tended to reverse this traditional Reformed condemnation of Roman doctrine and to obliterate any line of deep cleavage between Roman and Anglican doctrine. Newman's interpretation of the Articles in Tract XC. was put forth with the express object of endeavouring to prove that they were not necessarily condemnatory of distinctive Roman doctrine. It is little wonder that such a non-natural and casuistical attempt earned the stern censure of the Oxford Hebdomadal Board in 1841, which asserted " that modes of interpretation such as are suggested in the said Tract, evaded rather than explained the sense of the Articles, and reconciled subscription to them with the adoption of ' Roman Catholic ' errors which they were designed to counteract " ([19]).

This bold and startling Tractarian innovation ignored the great historical fact that the Articles belonged to an age in which Western Christendom was divided into two great camps the Roman and the Protestant, and that the Articles were a declaration that England took her place in the Protestant camp. That . . . camp . . . was agreed on accepting Scripture as the final authority on all matters of doctrine, on Justification by Faith as contrasted with Justification by Works or through the Church, on the fallibility of General Councils, on repudiating the doctrines of Transubstantiation, and on repudiation of the Mass as a propitiatory sacrifice, on the abolition of all worship of Images and on the renunciation of Papal authority ([20]).

The history of the Anglican Church during the past 100 years affords ample evidence that, in spite of the secession of Newman and others to the Church of Rome, Tractarian teaching has captivated the minds of an ever increasing number of Anglicans, so that many Churchmen to-day accept the exclusive and intolerant view, definitely repudiated by the Reformers, of " No Bishop, no church." This inverted emphasis on ' Order ' rather than on ' Faith ' has not only tended to weaken and seriously impair the historic friendship and fellowship with other Reformed Churches, but its effect is seen in the hostile attitude adopted by many Anglicans of this Tractarian school towards recent efforts put forth for Reunion with non-episcopalians, either at home or in the Mission field. This was very noticeable in 1913 in the ' Kikuyu Federation Scheme,' for closer co-operation and federation of Protestant Missionary Societies working in East Africa with a view to ultimate union of the Native Christian Churches. The United Conference for this purpose was concluded with a Corporate Communion Service at which the Bishops of Mombasa and Uganda officiated. As a result the Bishop of Zanzibar indicted these two bishops to the Archbishop of Canterbury for " heresy and schism," for administering the Sacrament to unconfirmed persons, and at the same time declared that the " very existence " of non-episcopal bodies was " hostile to Christ's Holy Church " ([21]).

A similar condemnation of non-episcopal ministries had been passed by Bishop Gore, who declared that Churches neglecting " the fundamental and Divine law of Christian fellowship "—the Apostolic Succession of bishops—were to be regarded as " rebels against a Divine law " ([22]).

In the Kikuyu ' Judgment,' however, the Archbishop of Canterbury reaffirmed the traditional Reformed position, as in practice, one of regarding the Anglican Confirmation rubric, as " the last of a series of rules laid down for the guidance of Church people with regard to *their* children," and therefore not applicable to members of other Churches. So that occasional admission to Communion of members of other Churches might be accepted as quite in harmony with the principles of the Church of England.

Another ' Proposed Scheme of Union ' of Churches in South India, which has been under serious and careful consideration since 1919, has also occasioned considerable adverse criticism, in view of Tractarian principles and prejudices. The Churches concerned, the Churches of India, Burma, and Ceylon, the South India United Church—and the South India Methodist Church—have all agreed (1929) on a Basis of Union, in which they accept the Holy Scriptures as the ultimate standard of Faith and accept the historic and constitutional episcopacy as a matter of Church order.

The historic reformation principles of fellowship with non-episcopal Churches are recognized by the provision that although episcopal ordination will be exclusively maintained in the United Church, all the existing ministers of the uniting Churches, whether episcopally or presbyterianly ordained " shall be acknowledged as ministers of the Word and Sacraments in the United Church " ([23]).

This last provision has been vigorously assailed by the Tractarian supporters of a rigid, narrow, and unhistorical view of episcopacy, which our Anglican Reformers definitely rejected. In this connection the present Bishop of Gloucester reaffirmed what we have seen to be the traditional Anglican Reformed position when he said :

I do not think that anything can justify us in saying that the sacraments of those who have not episcopal orders are invalid and no sacraments at all. I believe that the arguments in support of such a position are not for a moment tenable in face of any sincere historical criticism ([24]).

As we have seen Anglicans, especially since the Caroline period, regarded the English Dissenters who rejected or neglected episcopacy " where it could be had " in an entirely different light from the foreign non-episcopal churches. They looked on them as illegally defying the law of ' Church and realm,' and as wilfully creating a schism. The former charge was removed by the Toleration Act of 1689, and Churchmen to-day have no moral right to " visit the sins of the fathers on the children," even apart from the debatable question of the responsibility for the guilt of the original schisms. Schism has been well described as an alienation of affection amongst brethren, so that there may often be separation without schism and schism without separation. It is the unchristian censorious and divisive spirit which is really schismatic, and any body of Christians deliberately perpetuating this spirit is really guilty of an act of schism in the Church of Christ. It was the realisation of the mutually changed spirit and outlook on both sides, which led the Lambeth Conference in 1920 to make its memorable 'Appeal to all Christian People' for practical steps to be taken to restore the broken Fellowship of Christendom. In order to carry out this aim and objective, negotiations were commenced between Anglicans and the Orthodox Evangelical Free Churches to consider the possibility of closer fellowship or intercommunion if not actual reunion. In 1923 a joint statement on "the Status of the existing Free Church ministry," was issued by representatives of official Committees of Anglicans and Free Churchmen, and its main conclusion is in harmony with traditional Reformed principles of fellowship and intercommunion with non-episcopal churches. For it asserts that—

ministries which imply a sincere intention to preach Christ's Word and administer the Sacraments as Christ has ordained, and to which authority so to do has been solemnly given by the Church concerned, are real ministries of Christ's Word and Sacraments in the Universal Church [25].

Such a statement is certainly in harmony with the teaching and practice of the Church of the New Testament, which give no support "to any idea of a mechanical channel through which grace has come down from Apostolic channels, or to the idea that it is the Bishop who gives spiritual gifts " [26].* Yet in spite of this clear

---

*It is important to notice that the Report recently issued (1935) of the official Joint Conferences between Anglicans and Free Churchmen fully confirms this statement. In this suggested 'Sketch of a United Church' there is the proviso that "presbyters should be associated with the bishop in the act of ordination," and also that the Constitution " must leave room for and recognize as permissible various theories of the origin and nature of the episcopate."

acknowledgment of the value of non-episcopal ministries, Tractarian influences have so far prevented any practical illustrations of its admission in the realm of actual fellowship with the Free Churches through any officially authorised Intercommunion. It is, however, an encouraging sign to add that proposals for qualified and occasional acts of mutual intercommunion with Anglicans and Free Churchmen have been accepted since the last Lamberth Conference (1930) by the Anglican House of Bishops [27].

There is little question, however, that the practical realisation to-day of the principles of close fellowship based on the general doctrinal solidarity of all the Reformed Churches, which was so conspicuous during the Reformation period, is being seriously hindered by Tractarian teaching, which wishes to create " an organisation not of Christ " to " come between Christ and all non-epsicopal Churches and to demand as a condition of membership of the Body of Christ acceptance of Episcopacy " [28].

On the other hand, the official authorisation of free and full intercommunion with the ' Old Catholics,' in view of many of their unscriptural and unreformed doctrines and practices, has gone far to throw the Reformed Anglican Church, at least in appearance, on the Unreformed side of the great reformation ' watershed,' and line of ' deep cleavage.' We need, however, to bear in mind that not even the Resolutions of Lambeth Conferences can claim to affect or enunciate the authorised teaching of the Anglican Church. This point was made clear by Archbishop Longley, in his invitation to the first Conference in 1867, when he said, " Such a meeting would not be competent to make declarations or lay down definitions on points of doctrine " [29].

Again in 1875 Archbishop Tait, speaking in Convocation on April 16, declared—

there is no intention whatever on the part of anybody to gather together the Bishops of the Anglican Church for the sake of defining any matter of doctrine. Our doctrines are contained in our formularies, and our formularies are interpreted by the proper judicial authorities, and there is no intention whatever at any such gathering that questions of doctrine should be submitted for interpretation in any future Lambeth Conference.''

Neither do the declarations of bodies of clergy, or of individual leading Churchmen, affect more than their own personal opinions of Anglican teaching. It is necessary to make this point clear, because, although National life seems to tend more to ' collectivism,' Church life is becoming for more individualistic. Each one seems to do what is right in his own eyes, as regards the laws, customs and teaching of the Church. As the present Bishop of Durham recently reminded his ordinands—

there is not a solemn vow by which you publicly acknowledge yourself to be bound, which has not been emptied of all meaning by some sophistry and is not being openly repudiated by many clergymen . . . the English clergyman has in too many cases become a law to himself and fulfils his ministry in an Episcopal Church in the Spirit of individualistic sectarianism [30].

Therefore it is the official teaching of the Anglican Church, as set forth in the ' Declaration of Assent,' which is really authoritative. An anomalous and critical situation is, however, being created by the very large spread and acceptance of the main principles and the aims and ideals of Tractarianism. There is possibly a majority of the clergy to-day (although as was conspicuously evidenced by the rejection of the 1928 Prayer Book, not yet of the laity), who as far as the definite ' watershed ' which divides Reformed and Unreformed teaching is concerned, are definitely on the unreformed side. They are in their sympathies and convictions and outlook on the medieval, rather than on the Evangelical, side of the interpretation of Catholicity. But as we have seen, the Anglican Church, in its past history and teaching since the Reformation, stands distinctly on the Reformed side of a line of deep cleavage between Reformed and medieval theology. It would seem therefore to be urgently necessary for the Church of England to-day to see not only where it has stood doctrinally in the past, but where it stands as far as its official formularies are concerned, to-day, and where it wishes to stand in the future. It is clear that if the new school of divines, which has been created as the direct result of the Oxford Movement, should attempt to embody their special medieval views and doctrines in the official formularies of the Church, a very serious situation will be created. For such an attempt to achieve closer doctrinal Unity with Unreformed Christianity will at once threaten and probably precipitate an internal breach which will arrest, if not altogether destroy, the many sincere efforts which have recently been made for the healing of the breaches of Christendom.

On the other hand, much hope and encouragement may be drawn from an increasing number of clergy and especially of laity, in the Anglican Church to-day, who have inherited the liberal and catholic spirit displayed by Archbishops Sancroft and Wake, and who consequently yearn to see some outward and visible sign of the restoration of the Broken Fellowship of the Body of Christ. But, like Wake, they feel compelled to put the claims of Truth before those of Unity. They realize that a large measure of " agreement in the truths of God's Holy Word " is essential before we can hope that " all those who love Our Lord Jesus Christ in sincerity " will be able " to live together in Unity and godly love." And we do well to welcome the fact that the signs of the attainment of such a measure of agreement in essential truths are increasingly hopeful. In spite of the fascination which the dogmatic theology of medieval ' Catholicism ' exerts over many minds and certain temperaments, there is a growing impatience, especially amongst the younger generation, against the acceptance of rigid, exclusive and stereotyped views and theories. The old ' watchwords ' do not make the same clear-cut appeal, and are therefore not so fully accepted. There are also many surprisingly disconcerting reactions and cross-currents. Modern Christian thinkers refuse to be bound down rigidly to the ' orthodox ' enclosures and ' Divides ' of the past, and they are reviewing the history of Christian doctrinal controversies, not only with a more tolerant and charitable outlook, but with a wider perspective, and possibly also with a deeper and clearer understanding of the conflicting issues which were involved. While therefore in the maintenance of Truth we must not shut our eyes to the valuable lessons and landmarks of the past, yet it is probably true that the longed-for Reunion of the future will come " by the rediscovery of the old evangelical and catholic faith by all sections of Christendom in common," and thus there will be an " escape from the perversions and narrowings of Christianity, of which all sections of Christendom have been guilty, to the Gospel of God's redemption and to the richness of a Catholicism which is truly evangelical " [31].

But as we rejoice to day that this wider vision and this broader conception of the essential ' notes ' of the Christian Fellowship are far more generally accepted and widespread than they were three centuries ago ; let us not forget that even in the Reformation era there were some Christian sages and seers to whom had been revealed this " more excellent way " of peace and brotherhood. Certainly the main cause which so far continues to block the road towards Christian Reunion was just as clearly seen and expressed by Bishop Davenant, as it could be to-day. In his ' Good Counsells for the peace of the Reformed Churches,' he says,

Now the first and main obstacle that hinders those Churches which agree not in all points of Religion, from entertaining a Communion amongst themselves is the usurping and exercising of a tyrannical power and authority one over another. For if any one Church will take upon her to domineer and lord it over the faith of other Churches, so as not to acknowledge any for her brethren, nor admit of any into her fellowship and communion, but such only as will be content to *believe and speak just as she will have them*, all hope is then taken away of ever obtaining or preserving any agreement in any differences or disputes whatsoever. For the sacred Scriptures forbid us thus to enslave ourselves to any human authority, and our sole Lord and Master Christ Jesus forbids us to acknowledge any upon earth for a Lord over our Faith and Conscience, and that Church which enters into a Communion with another upon these terms doth not hereby purchase a Peace, but rather resigns herself up to a most unjust slavery [19].

When all those who love ' Our Lord Jesus Christ in

sincerity and truth ' have learned this fundamental lesson concerning Christian liberty and ' unity in diversity and diversity in unity,' the goal of Christlike harmony and fellowship will have been reached. And surely Hooker's pregnant assertion is far truer to-day than when he uttered it, that—" for the *preservation* of Christianity there is not anything more needful, than that such as are of the Visible Church should have mutual fellowship and society one with another " (' Eccles. Pol.' iii. 1. 14).

LISTS OF REFERENCES OF
QUOTATIONS UNDER CHAPTERS

CHAPTER I.

1. ROGER BACON, *Compendium Studii Philosphiae.*
2. ALLEN, *Erasmi Epistolae,* Vol. IV, 517-23.
3. ERASMUS, *Praise of Folly,* p. 170 (1887).
4. Quoted BEZOLD'S *Geschichte der Deutsche Reformation.*
5. DEMAUS, *Life of Latimer,* p. 137.
6. COULTON, G. G., *Five Centuries of Religion,* II, 228-9.
7. *Erasmi Epistolae,* p. 1041 (1641).
8. COULTON, *Five Centuries of Religion,* I, 291.
9. LUPTON, *Life of Colet,* p. 90, 134 (1887).
10. ERASMUS, *Praise of Folly,* p. 170.
11. *Protestant Dictionary,* p. 393 : Art. 'Ignatius Loyola' (1933).
12. ALLEN, *Erasmi Epistolae,* II, 185.
13. H. KNIGHTON, *Chronicon,* II, 191 (1889).
14. GAIRDNER, J., *Lollardy and the Reformation,* I, 100.
15. FOXE, J., *Acts and Monuments,* IV, 217-18 (1837).
16. HALL, T. C., *Religious Background of American Culture,* p. 45 (1930).

CHAPTER II.

1. GAIRDNER, *Lollardy and the Reformation,* I, 265.
2. GASQUET, Cardinal, *Eve of the Reformation,* p. 186 (1900).
3. *Ibid.,* p. 188.
4. FOXE, J., *Acts and Monuments,* V, 115 (1838).
5. *Ibid.,* V, 119.
6. DEMAUS, *Life of Tyndale,* p. 237.
7. LOVETT, *Printed English Bible,* p. 35.
8. TYNDALE, *Doctrinal Treatises,* p. 390 (Parker Society).
9. *Ibid.,* pp. 524, 525.
10. *Ibid.,* pp. 428, 414, 421, lii, 44.
11. TYNDALE, *Answer to More,* p. 236.
12. FOXE, *Acts and Monuments,* V, 12.
13. *Ibid.,* IV, 635.
14. COOPER, *Athen Cantab,* I, 42.
15. CRANMER, *Remains,* p. 218 (Parker Society).
16. CRANMER'S *Catechism,* Pref., VII, 208, 212.

17. CRANMER'S *Works*, I, 374.
18. LAURENCE, *Bampton Lectures*, *p.* 210.
19. *Original Letters*, 381-3 (Parker Society).
20. SOAMES, *Hist. of Reformation*, III, 72 (1826).
21. SMYTH, C. H., *Cranmer and the Reformation*, p. 70 (1926).
22. *Original Letters*, p. 72.
23. Quoted JACOBS, *Lutheran Movement in England*, p. 57 (1892).
24. FROUDE, *History of England*, III, 229.
25. BURNET, G., *Hist. of Reformation*, II, 422 (1825).
26. CRANMER'S *Letters*, p. 379.
27. BURNET, *Hist. of Reformation*, II, 422.
28. PIPER, *Die Zengen der Wahrheit*, Vol. III, 445.
29. BURNET, *Hist. of Reformation*, III, 139.
30. LUTHER'S *Works*, LXI, 304 : Erlanger Ed.

CHAPTER III.

1. BURNET, *Hist. of Reformation*, III, 33.
2. *Original Letters*, 524-6, 529.
3. LEVER, *Sermons*, ed. Arber, p. 122.
4. CARDWELL, *Two Liturgies of Edward VI*, Pref., XV sq.
5. Quoted BLAKENEY, R. P., *Introduction to the Book of Common Prayer*, p. 78.
6. STRYPE, *Cranmer*, p. 303-4 (1853).
7. *Ibid.*, II, 6.

All the other quotations in this Chapter are taken from the Original Letters of the Parker Society Edition.

CHAPTER IV.

1. *Original Letters*, pp. 102, 116, 73.
2. *Ibid.*, p. 514.
3. STRYPE, *Cranmer*, II, 76.
4. *Ibid.*, II, 77.
5. STRYPE, *Life of Grindal*, pp. 15-16 (1822).
6. *Ibid.*, p. 17.
7. *Original Letters*, p. 300.
8. *Ibid.*, p. 744.
9. ARBER, *Troubles at Frankfort*, p. 42.

CHAPTER V.

1. CREIGHTON, *Queen Elizabeth*, p. 60 (1900).
2. *Zürich Letters*, I, 321.
3. D'EWES, *Journal of Parliament*, p. 19.
4. ARBER, *Troubles at Frankfort*, 223-6.
5. GORHAM, *Reformation Gleanings*, 385, 390 (1857).
6. *Zürich Letters*, I, 100.
7. GORHAM, *Reformation Gleanings*, 403.
8. *Ibid.*, 410.
9. JEWEL, *Works*, III, 74, 70.

10. *Formularies of Faith*, p. 52 (1827).
11. HOOKER, *Ecclesiastical Polity*, iii, i.
12. *Post Communion Prayer* (Book of Common Prayer).
13. ARTICLE 8, Part I.
14. Chapter XVII.
15. HOOKER, *Eccles. Polity*, III, i, 34.
16. Quoted MACKINNON, *Luther and the Reformation*, IV, 156.
17. *Times*, Feb. 4, 1933.
18. BELL, *Documents of Christian Unity*, II, 28.
19. *The Christian East*, p. 34, Spring 1931.
20. CRANMER'S *Works*, II, 117.
21. BRADFORD, *Writings*, 505-9.
22. *Die Evangelischen Kirchenordnungen* I, 209f.
23. CALVIN *Institutes*, III, 77 (1846).
24. See BRAMHALL'S *Works*, III, 483 n. (1844).
25. JEWEL, *Works*, III, 59-60.
26. WHITGIFT, *Works*, I, 428, 368.
27. Hatfield House MSS., iii, 754.
28. STRYPE, *Life of Grindal*, p. 402 (1822).
29. STRYPE, *Annals of Reformation*, II, 71 (1725).
30. COSIN, *Works*, I, 2.
31. STRYPE, *Annals*, III, Appendix xxiii.
32. FULLER, *Church History*, III, 126 (1837).
33. PEARSON, *Thomas Cartwright*, p. 191 (1925).
34. *Ibid.*, p. 131.
35. Lansdowne MSS. 23, Art. 24, fol. 48.
36. STRYPE, *Life of Aylmer*, 183.
37. HOOKER, *Eccles. Polity*, V, 67, 6.
38. SANDYS, *Sermons*, 88-9.
39. COOPER, *Defense of the Truth*, 199 (1850).
40. JEWEL, *Works*, II, 1120.
41. SCHAFF, *Creeds of Evan. Prot. Churches*, 137-40 (1877).
42. CALVIN'S *Institutes*, III, 434, 430-2 (1846).
43. SCHAFF, *Creeds of Evan. Prot. Churches*, 469.
44. At the Diet of RATISBON L. A. COX, *Life of Melanchthon*, 427 (1815).
45. KIDD, B. J., *Documents of the Continental Reformation*, 225.
46. SCHAFF, *Creeds of Evan. Prot. Churches*, 472.
47. HALL, *Harmony of Protestant Confessions of Faith*, 328 (1844).
48. CRANMER'S *Remains*, 172.
49. SPARROW, *Rationale of the Book of Common Prayer*, 349-50 (1661).
50. JEWEL, *Works*, III, 64.
51. BILSON, *The True Difference*, Pt. iv, 706 (1585).
52. *The Christian East*, Spring 1931, p. 37.
53. COSIN, *Works*, V, 356.
54. COSIN, *Hist. of Popish Transubstantiation*, p. 61.
55. *The Archbishop of Canterbury on Reservation of the Sacrament*, p. 8 (1900).
56. SCHAFF, *Creeds of Evan. Prot. Churches*, 142.

57. *Ibid.*, 295.
58. KIDD, *Eucharistic Sacrifice*, 23, 22.
59. BICKNELL, *Thirty-Nine Articles*, 525.
60. BREEN, *Church of Old England*, 47.
61. *Homilies and Canons*, p. 414 (1844).
62. STRYPE, *Annals of Reformation*, I, 161-2.
63. FRERE, *Hist. of English Church*, p. 98.
64. Quoted ROUND, *XIXth Century*, May 1897 Art., ' Sacrifice of Mass.'
65. *Zürich Letters*, I, 24.
66. DUGDALE, *Life of Guest*, 133.
67. CARDWELL, *Synodalia*, I, 404.
68. BICKNELL, *Thirty-Nine Articles*, p. 518-9.
69. COVEL, *The Greek Church*, p. 55 (1722).
70. WINER, *The Confessions of Christendom*, 282 (1873).
71. CONSTANDINIDES, M., *The Orthodox Church*, p. 160.
72. *Catech. Concil. Trident*, pars. ii, Ch. IV, xxxi.
73. DEANESLEY, M., *The Lollard Bible*, p. 221-2.
74. KNIGHTON, H., *Chronicon*, Vol. II, 151-2.
75. WORKMAN, *John Wyclif*, II, Ch. V.
76. MORE'S *English Works*, p. 678 (1557).
77. COULTON, *Five Centuries of Religion*, I, 291.
78. WYCLIF, *De Veritate*, I, xxxvii.
79. WORKMAN, *John Wyclif*, II, 51.
80. *Ibid.*, II, 150.
81. LUTHER, *Werke*, II, 279.
82. *Corpus Reformatorium*, Vol. XXI, 453 : Brunswick (1834).
83. SCHAFF, *Creeds of Evan. Prot. Churches*, 362.
84. FOXE, *Acts and Monuments*, VI, 532.
85. RIDLEY, *Works*, p. 14.
86. TAYLOR, J., *Works*, X, 412-3, 438 (1822).
87. JEWEL, *Apology*, Pt. II, Ch. IX, 28 (1852).
88. FIELD, *Of the Church*, Vol. II, 444.
89. *Three Letters of Peter du Moulin Answered*, ed. 1647.
90. CARDWELL, *Synodalia*, I, 126.
91. *Ibid.*, I, 275.
92. Session IV, Canon I, Conc. XIV, 746.
93. CONSTANDINIDES, M., *The Orthodox Church*, 148.
94. BELL, *Docts. of Christian Unity*, II, 27.
95. *Homilies and Canons*, p. 6 (1844).
96. *Malines Conversations*, p. 77 (1927).

CHAPTER VI.

1. STONE, D. *The Faith of an English Catholic*, p. 35.
2. *Parker's Correspondence*, 224-6.
3. *Zürich Letters*, I, 149.
4. MACMILLAN, W., *Worship of the Scottish Reformed Church*, p. 33.
5. *Ibid.*, p. 31.
6. *Ibid.*, p. 40.

7. STRYPE, *Life of Grindal*, I, 403.
8. *Zürich Letters*, I, 228.
9. Cf. MACKINNON, *Luther and the Reformation*, IV, 156.
10. KIDD, B., *Documents of the Continental Reformation*, 445-7.
11. *Calvin's Tracts*, Vol. II, 307 (Edin., 1849).
12. Blakeney, *The Book of Common Prayer*, 195-6.
13. *Zürich Letters*, 339.
14. BINGHAM, *Origines Ecclesiasticae*, Vol. VIII, Pref., X.
15. *Ibid.*, Vol. VIII, 32.
16. *Of Episcopacy—Three Letters to Peter du Moulin Answered*, 1647.
17. BINGHAM, *Origines Ecclesiasticae*, Vol. VIII, 100.

CHAPTER VII.

1. *Zürich Letters*, I, 318, 126, 23.
2. *Ibid.*, I, 38, 100.
3. *Ibid.*, I, 58.
4. STRYPE, *Annals*, I, 273-4 (1725).
5. *Zürich Letters*, I, 296, 152, 363-4.
6. *Ibid.*, II, 332.
7. *Ibid.*, I, 291.
8. STRYPE, *Annals*, No. CXLVIII, Vol. 4, p. 214.
9. SARAVIA, *De Diversis gradibus Ministrorum Evangelii*, p. 18, 32-3 ; Latin Works, 1601.
10. SPOTTISWOOD, *Church History*, Bk. VII, 514.
11. COLLIER, *Ecclesiastical History*, VII, 120.
12. *Responsio Saravia*, Chs. XXI and XVIII.
13. *Three Letters to Peter du Moulin Answered*, ed. 1647.
14. BRAMHALL'S *Works*, III, 517-8.
15. HALL'S *Works*, V, 56.
16. FIELD, *Of the Church*, Vol. I, 82-3 (1847).
17. J. BROWN, *Pilgrim Fathers of New England*, p. 178 (1897).
18. LAUD'S *Works*, Vol. VII, 112, and VI, 410 (1857).
19. COSIN'S *Works*, Vol. IV, 337.
20. *Cosin Correspondence*, II, p. viii.
21. COSIN'S *Works*, I, 2-4.
22. Quoted FLETCHER, *Some Troubles of Archbishop Sancroft* (1926).
23. HALL'S *Works*, IX, 517.
24. BURNET, *Vindication*, pp. 84-5 (1696).
25. CARDWELL, *Hist. of Conferences*, 412.
26. MAURICE H., *Defense of Diocesan Episcopacy*, 452-3 (1700).
27. MOSHEIM, *Eccles. Hist.*, V, 169 (Maclaine).
28. WALL, *Hist. of Infant Baptism*, Part II, Ch. XI, pp. 669-71 (1862).
29. *East and West*, p. 50 (1922).
30. FULLER, *Church History*, III, 296-305 (1837).
31. NEAL, *Hist. of Puritans*, II, 353 (1822).
32. MOSHEIM, *Eccles. Hist.*, p. 873, n. 1 (Murdoch).
33. *Doddridge's Correspondence*, III, 264.

34. BENHAM, *Memoirs of James Hutton*, p. 24 (1886).
35. HUTTON, *Short Hist. of Moravian Church*, 211-12 (1895).
36. MOSHEIM, *Eccles. Hist.*, Vol. III, Appen. III, Letters iii, iv, vi and viii (1810).
37. COURAYER, *English Ordinations*, p. lix.
38. LATHBURY, *Hist. of Non-Jurors*, 310-50 (1897).

CHAPTER VIII.

1. BAXTER, R., *Under the Cross*, p. 277.
2. D'OYLEY, *Life of Sancroft*, I, 325.
3. LUTHER'S *Primary Works*, p. 164 (Wace and Bucheim).
4. HEADLAM, *What it Means to be a Christian*, p. 192.
5. BELLARMINE, *De Verb Dei*, lib. IV, c. 3.
6. SCHAFF, *Creeds of Evan. Prot. Churches*, 94, 96.
7. TAYLOR, J., *Works*, X, 268 (1822).
8. CARDWELL, *Synodalia*, I, 127 (1842).
9. Sess. IV, Canon I.
10. *Kikuyu*, p. 28.
11. *Lambeth Conference Report*, 1930, p. 141, 49.
12. JACKSON, T., *Works*, XII, 183-4 (1844).
13. *Catechism Catholique, Historique, et Dogmatique*, p. 55.
14. *Old Catholic Missal and Ritual*, p. 14.
15. KNOX, E. A., *The Tractarian Movement*, 293-4.
16. *Ibid.*, 133.
17. *Homilies and Canons*, p. 231, 418, 415 (1842).
18. CARDWELL, *Synodalia*, I, 404 (1842).
19. *Tract XC*, p. xiv and xviii.
20. KNOX, *Tractarian Movement*, p. 259.
21. *Open Letter to Bishop of St. Albans*.
22. GORE, *Orders and Unity*, 183-5.
23. BELL, *Docts. of Christian Unity*, II, 147-8.
24. *Times*, Feb. 4, 1933.
25. BELL *Docts. of Christian Unity*, I. 159.
26. HEADLAM, *What it Means to be a Christian*, 196.
27. *Ibid.*, 174.
28. KNOX, *Tractarian Movement*, 377.
29. *Five Lambeth Conferences*, p. 6 (S.P.C.K.).
30. HENSON, *Church and Parson in England*, p. 98 (1927).
31. AULEN, *Christus Victor*, Pref. p. x, by A. E. Hebert (1931).

BIBLIOGRAPHY

The following books, amongst others, have been consulted for this Treatise :—

ALLEN, P. S. : *Erasmi Epistolae* (1906).
ANDREWES, Bp. L. : *Three Letters to Peter du Moulin Answered*, ed. 1647.
Anglican Essays by Archbishop of Armagh and others.
ANRICH, G. : *Martin Bucer*, Strasburg, 1914.
ARBER, E. : *The Troubles at Frankfort*.
ARROWSMITH, R. S. : *Prelude to the Reformation*.
AULEN, G. : *Christus Victor* (S.P.C.K.).

BARNES, A. S. : *Bishop Barlow and Anglican Orders*.
BAXTER, R. : *Under the Cross*.
BAYNE, C. G. : *Anglo-Roman Relations, 1558-1565* (1913).
BEARD, C. : *Hibbert Lectures*, 1883.
BELL, G. K. A. : *Documents of Christian Unity*.
BENRATH, K. : *Bernardino Ochino of Siena* (English Translation, London, 1876).
BENHAM, D. : *Memoirs of J. Hutton*.
Beza Icones (R. T. S.).
BEZA, T. : *Responsio Saravia*.
BEZOLD : *Geschichte der Deutsche Reformation*.
BICKNELL : E. J., *Thirty-Nine Articles*.
BILSON, J. : *The True Difference* (1585).
BINGHAM, J. : *Origines Ecclesiasticae* (1834).
BIRT, H. N. : *The Elizabethan Religious Settlement*.
BLAKENEY, R. P. : *The Book of Common Prayer*.
BRAMHALL, Archbp. : *Works*.
BRIGHTMAN, F. E. : *The English Rite* (1915).
BRILIOTH, Y. : *Eucharistic Faith and Practice* (S.P.C.K.) (1930).
BROGDEN, J. : *Illustrations of the Liturgy and Ritual* (1842). *Catholic Safeguards* (1851).
BROWN, J. : *The Pilgrim Fathers of New England* (1897).
BURNET, Bishop G. : *History of the Reformation* (1825). *History of His Own Times* (1875). *Thirty-Nine Articles* (1831).
BURRAGE, C. : *The Early English Dissenters*.

CALVIN, J. : *Institutes of the Christian Religion* (1846).
 Commentaries (1844).
Cambridge Modern History, Vols. I and II.
CARDWELL, E. : *Documentary Annals.*
 History of Conferences.
 Two Liturgies of Edward VI.
 Reformatio Legum Ecclesiasticarum (1850).
 Synodalia.
CARTER, C. S. : *The Anglican Via Media.*
 The English Church and the Reformation.
 The English Church in the XVIIIth Century.
 Ministerial Commission.
 The Reformers and Holy Scripture.
COLLIER, J., Bp. : *Ecclesiastical History* (1840).
CONSTANDINIDES, M., *The Orthodox Church.*
COOPER, Bp. : *Defence of the Truth* (1850).
COSIN, J., Bp. : *Correspondence.*
 Works.
 History of Popish Transubstantiation.
COULTON, G. : *Medieval Studies.*
 Five Centuries of Religion.
COURAYER, Fr. : *English Ordinations.*
COVEL, J. : *The Greek Church* (1722).
COX, F. A. : *Life of Melanchthon* (1815).
CREIGHTON, Bp. : *Queen Elizabeth.*

DALTON, H. : *John à Lasco*, London, 1886.
DAVENANT, Bp. J. : *An Exhortation to Brotherly Communion
 betwixt the Protestant Churches*, London, 1641.
DAVIDSON, Archbp. R. T. : *Kikuyu.*
D'AUBIGNE, M. : *History of the Reformation.*
DEMAUS, R. : *Life of Latimer.*
DEANESLEY, M. : *The Lollard Bible.*
DENNEY, J. : *The English Church and the Ministry of the Reformed
 Churches.*
DICTIONARY OF NATIONAL BIOGRAPHY—Special Articles.
DIMOCK, N. : *Dangerous Deceits.*
 Missarum Sacrficia.
D'OYLEY : *Life of Sancroft.*
DIXON, R. W. : *History of the Church of England.*
DUGDALE : *Life of Guest.*
DUTCH REFORMED CHURCH PSALM AND PRAYER BOOK, 1609.
 Dordrecht.

ERASMUS, D. : *Praise of Folly* (1887).

FAREL, W. : *La Maniere et Fasson quon tient es lieux que sa Grace
 a visites*, ed. Baun, Strasburg, 1859.
FIELD, Dean : *Of the Church.*
FIVE LAMBETH CONFERENCES (S.P.C.K.).
FLETCHER : *Some Troubles of Archbishop Sancroft* (1926).

Frere, Bp. W. H. : *History of the English Church.*
Foxe, J. : *Acts and Monuments* (1838).
Froude, J. A. : *History of England.*
Fuller, T. : *Church History* (1837).

Gairdner, J. : *Lollardy and the Reformation.*
Gasquet, F. A. : *The Eve of the Reformation* (1900).
Gasquet, F. A., and Bishop E. : *Edward VI and the Book of Common Prayer.*
Gee and Hardy : *Documents Illustrative of English Church History.*
Good Counsells for the Peace of the Reformed Churches. By some reverend and learned Bishops and divines, Oxford, 1641.
Gore, Bp. C. : *Orders and Unity.*
The Christian Ministry.
Gorham, G. C. : *Reformation Gleanings.*

Hall, Bp. J. : *Works.*
Hall, P. : *Harmony of Protestant Confessions of Faith.*
Hall, T. C.: *The Religious Background of American Culture* (1930).
Hardwick, C. : *History of the Articles.*
Church History—Reformation.
Hauck, A. : *Deutschland und England in ihren Kircklie hen Beziehungen.* Acht Vorlesusigen in Oktober, 1916, an der Universat Upsala gehalten von Albert Hauck (Professor in Leipsic).
Headlam, Bp. A. C. : *Doctrine of the Church and Christian Reunion.*
What it means to be a Christian.
Henson, Bp. H. : *Church and Parson in England* (1927).
Homilies and Canons (1844).
Hooker, R. : *Laws of Ecclesiastical Polity.*
Huguenot Society of London—Proceedings of, Vol. XIV.
Hutton, J. E. : *Short History of Moravian Church* (1895).
Hutton, W. H. : *John Bunyan.*

Jackson, Dean T. : *Works* (1844).
Jacobs, H. E. : *The Lutheran Movement in England* (1892).
Jewel, Bp. J. : *Works.*
Apology.
Johnson, A. H. : *Europe in the XVIth Century.*

Kidd, B. : *The Thirty-Nine Articles.*
The Later Medieval Doctrine of the Eucharistic Sacrifice.
Documents of the Continental Reformation.
Knighton, H. : *Chronicon,* by Lumley, J. R. Rolls Series (1889).
Knox, Bp. E. A. : *The Tractarian Movement.*
Knox, J. : *Works,* Collected and Edited by David Laing, Edin., 1855.

LAMBETH CONFERENCE REPORT (1930).
LATHBURY, J. : *History of the Non Jurors* (1845).
LAUD, Bp. W. : *Works*.
LAURENCE, Archbp. : *Bampton Lectures*.
LEVER, T. : *Sermons*, ed. Arber.
LEWIS, J. : *Reformation Settlement*.
LORIMER, H. : *John Knox and the Church of England*.
LUPTON, E. : *Life of Colet* (1887).
LUTHER'S Primary Works—Wace and Bucheim (1896).

MACDONALD, A. J. : and Others, *Evangelical Doctrine of Holy Communion*.
MACKINNON, J. : *Luther and the Reformation* (1925).
MACMILLAN, W. : *Worship of the Scottish Reformed Church* (1931).
MACOLL, M. : *Reformation Settlement*.
MASON, A. J. : *The Church of England and Episcopacy*.
MASSINGBERD, F. C. : *The English Reformation*.
MAURICE, Dr. H.: *Defense of Diocesan Episcopacy*, London, 1900.
MORE, Sir T. : *English Works*.
MORTON, Bp. J. : *De Pace Ecclesiastica Sententia*, London, 1638.
MERRIMAN, R. B. : *Life and Letters of Thomas Cromwell*.
MOSHEIM, J. L., VON : *Ecclesiastical History*, by Murdoch and by Maclaine.

Narratives of the Reformation (Camden Society) (1850).
NEANDER, A. : *Church History* (1856).
NEAL, J. : *History of the Puritans* (1822).
NEALE, J. M. : *History of the Holy Eastern Church* (1847).
LE NOUVEAU TESTAMENT, LES PSEAVMES DE DAVID ET PRIERES ECCLESIASTIQUES. Amsterdam, 1690.

OMAN, J. : *The Church and the Divine Order*.
Original Letters of the English Reformation (Parker Society).
OWST, G. R.: *Literature and Pulpit in Medieval England* (1933).

PARKER SOCIETY WORKS—*Passim*.
PASCAL, G. : *Jean de Lasco*, Paris, 1894.
PEARSON, A. F. S.: *Thomas Cartwright and English Puritanism*.
PLUMMER, J. : *The Continental Reformation*.
POLLARD, A. F. : *Henry VIII*.
  Thomas Cranmer.
POCOCK, N. : *Records of the Reformation* (1870).
PRAYER BOOK DICTIONARY, 1925.
PROCTER and FRERE : *New History of the Book of Common Prayer*.
PROTESTANT DICTIONARY, Revised Edition, 1933.
PROTHERO, G. W. : *Statutes and Constitutional Documents*.

ROGERS, T. : *The Catholic Doctrine of the Church of England*.

SARAVIA, A.: *De Diversis gradibus Ministrorum Evangelii*, Latin
Works, 1601.
SCHAFF, P. : *Creeds of the Evangelical Protestant Churches.*
SMITH, A. L. : *Church and State in the Middle Ages.*
SMITH, T. : *Miscellanea*, London, 1686.
SMITHEN, F. J.: *Continental Protestantism and the English
Reformation.*
SOAMES, H. : *Elizabethan Religious History.*
   History of the Reformation (1826).
SPARROW, Bp. A.: *Rationale of the Book of Common Prayer* (1661).
STANLEY, A. P. : *History of the Eastern Church* (1894).
STRYPE, J. : *Memorials of the Reformation.*
   Annals of the Reformation.
   Life of Grindal.
   Life of Parker.
   Life of Aylmer.
   Life of Whitgift.

TAYLOR, Bp. J. : *Practical Works* (1822).
THOMAS, W. H. G. : *Principles of Theology.*
TWO TREAATISES ON THE CHURCH (Jackson and Sanderson)
   (1901).
TYNDALE, W. : *Doctrinal Treatises.*
   Answer to More.

USHER, R. G. : *The Reconstruction of the English Church.*

VIENOT, J. : *Histoire de la Reforme Française* (1926).
VON HASSE KARL : *Handbook to the Controversy with Rome.*

WALL, W. : *History of Infant Baptism* (1862).
Westcott's Fear.
WESTON, Bp. F. : *Open Letter to the Bishop of St. Albans.*
WINER, G. B.: *The Doctrines and Confessions of Christendom*,
   English translation, 1873.
WORDSWORTH, Bp. J.: *The National Church of Sweden.*
WORDSWORTH, C. : *Ecclesiastical Biography.*
WORKMAN, H. B. : *John Wyclif.*
WOUDSTRA, M.: *De Hollandsche Vreemdelingen Gemeents Te
Londen* (1908).
WRIGHT, Dr. C. H. H. : *The Service of the Mass in the Greek and
Roman Churches.*
WYCLIF, J. : *De Veritate Sacrae Scripturae*, ed. R. Buddenseig,
   Leipzig, 1904.
WYCLIFFE, JOHN DE : *Tracts and Treatises* (1845).
WYLIE, J. : *History of Protestantism.*

ZÜRICH LETTERS (Parker Society).

INDEX

Q

231

which continued the negotiations with the ' Old Catholics,' and it apparently created ' impediments to union.' Terms of ' Intercommunion ' were, however, agreed upon in July, 1931, but these definitely excluded " the acceptance of all doctrinal opinion, sacramental devotion or liturgical practice " of the other Church. These terms were ratified later by the Anglican Convocations and full intercommunion was thus establshed between the ' Old Catholics ' and the Church of England. There seems little question that the Concordat thus reached, however desirable on grounds of Christian charity and comity, with a Church that must rank rather on the Unreformed than on the Reformed side marks a new departure in Reformed Anglican tradition. It would seem almost to be driving a wedge into that great historic doctrinal solidarity which, as we have seen, has existed amongst all the great Reformed Churches, including the Anglican, since the Reformation. For hitherto Reformed Anglicans have always regarded " *Faith*," or pure Scriptural doctrine, as the one great essential, and " Order " as a secondary, although not unimportant non-essential. But now full Intercommunion is officially authorised between two Churches which possess indeed a common " Order " but differ seriously in " Faith," while the Anglican Church still denies a similar concordat with members of non-episcopal ' Free Churches ' who only differ on the question of Church polity or Order. For it should not be forgotten that the Toleration Act of 1689, which legalised orthodox Nonconformist worship, required all Dissenting Ministers, as a proof of their orthodox faith, to accept all the *doctrinal* Articles of the Church of England. This regulation was enforced for the next 80 years, in order to exclude Unitarians and Roman Catholics according to the terms of the Toleration Act.

What, we may well inquire, has caused this changed emphasis and this changing orientation ? In so far as it has been accepted by Anglican thinkers it is safe to assert that it has been done so, almost entirely as the result of the teaching of the Tractarian Movement which started in 1833. Up